Milicianas

Milicianas

Women in Combat in the Spanish Civil War

Lisa Margaret Lines

LEXINGTON BOOKS
Lanham • Boulder • New York • Toronto • Plymouth, UK

Published by Lexington Books
A wholly owned subsidiary of The Rowman & Littlefield Publishing Group, Inc.
4501 Forbes Boulevard, Suite 200, Lanham, Maryland 20706
www.lexingtonbooks.com

Estover Road, Plymouth PL6 7PY, United Kingdom

British Library Cataloguing in Publication Information Available

Library of Congress Cataloging-in-Publication Data

Lines, Lisa Margaret, 1980-
Women in combat in the Spanish Civil War / Lisa Margaret Lines.
p. cm.
Includes bibliographical references and index.
ISBN 978-0-7391-6492-1 (hbk. : alk. paper) -- ISBN 978-0-7391-6494-5 (electronic)
1. Spain--History--Civil War, 1936-1939--Participation, Female. 2. Spain--History--Civil War, 1936-
1939--Women. 3. Women in combat--Spain--History--20th century. 4. Spain--Militia--History--20th
century. 5. Women revolutionaries--Spain. I. Title.
DP269.L5155 2012
946.081'4082--dc23
2011041369

♾™ The paper used in this publication meets the minimum requirements of American
National Standard for Information Sciences Permanence of Paper for Printed Library
Materials, ANSI/NISO Z39.48-1992.

Printed in the United States of America

This book is dedicated to Kody, my best friend. I love you and miss you. You will be in my heart forever.

Contents

Acknowledgments

This book is based on my PhD Social Sciences thesis, and consequently I would like to sincerely thank all those who assisted me in my journey to complete the degree, including Associate Professor Peter Monteath, Dr. David Lockwood, Paul Sharkey and Dr. Renfrey Clarke.

I am forever grateful to my mother Wendy, my brother Beaudean and my nanna Joni for their love, support and understanding throughout my education. I am also grateful for the love and support I have received from my parents-in-law, Sophie and Brian. My family and friends are invaluable and I would be lost without them.

Most importantly, I want to thank my husband Nick. He has absolutely been my rock. Nick is my strongest supporter and the most understanding, kind and patient person I have ever known. He has helped me through these long, hard years in every way he could, and I could not have done it nearly as well without him.

A Note on the Text

The following Spanish place-names have been translated and appear in the text in English:

Andalucía: Andalusia
Aragón: Aragon
Cataluña: Catalonia
Extremadura: Estremadura
Mallorca: Majorca
Sevilla: Seville
Zaragoza: Saragossa

Where no common English translation exists, the Spanish name has been used for locations. In general, Catalan names have been written in Spanish. For example, "Conxa Pérez Collado" is referred to as "Concha Pérez Collado." Unless otherwise noted, all Spanish translations that appear in this book have been translated by the author.

The warring parties have generally been referred to as the Republicans and the Nationalists for convenience (despite the fact that these terms are not direct translations of the Spanish terms *Republicano* and *Nacional*). However, these groups are also variously known by other names, such as "loyalists" (for the Republicans) and "fascists," "rebels" or "insurgents" (for the Nationalists).

List of Political Organizations and Their Abbreviations

AMA *Asociación de Mujeres Antifascistas*, (Association of Anti-fascist Women). Communist women's organization.

CEDA *Confederación Española de Derechas Autónomas*, (Spanish Confederation of Autonomous Rights). The Catholic Party.

CNFGF *Comité Nacional Femenino contra la Guerra y el Fascismo*, (National Women's Committee against the War and Fascism). A communist women's committee.

CNT *Confederación Nacional del Trabajo*, (National Confederation of Labour). The anarcho-syndicalist trade union.

FAI *Federación Anarquista Ibérica*, (Iberian Anarchist Federation). The anarchist political party.

FIJL *Federación Ibérica de Juventudes Libertarias*, (Iberian Federation of Libertarian Youth). The anarchist youth group.

JCI *Juventud Comunista Ibérica*, (Iberian Communist Youth). The POUM youth group.

JSU *Juventudes Socialistas Unificadas*, (United Socialist Youth). The united communist and socialist youth group.

MFAC *Milícies Femenines Antifeixistes de Catalunya*, (Women's Anti-fascist Militias of Catalonia).

PCE *Partido Comunista de España*, (Communist Party of Spain).

POUM *Partido Obrero de Unificación Marxista*, (Workers' Party of Marxist Unification). The dissident Marxist (or anti-Stalinist) communist party.

PSOE *Partido Socialista Obrero Español*, (Spanish Socialist Workers' Party).

PSUC *Partido Socialista Unificado de Cataluña*, (United Socialist Party of Catalonia). The communist party in Catalonia.

UGT *Unión General de Trabajadores*, (General Union of Workers). The socialist trade union that came to be dominated by the communists.

Introduction

From the instant the Nationalist insurrection began on 17 July 1936,[1] and during the days that followed, women played an integral role in the spontaneous uprising that prevented the immediate success of the Nationalist military revolt. Around 1,000 of these Spanish women went on to enlist in the militias that fought on the front lines, and they were joined by a small number of female international volunteers. Women also played an important role in the defense of cities, with several thousand more women forming sections of the armed rearguard, most notably in Madrid. As a result of the advances made by women during the Second Republic, and the speed with which these rights and opportunities were enhanced by the social revolution that began at the same time as the civil war, women were able to play a military role in the conflict that would have otherwise been unimaginable for them. Women's participation in the anti-Nationalist resistance constituted one of the most significant mass political mobilizations of women in Spain's history.

Rosario Sánchez de la Mora was only seventeen years old in 1936. She was living away from her parents and staying in Madrid with relatives in order to attend classes.[2] She was a political activist and member of the united communist and socialist youth group. On 20 July, a group of young communist men visited her school looking for volunteers to join the militias fighting against the Nationalists. Sánchez de la Mora promptly signed up. The next morning at eight, she climbed on a truck that took her to the front.[3] When Sánchez de la Mora volunteered for the militia, she did so understanding that she would be required to participate in combat.

Sánchez de la Mora was first stationed at Buitrago, south of the Ebro River, as a member of the first shock group of the 46th Division.[4] She fought on the front line of what was a very important sector, since the Ebro River provided water to Madrid and it was imperative to safeguard this water supply. She explained, "we had to shoot continually in order that the fascists would note that we were presenting a strong resistance." She related that her position was always "the same hell. We shot day and night, of course thanks to this I learnt very quickly how to fight."[5]

After several months in the trenches at Buitrago, Sánchez de la Mora was transferred into the dynamite section of a mobile shock troop. She received training in the construction of bombs, and learned how to use them in various methods of attack. Even during her training, Sánchez de

1

la Mora made bombs for use in combat, and shortly she became an expert. After September 1936, due to an accident in which she lost her hand trying to protect the members of her troop, Sánchez de la Mora was transformed from an ordinary militiawoman to a war legend. She was celebrated throughout the Republic in the communist and independent press, in poems, and in speeches.

At the outbreak of the war, Concha Pérez Collado, an anarchist from Barcelona, was armed and ready. The members of her anarchist group had been prepared for several days before the uprising, knowing that it would begin at any moment. During the first few days of the fighting, Pérez Collado participated in the attack on the Model Prison to liberate the political prisoners held there.[6] She was involved in the requisitioning of a convent, and in building barricades around her neighborhood.[7] In the back of a truck covered with a mattress, and with only four weapons, Pérez Collado and her comrades went to the Pedralbes Barracks and took part in the fighting there, where they managed to obtain more weapons.[8] It was after this that the group decided they could best aid the cause by going to the Aragon front.

Pérez Collado traveled to Caspe on the Aragon front where she joined the Ortíz Column.[9] Her unit then moved on to Azaida, where they remained until the attack on Belchite, in which Pérez Collado and her militia took part, began on 24 August.[10] In December, after fighting for more than four months on the Aragon front, Pérez Collado traveled to Huesca to fight.[11] Pérez Collado spent several more months fighting in the Tardienta sector before *milicianas* (militiawomen) began to be removed from their combat positions. She returned, voluntarily, to Barcelona, where she worked in a collectivized munitions factory.[12]

Between July and December 1936, the *miliciana* was a Republican icon for the people's fight against fascism.[13] Photographs and posters of armed women on the front lines appeared in the press both in the Republican zone and internationally. These images represented a significant challenge to the traditional Spanish gender roles for women. However, by late 1936 attitudes toward women in combat had begun to change drastically again. The Republican government's slogan became "Men to the Front, Women to the Home front". In March 1937, the majority of militiawomen were removed from the fronts or forced to undertake purely auxiliary roles. Though many *milicianas* objected to this decision, no organized protest was made by them or any anti-fascist women's organization.

MILICIANAS *MISSING FROM HISTORY*

The history of this military participation of women during the Spanish Civil War has thus far been neglected, underestimated, or downplayed.

During the Spanish Civil War, thousands of women broke free of their traditionally defined gender role to take up arms and actively fight for the survival of the Republic. This behavior was highly irregular for twentieth century Europe, let alone Spain due to the strong influence of the Catholic Church. Yet despite this, the published history of the Spanish Civil War does not adequately reflect the significance of this occurrence. The women who fought for the Republic during the war have been silenced and ignored, and their military contribution has been under-reported and downplayed. There are several important reasons for this gap.

Catherine Coleman, one of the historians who has dealt with the subject, makes a connection between how women are treated in contemporary literature and the attitudes toward women that were held during the Spanish Civil War. She explains that due to sexism women's issues were considered unimportant during the civil war, and were consequently left out of many of the histories written during and after the conflict.[14] This attitude that women's issues and activities are less important than male-dominated issues and histories has prevailed. Women's history is treated as merely a collection of stories, a side issue, or a special interest category. But men's history is "general"; it is the history of us all. Coleman goes on to state that despite the available primary sources that testify to women's significant participation in the conflict, historians have chosen either to ignore or underestimate their involvement.[15]

Another explanation is the old adage that it is the winners who write history, and the Nationalists had certainly not been supporters of the struggle for women's liberation. The subject of women in combat has been given even *less* attention than the subject of women's general participation in the Republican war effort, because the *milicianas* actively took on roles that were considered inappropriate for women. Consequently, the *milicianas* have been effectively erased from history because they dared to enter the supposedly male arena of front line warfare.

Winners write history because they can suppress and censor the history of the losers, in this case the Republicans and in particular women. Shirley Mangini cites the impact that Francisco Franco's regime had on the defeated Republican and revolutionary women as a major reason for the lack of sources concerning their actions during the war. She relates that Francoist propaganda ridiculed the *milicianas* to such a degree that no one spoke of them, and that the women themselves hid their involvement out of shame or from fear of further reprisals.[16] A large number of the *milicianas* were imprisoned and tortured for years, even decades. Upon their release, these women often did not wish to relive those experiences, or found the pain of doing so unbearable.[17]

There also exist other possible explanations for the disappearance of the *milicianas* from history, such as illiteracy on their part, restrictions involved in their status as political exiles in France for those who escaped

Spain after the war, and prejudices and sexism within the groups, such as the Communist Party and anarchist groups, to which the militiawomen belonged.

The subject of the *milicianas* had never been openly dealt with in Spain itself until a series of conferences on the subject of women in the Spanish Civil War was held in Salamanca in 1989.[18] The history since written on the subject remains incomplete. Mangini in her discussion on the subject asserts that, "the *miliciana* phenomenon has never been adequately addressed."[19] By piecing these resources together, the reader can gain a fuller understanding of the subject, but there remain aspects that have not been dealt with and questions that have not been answered. More importantly, the significance of the *miliciana* phenomenon has never been fully recognized.

Clearly, a lack of primary sources pertaining to the *milicianas* has had an effect on the ability of historians to carry out in-depth analysis. This was the case immediately after the civil war, and the problem has been exacerbated with each passing decade. Even the most dedicated and willing historian may still find herself unable to examine, in as much detail as first hoped, the *miliciana* phenomenon for the simple reason that many sources have disappeared, been destroyed, or perhaps never existed in tangible form. In addition, the passage of time now makes the collection of original oral testimonies virtually impossible. In 2010, there remain very few living female participants in the Spanish Civil War.

As is common practice at the end of a war, many documents were destroyed by Republicans who feared violent retribution. Women who had fought on the Republican side attempted to conceal that fact by any means possible, knowing that they would face terrible humiliation, prison, and even death if caught. Even before the end of the war, many documents and evidence pertaining to the Republican military effort were lost through the very act of war itself. The constant bombardment of Madrid had a significant impact on the amount of surviving material.

Despite the shortage of primary sources and the virtual impossibility of conducting new interviews with participants, it is nonetheless still possible to make an original contribution to the subject, as this book aims to do. The interest of the historian does not diminish with the passage of time, and new interpretations and innovative methods of inquiry are still able to provide new insight into the subject of women's participation in combat during the Spanish Civil War.

THE SIGNIFICANCE OF THE MILICIANA

This book demonstrates the full extent of women's self-motivation and military participation in the civil war, and so asserts the significance of their role in the conflict. The role played by the women who took up arms against the Nationalists during the war was far more important than many historians would have us believe. Due recognition has not yet been given to the commitment of these women and the fact that they played a significant role in driving this process. The *miliciana* phenomenon was highly influential in terms of changing gender roles and accepted codes of behavior for women in Spain, even if only for a short time. The presence of a substantial number of women in combat roles in the front lines and rearguard, a phenomenon that in 1936 was unique in the history of Spain, was meaningful both in quantitative and qualitative terms.

While there exists a rich history of women warriors beginning in ancient times,[20] the uniqueness of the *milicianas* lies in the fact that before 1936 there had not been a significant mobilization of women to fight in a modern war on equal terms with men in Spain. While it is true that individual women have taken part in almost every military conflict either as notable exceptions, or by disguising themselves as men, Spanish women had never been incorporated on a large scale into any fighting force. Prior to the Spanish Civil War there had already been a number of iconic women warriors, such as Agustina de Aragón who participated in the resistance to Napoleon,[21] and Aida Lafuente who fought in the general strike in Asturias in October 1934.[22] However, these women stood out because they were the *exceptions* to the rule that women did not take part in combat on equal terms with men. The *milicianas* were unique not only because there was a much larger number of them, but also because they served both in women's battalions *and* alongside men in mixed gender militias. Their presence in battle is not noteworthy because they were highly conspicuous on the front lines; rather, it is so important because, through the eyes of their male comrades, it was considered unexceptional.

Part of the significance of the *milicianas* lies in the fact that their motivations were not as frivolous or subservient as the majority of the published history supposes. These women did not volunteer for combat because they were ordered to do so, or merely to support their men. They did so with revolutionary fervor and enthusiasm because they believed they could have an impact on the course of the war and revolution. While it is true that a small minority of *milicianas* did volunteer for less than altruistic reasons, this should not detract from the fact that the overwhelming majority of militiawomen took up arms with the purpose of defeating the Nationalists and protecting the Republic, and to further the social revolution. Further, while a minority of women followed their fathers, husbands or even sons into battle, the vast majority went into combat for reasons that were their own. A relative proportion of the young men who volunteered to serve in the militias may have also held unrealistic ideas of what war would be like, or gone to the front purely because they saw it as a heroic adventure. However, the motivations of these men are never questioned—and they are certainly never used to detract from the political and loyalist motives that drove hundreds of thousands of Republican men into battle.

The *miliciana* phenomenon in highly significant because the militia-women on the front lines took part in combat on equal terms with their male comrades. It is true that women often suffered a "double burden"[23] in the front lines, undertaking both combat and auxiliary tasks (while most men did not), in much the same way as women continue to do today, through undertaking both paid employment and unpaid domestic labor (while men on the whole do not). There is also evidence, however, that shows that in some militias there was an equal distribution of labor, and that the militiamen completed domestic tasks equally with the women of their unit. This book will provide a realistic picture of the lives of these women during the war.

In late 1936, attitudes toward the *milicianas* began to shift. Propaganda that once glorified these fighting women now called for a return to more traditional gender roles. The number of images in the media and propaganda featuring uniformed women armed with rifles declined sharply. Propaganda instead began to feature images of women undertaking auxiliary tasks like sewing, or encouraging men to enlist. Newspapers in the Republican zone still featured photographs of militiawomen in their uniforms, but instead of wielding rifles, they were cooking, cleaning or washing clothes. Over a period of several months in 1937, militiawomen were removed from the war fronts, in some cases forcibly. The women who remained at the front were stripped of their weapons and allowed only to become nurses, or to cook, clean, and wash for the men they had once fought beside. There were some exceptions. There are cases of women who remained at the front and retained their combat positions after the majority of women had returned to the home front. These women continued to fight for the Republic until their deaths or the end of the war.

The removal of women from combat was linked to the fate of the social revolution, which had begun in the Republican zone in Spain at the same time as the civil war in July 1936. Led by anarchists, dissident Marxists, and left-wing socialists, this revolution saw the beginnings of the collectivization of land, workers' control of factories, and advances in workers' and women's rights. However, roughly eight months after it had begun, the social revolution failed.[24] This meant the reversal of the many gains that the social revolution had made. It was in this context that the removal of women from their positions of combat took place.

While it is widely accepted that a decision of some kind was taken to remove women from their combat positions forcibly, and to reassign them to tasks on the home front, there is no consensus among historians or participants in the war as to who made this decision, when it was made, or what reasons were behind it. It may even have been a series of decisions made by various people that effected the removal of different groups of women from the front. Due to the absence of key documents, this question may never be answered fully. What is clear, however, is that some form of decision (or series of decisions) was made. This book will analyze the reaction of the women to this turn of events.

An interesting aspect of the reversal of women's ability to participate in combat is that a consensus on the issue was achieved across all of the left-wing political groups within the Republican zone. (This consensus was shared at least by the essentially male leadership of these political parties.) Communists, anarchists, dissident Marxists, and socialists all appeared to agree on one point—that a woman's place was not at the war front, but on the home front. This book will look systematically at the actions and response of each of the left-wing political groups to this question of the removal of women from combat positions, in order to demonstrate this consensus.

However, while an accord may have existed among the essentially male leadership of left-wing groups, it is clear that the militiawomen viewed the decision to remove them from combat in a very different light. The predominantly male leadership of these groups saw the removal of women from the front as a positive and necessary step toward the professionalization of the military and (they hoped) an improvement in Republican military success. Conversely, many of the militiawomen held deep reservations about this decision, and clearly viewed this tactic as a reversal of the gains that had been made for women as a result of the civil war and social revolution. The militiawomen believed that their removal from combat roles reflected a return to more traditional roles for women in Spanish society. This was clearly not something that they welcomed.

Finally, the significance of the *milicianas* and their contribution to the war will be demonstrated through an analysis of the representation of the militiawomen in the press and propaganda in the Republican zone. The many photographs, posters and other images of the *milicianas* that were produced and widely distributed during the war reveal interesting information about the changing gender roles in Spanish society, the popular perception of these fighting women, and the attitudes of both the press and the public toward them.

A GRASSROOTS, FEMINIST HISTORY

The aim of this book is to provide a grassroots history of the women who fought during the Spanish Civil War. It is not a "history from above", which serves only to outline the actions of the principally male government, armed forces and political parties. Rather, it is a "history from below", which will primarily examine the *milicianas'* own experiences of combat. It is for this reason that the sources of most importance to this book are those that have come from the women themselves, such as

interviews, testimonies, records and memoirs. While the book also uti-
lizes sources that have come from observers, journalists, historians, political parties, and the Republican government, it does so always with a
focus on relating the history of the militiawomen themselves.

This approach will provide a view of the civil war that lies outside the
mainstream historical perspective. War histories and narratives are most
often histories of the *male experience* of war. A grassroots history that
serves to highlight the female experience of war and revolution, from the
unique perspective of those women who actually played a military role,
thus allows the opportunity for a very different reading of the Spanish
Civil War.

This book has been written from a feminist viewpoint, which also
allows an alternate understanding of the civil war. This particular feminist perspective views the equal participation of women in combat as a
positive advance toward the liberation of women, and consequently
views the disarming of these women as a regressive policy and a reversal
of the gains that women had previously enjoyed. This fact alone means
that the argument presented in this book stands in opposition to many of
the conventional narratives on the *miliciana* phenomenon.

This feminist examination of the Spanish Civil War, focusing on the
experiences of the women who took part in the fighting, presents an
alternative narrative of the conflict because a male history of war, as
Miriam Cooke argues in *Women and the War Story*, is generally orderly
and mythological. Male histories "endlessly repeat . . . tales of roles and
experiences in which war mirrors the experience of its predecessors,"[25]
whereas women's war stories "allow for the narration of war's dyna-
mism and incomprehensibility,"[26] thus reflecting the true messiness and
confusion of war. Cooke describes herself as an "internationalist feminist",[27] and her work emphasizes the importance of women relating their
own war stories. She explains, "women like Rosie the Riveter in America
and the Algerian Jamilas learned too late that actions do not carry their
own rewards, but that they must be remembered and repeated so as not
to be erased."[28] Like many of the works of other female historians who
have begun writing about the Spanish Civil War since the early 1990s,
this book aims to challenge the conventional narrative of a war fought
and experienced only by men.

The fact that this book has been written from a feminist viewpoint is
integral. Since the argument presented here is that sexism has played a
key role in historians' ignoring or diminishing the significance of the
milicianas, a belief in the absolute equality between women and men is
necessary in order to overcome this barrier and assert the significance of
the militiawomen. A simple belief in absolute equality is a prerequisite to
understanding the importance of the *milicianas*. Clearly, those who view
women and women's issues as less important than men and male con-

cerns will not grasp the importance of the military role played by women during the civil war.

WARTIME ADVANCEMENTS FOR WOMEN: PERMANENT OR "FOR THE DURATION"?

In times of war, it is often the case that the rights of women are rapidly advanced and gender roles are challenged, allowing women to fulfill social and economic roles previously denied to them.[29] The most obvious cause of this is women's mass entrance into the workforce to solve the problem of the sudden and extensive labor shortage produced by hundreds of thousands of men leaving for the front.[30] This phenomenon has been widely discussed, in particular in relation to World Wars I and II (WWI and WWII).[31] As a result of war, women are needed not only in the workforce, but also more generally in the public sphere and in leadership roles. Consequently, they enjoy new rights and opportunities. The Spanish Civil War was no exception to this rule.

However, at the end of a war, most often, these progressive gains for women are reversed and the majority of newly-won rights are lost. Men return home from the war to take up their former positions in both the workforce and society, and women are expected to return to their homes and domestic responsibilities. Alan Milward and Angus Calder argue that this regression takes place because wars do not cause any social or economic changes; instead, they only highlight or accelerate processes that already exist within society.[32] Consequently, women's experiences during the war do not come as a result of genuine change, but are in fact merely an aberration from "normal" relations between the genders, which return once the war is over.[33] Cynthia Enloe, a prominent historian in the field of women and war, agrees with this theory. In her chapter "Rosie the Riveter," Enloe examines the situation of those women who were called upon to take up new roles in the labor force during both world wars, but only "for the duration." She refers to the gains made by women in wartime as "temporary, expedient and reversible."[34]

In addition to changes in gender roles brought on by the war, Spanish society in the Republican zone in 1936 was also transformed by a social revolution that occurred simultaneously. During wartime, women's roles are transformed for the most part out of economic necessity, rather than as a result of any deliberate program of reform or campaign to achieve sexual equality. In contrast, most progressive revolutions espouse an ideology of women's liberation and bring with them more radical and deliberate changes to gender roles.[35] It was the conditions created by the simultaneous social revolution that allowed for more radical transformations, such as the military participation of women.[36] It is of course impossible to make a clear distinction between specific gains made as a result of the war and those caused by the revolution. However, some division can be made since, while the end of the social revolution in March 1937 brought with it a retreat from *some* of the new and enhanced rights and opportunities for women, such as their participation in combat, women continued to enjoy other progressive gains until the close of the war, for example expanded opportunities in the labor force and, consequently, in training and education.

Similar to those improvements in women's rights during times of war, advancements for women caused by a social revolution will also necessarily be temporary, in the event of the failure of the revolution. Any gains made for women during a revolutionary period are reversed at its end when social, political, and economic norms, and with them traditional gender roles, are reasserted. This was the case for the social revolution that took place concurrently with the Spanish Civil War. The revolution in the Republican zone did initially cause swift and profound social and economic changes in many areas, particularly those primarily under anarchist influence such as Catalonia. However, these changes were implemented sporadically, were more successful in some areas than others, and in any case were short-lived. The social revolution began to falter in late 1936 and came to a decisive end during the May Days in 1937.

It is also necessary to refer briefly to the beginnings of positive change for women ushered in by the Second Republic. Though this period saw significant advances in women's rights, five years was too brief to produce deep-rooted transformations in gender issues, particularly since the conservative bloc won the election in 1933 and during their two years in power reversed many of the progressive gains made for women. Thus, the failure to achieve women's liberation during the civil war period stemmed at least in part from the inadequacy of preparation for emancipation in the pre-war period. Further, this inadequacy was evident across the full range of the political spectrum, though perhaps with some small but notable exceptions.

Marxist theory explains why it is that the advancements for women during times of war and revolutionary periods that ultimately fail can only be temporary, unless they are accompanied by fundamental and lasting social, political, and *economic* change. August Bebel and Friedrich Engels were two key theorists in the development of Marxist theory about women's liberation. In 1878, Bebel published *Woman Under Socialism*,[37] which was the first work to outline socialist theory on the "woman question." Bebel also highlighted the importance of women's participation in the revolution and the construction of a socialist society, asserting, "there can be no emancipation of humanity without the social independence and equality of the sexes."[38]

Engels explained in his 1884 work *On the Origins of the Family, Private Property and the State*[39] his theory to explain the original causes of women's oppression. He argued that the "world historical defeat of the female sex"[40] was brought about by the domestication and herding of animals that brought into existence private property and consequently class society. Prior to this, Engels argued, human society was egalitarian and collectivist, neither sex was subordinate to the other, and indeed the material conditions for such subordination did not exist. The central argument shared by both Bebel and Engels was that women's oppression was caused by the existence of both class society and private property, and thus genuine gender equality cannot be achieved until these preconditions are removed by a revolution and the subsequent creation of a socialist society. Contemporary Marxists point out that despite some advances toward women's emancipation in the nineteenth and twentieth centuries, women's position has not substantially improved, because these legal changes did not affect the structural forms of inequality enshrined in the rule of capital.[41] István Mészarós argues that there can be no "special space" for women within the existing political-economic order, upholding the position of Bebel and Engel that the empowerment of women must necessarily come as part of the empowerment of all human beings, as part of the adoption of a comprehensively different system of production and reproduction.[42]

Later Marxist theorists such as Evelyn Reid have updated Engels' theory based on newly discovered anthropological and archaeological evidence.[43] Reid's work confirms Engels' contentions about the egalitarian nature of early human societies; however, it also makes use of new scientific evidence to fill several gaps in Engels' explanation of the transition from pre-class to class society. More recently, the Marxist sociologist Pat Brewer has published findings that support Reid's theories.[44]

Similarly, contemporary feminist theorists have also added to Engels' account of women's exploitation under capital and the transformative potential of gender relations under socialism. While the central thesis of Engels and Bebel remains fundamental to Marxist theory on women's liberation today, socialist feminist critiques have nevertheless questioned understandings of gender politics within Marxist theory.[45] Nancy Holstrom has argued that while feminists have criticized Marxism for inadequately accounting for women's oppression within gender hierarchies, the integration of Marxist and feminist theories can nevertheless be a source of fruitful and necessary insight into defining and elucidating the characteristics of a genuine socialist democracy.[46] Holstrom contends that it is imperative for socialist theory and practice today to take gender and race politics into account.[47] This investigation therefore answers Holstrom's call for an integration of these perspectives, by offering a nuanced understanding of the operation of gender dynamics within socialist revolutionary politics during the Spanish Civil War.

The theory of Marxism reveals that during times of war and revolution, gender relations are blurred but not definitively changed. At the end of the war or the revolution, regardless of who wins, women will not be completely liberated unless there is a successful political, social, and economic revolution to overthrow the conditions that were the underlying cause of women's oppression.[48] Once the extraordinary period of war or revolution has passed and the process of rebuilding society has begun, women will be returned to their "normal" subjugated position unless the economic causes of women's oppression have been removed.

This book views the events of the Spanish Civil War from a Marxist perspective, and contends that the gains made for women as a result of both the war and the short-lived revolutionary period were necessarily reversed as a consequence of the failure of the social revolution, which meant that no fundamental or lasting economic change was realized. Republican Spain saw the partial reassertion of traditional social, political and economic norms in March 1937 at the end of the social revolution, and the process was completed at the close of the civil war in 1939, when Franco ensured the reversal of all progressive gains made during the war.

LEFT-WING GROUPS AND WOMEN'S LIBERATION

While Marxist theory dictates that the gains made for women during the Spanish Civil War were necessarily temporary, the relationship between left-wing political parties in the Republican zone and gender issues is nonetheless significant in relation to the reversal of women's rights that occurred. The failure of the revolution, and the resultant reversal of many of women's advancements, was largely caused by the regressive role played by the PCE. However, it is clear that the lack of commitment to gender equality, as demonstrated by the persistence of conservative thinking within progressive political groups, played a role in determining both the timing and nature of this retreat.

In order to understand the connection between women's issues and progressive groups in Spain, it is useful to examine theories on gender and revolution. Valentine Moghadam, who has made a valuable contribution to this field, maintains that there are two categories of revolution, the "woman in the family" revolution, also referred to by Moghadam as the patriarchal model, and the "women's emancipation" or modernizing model.[49] The former is a revolutionary ideology that:

> Excludes or marginalizes women from definitions and constructions of independence, liberation and liberty. It frequently constructs an ideological linkage between patriarchal values, nationalism, and the religious order. It assigns women the role of wife and mother, and associates women not only with family but with tradition, culture and religion.[50]

Conversely, Moghadam explains that the "women's emancipation" model of revolution espouses an ideology where:

> The emancipation of women is an essential part of the revolution or project of social transformation. It constructs Woman as part of the productive forces and citizenry, to be mobilized for economic and political purposes; she is to be liberated from patriarchal controls expressly for that purpose.[51]

However, the social revolution that took place in Spain in 1936 cannot simply be classified as one or the other model, since it was not led by a singular political group or ideology. The various left-wing political groups in the Republican zone each had their own history and relationship with gender issues. More radical groups, such as the anarchists, *Mujeres Libres,* and the POUM had an ideology that could be classified as the "women's emancipation" model. In contrast, more moderate forces, such as the communists and socialists, promoted ideology more in line with the "woman in the family" model. The issue is further complicated by the fact that the membership of some groups, the anarchists in particular, demonstrated various and conflicting opinions on the subject of women's liberation.[52] These varying attitudes meant that at different times the anarchists demonstrated both the "women's emancipation" and "woman in the family" models. What is significant about Moghadam's theory in terms of the Spanish example is it demonstrates that broad ideological radicalism does not necessarily equate to an enduring commitment to full sexual equality.

Despite the advancements toward sexual equality that were made after the outbreak of the civil war, sexism pervaded the policies and practices of the male-dominated left-wing groups in the Republican zone. Historians such as Cynthia Enloe and Karen Kampwirth argue that the attitudes toward women among left-wing groups prior to a revolution dictate what happens to women and their issues both during the revolution, and in the society that is constructed afterwards.[53] In the case of the Spanish Civil War, the situation is more complex because the revolution failed. It cannot be simply argued that left-wing groups abandoned only the issue of women's rights and not others, since the entire revolutionary process ended.

However, it could be argued that if the left-wing groups had not been so backward about the question of women's liberation prior to the revolution, perhaps they would not have accepted this reversal, and consequently forced the removal of women from combat roles so soon, without any protest, and in such a united way. For example, the anarchists did not abandon the idea of the collectivization of land so easily. It is impossible to judge if the attitudes of left-wing groups toward gender issues would have improved had the social revolution been successful. However, their treatment of women's issues during the revolution certainly follows the general pattern outlined by Enloe, in which male-dominated political groups, despite their progressive ideology, subordinate the needs and rights of women to larger aims.[54] The experience of *milicianas* during the Spanish Civil War fits within this larger context and theoretical framework.

OVERVIEW OF THIS BOOK

This book is primarily concerned with the period between July 1936 and July 1937, the initial period of revolutionary enthusiasm and the era in which the *miliciana* played her most significant role. For the most part, the book has been organized chronologically. Where there is an overlap in periods, the *actions* of the militia women will be discussed first in chapters 3 and 4, and the *attitudes* of others toward these fighting women will be discussed second, in chapters 5 and 6.

Organizing the chapters chronologically allows the reader to gain insight into the significance of the militia women by relaying the information in the sequence in which the women themselves experienced it. The book will demonstrate how drastically roles changed for women at the beginning of the civil war, show how the women experienced this for approximately eight months, and then reveal how society later reverted to more traditional gender roles.

Chapters 1 and 2 provide the historical and political context for the book. Chapter 1 includes a discussion on the social, political and economic position of women in Spanish society during the period 1800 to 1931, and during the early years of the Second Republic, 1931 to 1936. The record of left-wing groups in relation to gender issues prior to the civil war is also examined. Chapter 2 examines the period beginning with the outbreak of the civil war, and discusses the impact on Spanish women of both the war and social revolution. Knowledge of these issues is imperative to understanding the experience of the *milicianas*.

The view presented in this book will provide an alternative to the one that is most often found in other books on this topic, through demonstrating that the contribution of the militia women was in fact integral, especially in the early stages of the conflict. The *milicianas* were important both quantitatively and qualitatively, as chapter 3 will demonstrate. Chapter 3 will show that women's participation in the street fighting and resistance to the Nationalist uprising was vital to initial Republican successes. The chapter will then go on to examine the motivations of the *milicianas* for volunteering for the militias that went on to fight in the front lines. It will be shown that these women did not volunteer for combat simply because they were ordered to, or to follow their men to the front. They were highly self-motivated, and joined the militias as a result of their revolutionary fervor and commitment.

This chapter will also deal with the issue of how many *milicianas* fought in the front lines and in the rearguard, since in the past some historians have underestimated their numbers. Chapter 3 will present the figure of around 1,000 as a well-researched estimate of how many Spanish and foreign women actually took part in armed combat in the front lines, and will also demonstrate that another several thousand armed women played an important role in the military defense of towns and cities in the rearguard.

Chapter 4 will then examine the actions of the *milicianas*, and the military roles they played, from the beginning of the war until July 1937 when the majority of women had been removed from combat. Many other books attempt to dismiss the military contribution of the *milicianas* by arguing that women did not participate in combat on equal terms with men. Instead, they focus on the domestic and auxiliary tasks performed by the militia women at the front. This chapter will show that in fact women did participate in combat on equal terms with men. Using primary sources, in particular the various memoirs written by *milicianas* or their oral testimonies, chapter 4 will discuss the type of combat duties women undertook and the battles in which they were involved. The chapter will demonstrate that the *milicianas* did make a significant contribution to the Republican war effort.

While chapters 3 and 4 deal specifically with the actions of the militia women themselves, chapters 5 and 6 deal more specifically with the attitudes of others toward the *milicianas* and the controversy that surrounded their existence. This separation has been made in order to demonstrate that the *milicianas* were not exclusively active participants or passive subjects during the war, but were in fact both. Not only were these women actively involved in the armed anti-fascist resistance, they were also used as symbols, and their existence was discussed, examined, and disputed by many different groups during the war.

Chapter 5 deals with attitudes of both the public and left-wing political groups toward the *milicianas*, and how these were received by the militia women themselves. This chapter will first relate how the initial attitudes toward the militia women were positive, and will then examine the change in attitudes toward the *milicianas* that began to take place beginning in December 1936. Some historians refer to this change in attitude taking place earlier in the year, which serves only to downplay the significance of the *milicianas* by shortening the period in which they played a prominent and positive role in the public eye. Further, some historians seem to view this change in attitude toward the *milicianas* as an isolated development of relevance solely to women in combat, and fail to place it in its proper context in relation to the end of the social revolution, which began to falter in December 1936 and ended completely with the defeat of the anarchists in March 1937. This chapter will attempt to correct this misconception.

Chapter 5 will also outline the arguments put forward by the Republican government and left-wing political groups as they sought to show that women were not suitable for combat, and should be obliged to fulfill non-military roles on the home front. This chapter will focus on how the *milicianas* perceived these arguments, and show that they believed them to be nothing more than pretexts.

Part two of chapter 5 discusses the resulting decision to remove women forcibly from combat, and the effects of this decision on the *milicianas*. Historians have given varied accounts of when the formal decision to remove women from the fronts was made. While some claim that the socialist Prime Minister Francisco Largo Caballero passed the sanction in the late autumn of 1936,[55] other historians argue that the decision was not taken until later, in March 1937.[56] While the latter is more likely the case, a definitive answer may never be found. It is possible that the decision to remove women from combat actually took the form of a series of decisions, made by various political leaders at different times and affecting different groups of female combatants.

What is significant about the decision(s) to remove women from combat in the civil war is that while the male leaders of the Republic all agreed with this move, the women themselves saw it in a very different light. Systematically examining each political group, part two of chapter 5 will show that the predominantly male leadership of left-wing groups agreed on the necessity of removing the *milicianas* from the front lines and disarming women in the rearguard. However, what is also clear is that the *milicianas* themselves saw this return to traditional gender roles as a retreat from the gains they had made as a result of the war and the social revolution. Militia women saw that the unwillingness to continue allowing them to perform a role that was outside traditional gender boundaries was not an isolated incident. Rather, it was part of a general reversal of progressive ideas and practices that came with the defeat of the social revolution. Chapter 5 is relevant to the discussion on the connection between gender issues and left-wing groups, and the impact of this relationship on outcomes for women in times of war and revolution.

Lastly, chapter 6 will analyze the symbolism and imagery surrounding the *milicianas* in the press and propaganda in the Republican zone, in a further attempt to demonstrate the significance of the militia women in terms of challenging conservative gender roles and creating new opportunities and accepted codes of behavior for women. This chapter deals with the whole period examined in the book, from July 1936 to July 1937. This discussion has been left until last since its main focus is not on the experiences of the *milicianas* themselves, but rather on examining how these women were represented in the press. A study of how *milicianas* were represented is interesting because the press during the civil war not only reflected reality, but also helped shape it. As wartime propaganda, its role was not only to report the news but also to influence beliefs and attitudes among the public.

Chapter 6 analyzes the primary sources systematically, examining the press and propaganda of each left-wing political group within the Republican government. The chapter will show that between July and December 1936 the *miliciana* was a Republican icon for the people's fight against fascism. Photographs and posters of armed women on the front lines appeared in the press both in the Republican zone and internationally. They featured women wearing blue *monos* (overalls), shouldering rifles with the anti-fascist red kerchief tied around their necks. Often these women were portrayed leading men into battle. These images represented a very significant aspect of the challenge to the traditional gender roles for women. Further, it is interesting to examine the change in attitudes toward the *milicianas* and the reversal of gains made for women as they are reflected in the media.

In order to grasp how extraordinary the phenomenon of thousands of women taking up arms to fight in Spain in 1936 actually was, however, it is first necessary to gain an appreciation of the social, economic and political position of women in Spain prior to the outbreak of the civil war.

NOTES

1. Gabriel Jackson, *A Concise History of the Spanish Civil War*, Thames and Hudson, London, 1974, 43. The insurrection began in Morocco on 17 July and on the mainland on 18 July 1936.
2. Mangini, *Memories of Resistance*, 82.
3. Panes in Strobl, *Partisanas*, 39.
4. Mónica Carabias Álvaro, *Rosario Sánchez Mora (1919)*, Ediciones del Orto, Madrid, 2001, 25-28.
5. Strobl, *Partisanas*, 70.
6. Dolors Marín, "Las Libertarias," in Strobl, 354.
7. Lisa Lines, "Interview with Concha Pérez Collado," Barcelona, 13 February 2005.
8. Marín, "Libertarias," 354.
9. Mateo Rello, "Concha Pérez and Anarchy," *Solidaridad Obrera*, 17 July 2006.
10. Hugh Thomas, *The Spanish Civil War*, 4th edition, Penguin, London, 2003, 704.
11. Marín, "Libertarias," 355.
12. Marín, "Libertarias," 356.
13. The direct translation of *miliciana* is "militiawoman". The definition of *miliciana* in the context of the Spanish Civil War is an unprofessional or irregular combatant in the service of the Republic, the revolution or an ideological or political faction.
14. Coleman, "Women in the Spanish Civil War," 51.
15. Coleman, "Women in the Spanish Civil War," 51.
16. Mangini, *Memories of Resistance*, 81.
17. Mangini, *Memories of Resistance*, 130.
18. Nash, *Defying*, 43 and Coleman, "Women in the Spanish Civil War," 52n.
19. Mangini, *Memories of Resistance*, 80.
20. See for example David E. Jones, *Women Warriors: A history*, Brassey's, London, 1997 and Reina Pennington, *Amazons to Fighter Pilots: A biographical dictionary of military women*, Greenwood Press, Westport, 2003.
21. John Lawrence Tone, "Spanish Women in the Resistance to Napoleon, 1808–1814," in Victoria Lorée Enders and Pamela Beth Radcliff (eds.), *Constructing*

Spanish Womanhood: Female identity in modern Spain, University of New York Press, Albany, 1999, 259–282.

22. Brian D. Bunk, "Revolutionary Women and Gendered Icon: Aida Lafuente and the Spanish Revolution of 1934," *Journal of Women's History*, vol 15, no 2, Summer 2003, 99–105.

23. The "double burden" refers to the extra responsibility carried by women who work in paid employment but remain solely or mostly responsible for unpaid domestic duties in the household, including responsibilities associated with bearing and raising children. See Chapter 6, "The Double Burden: Marriage, motherhood and employment in the interwar years," in Ann Allen, *Feminism and Motherhood in Western Europe 1890–1970: The maternal dilemma*, Palgrave Macmillan, New York, 2005, 137–160.

24. This book takes the May Day events as the decisive moment for the failure of the social revolution.

25. Miriam Cooke, *Women and the War Story*, University of California Press, Berkeley, 1996, 40.

26. Cooke, *Women and the War Story*, 40.

27. Judith Gabriel, "Challenging the Masculine War Myth," *Al Jadid Magazine*, vol 5, no 28, Summer 1999. http://www.aljadid.com/reviews/0528gabriel.html Accessed on Wednesday 17 July 2006, 9:00AM.

28. Gabriel, "Challenging."

29. Margaret R. Higonnet and Patrice L. R. Higonnet, "The Double Helix," in Margaret Randolph Higonnet, Jane Jenson, Sonya Michel and Margaret Collins Weitz (eds), *Behind the Lines: Gender and the two World Wars*, Yale University Press, New Haven, 1987, 31.

30. Maurine Weiner Greenwald, *Women, War and Work: The impact of World War I on women workers in the United States*, Cornell University Press, Ithaca, 1990, x and Chester W. Gregory, *Women in Defense Work during World War II: An analysis of the labor problem and women's rights*, Exposition Press, New York, 1974, xvi.

31. See for example Chapter 7, "Rosie the Riveter: Women in defence industries," in Cynthia Enloe, *Does Khaki Become You? The militarisation of women"s lives*, South End Press, London, 1983, 173–206, Greenwald, *Women, War and Work* and Gregory, *Women in Defense Work*.

32. Alan Milward, *War, Economy and Society, 1939–45*, Allen Lane, London, 1977 and Angus Calder, *The People's War: Britain 1939–45*, Cape, London, 1969, cited in Higonnet and Higonnet, "Double Helix," 31.

33. Higonnet and Higonnet, "Double Helix," 31.

34. Enloe, *Does Khaki Become You?*, 190.

35. Valentine Moghadam, "Gender and Revolutions," in John Foran (ed.), *Theorizing Revolutions*, Routledge, London, 1997, 152.

36. This might explain why women had not participated in combat to such a degree during other times of war and conflict in Spain"s history, as these wars were not accompanied by a revolution.

37. August Bebel, *Woman Under Socialism*, translated by D. de Leon, New York Labor Press, New York, 1904.

38. Bebel, *Woman Under Socialism*, 6.

39. Friedrich Engels, *On the Origins of the Family, Private Property and the State*, Foreign Languages Press, Peking, 1978.

40. Engels, *On the Origins*, 65.

41. István Mészáros, *Beyond Capital: Toward a theory of transition*, Merlin Press, London, 1995, 191.

42. Mészáros, *Beyond Capital*, 203.

43. Evelyn Reid, *Sexism and Science*, Pathfinder Press, New York, 1978 and *Women's Evolution from Matriarchal Clans to Patriarchal Family*, Pathfinder Press, New York, 1974.

44. Pat Brewer, *The Dispossession of Women*, Resistance Books, Chippendale, 2000.

45. Nancy Holstrom, "The Socialist Feminist Project," *Monthly Review*, vol. 54, no. 10, 2003, 38–49.

46. Holstrom, "Socialist Feminist Project," 46.

47. Holstrom, "Socialist Feminist Project," 48.

48. Holstrom, "Socialist Feminist Project," 38.

49. Moghadam, "Gender and Revolutions," 137.

50. Moghadam, "Gender and Revolutions," 143.

51. Moghadam, "Gender and Revolutions," 152.

52. See Ackelsberg, "Separate and Equal?" 66.

53. For an in-depth study of this issue, in particular in relation to women who participated in the wars fought by liberation armies, and their consequent treatment by the new state once the revolutionary war is successful, see Chapter 6, "Women in Liberation Armies", Enloe, *Does Khaki Become You?*, 160–172. See also Karen Kampwirth, *Feminism and the Legacy of Revolution: Nicaragua, El Salvador, Chiapas*, Ohio University Press, Athens, 2004 and "From Feminine Guerrillas to Feminist Revolutionaries: Nicaragua, El Salvador, Chiapas," Paper presented at the Latin American Studies Association Conference, Guadalajara, April, 1997, though Kampwirth's focus is on how a lack of commitment to gender issues within revolutionary groups serves to develop the women within them as feminists in post-revolutionary societies.

54. Enloe, *Does Khaki Become You*, 160–172.

55. Nash, *Defying*, 110.

56. Fraser, *Blood of Spain*, 287 and Coleman, "Women in the Spanish Civil War," 50.

ONE

Women in Spain, 1800–1936

In order to gain a full understanding of the significance of the *miliciana* phenomenon, it is first necessary to appreciate the political, social and economic position of women in Spanish society prior to the outbreak of the civil war in July 1936. For this reason, this chapter paints the picture of both the period from 1800 to 1931, during which women were severely oppressed by both the church and state, and of the years during the Second Republic from 1931 to 1936, when advances in women's rights began to be made. Women's roles in various social and political movements during both these periods will also be examined.

The reversion to more traditional gender roles during the war reflected the persistence of conservative thinking on gender issues even within progressive political organizations. In some ways, the continuance of traditional ideas within left-wing groups contributed more to the failure to achieve sexual equality than did the persistence of those ideas in other sectors, since it was these progressive forces that had previously set the agenda for the advancing of women's rights. For this reason, it is important to understand the policies and practices on gender issues prior to the war of each of the significant left-wing political groups: communist, anarchist, dissident Marxist and socialist.

The Spanish Civil War, and the social revolution that accompanied it, provided an opportunity for women to step outside their traditional gender roles and create new ones. This change in gender roles took place largely among the women and men of left-wing Republican and revolutionary groups. It was also in this setting that women took on military roles in the war, both in a front-line and rearguard capacity. These left-wing groups appeared to offer women the chance to achieve tangible advances in their rights and position in society, as women were given the opportunity to take up roles and leadership positions in the public sphere that had previously been denied to them; it was even seen as acceptable for women to join directly in the fighting. However, these initial hopes of achieving equality were dashed, as Spanish society in the Republican zone reverted to traditional gender roles within eight months after the war had begun. The Spanish Civil War led to new and exciting opportunities opening up for women, then saw severe limitations placed on women as progressive ideology succumbed to traditional customs and discourse. In order to depict this contradictory process, in which rapid advance was succeeded by steady retreat, the present chapter will examine the course of the social revolution in relation to gender issues.

The aim of this chapter is not to provide a detailed examination of each of the topics raised here, and it does not bring to light any new evidence. The subjects involved have been thoroughly examined and discussed in many other historical works. Rather, the aim is to introduce the relevant issues in order to provide a historical and political context for the book. This chapter will provide information on the major themes and issues that are integral to gaining a full understanding of the experience of the militia women during the civil war. Providing this context will also demonstrate how the subject of women in combat during the Spanish Civil War fits into a larger discussion on the issue of gender relations within the Spanish Second Republic, Spanish history more generally and the wider issue of women in war and revolution globally. Establishing these links will allow the book to draw broader conclusions from the experiences of the *milicianas*.

WOMEN IN SPANISH SOCIETY, 1800 – 1931

In the nineteenth and early twentieth centuries, Spanish women were severely oppressed, and Catholicism ensured their subjugation. The deeply ingrained sexism in Spanish society ensured that women possessed no independence, and instead were controlled by their fathers, husbands and priests. This can be seen clearly through an examination of the political, social and economic position of women in Spanish society from 1800 to 1931.

Prior to the formation of the Second Republic in 1931, Spanish women were not the legal equals of men. Unmarried women were in a slightly better legal position than were married women, since once they reached the age of 23, they possessed some legal rights, such as the right to sign contracts and conduct business.[1] However, unmarried women still did not possess full legal rights. Some of the rights denied to all women included voting or being elected to any public office, or being employed as a civil servant.[2] Women lost what few legal rights they had on their wedding day. A married woman could not conduct business, own or manage property, change her place of residence, or accept an inheritance without the approval and involvement of her husband. Until 1931, it was illegal for wives to disobey their husbands. Any form of adultery committed by women was illegal; however, men's adulterous actions were not against the law unless they also caused a "public scandal." Divorce was illegal.[3]

Beyond the legal constraints for women, social conditioning (largely controlled by religious ideology) played a crucial role in ensuring the oppression of women. Catholic Spain presented young girls with strict gender roles to which they learned to adhere as they grew older. The only acceptable path for women was to marry, raise children and aspire to be a good wife and mother.[4] The domestic sphere was the only possible realm in which middle- and upper-class women were allowed to exist, and José Alvarez Junco relates that family life was characterized by "traditional patriarchal tyranny, often expressed through violence toward women."[5] Some women from the lower classes did enter the public sphere, albeit in a limited role, as unskilled laborers.

Given these severely restricted roles for women, the provision of education was seen as unnecessary. In the nineteenth century, the vast majority of Spanish women received no formal education. In the year 1900, most women had still not attended even primary school, and the rate of female illiteracy was as high as 90 percent.[6] Consequently, the numbers of women in secondary and tertiary education were close to nil. Junco, in his detailed study of the history of education and gender equality, mentions only one woman, María Goyri, who earned a university degree in the 1890s.[7] When there were calls for improved educational opportunities for women, they came in the context of the aim of improving women's domestic roles. Sofía Tartilán's *Páginas para la Educación Popular* argued that better education for women was necessary to improve their ability to educate their children and please their husbands.[8] Educational opportunities for women did improve in the early twentieth century. By 1930, the female illiteracy rate had fallen to 38 percent, and the number of boys and girls in primary education by this time was almost equal.[9] Nonetheless, the gender disparity in higher education continued. In 1928, women made up only 4.2 percent of university students.[10]

Women of the middle and upper classes thus exclusively fulfilled the role of wife, mother and guardian of the home. Meanwhile, despite the fact that women from the lower class were also considered fit only to be housewives, for economic reasons some were forced to take jobs where they worked for the lowest pay, under the worst conditions. The number of women in this situation began to decline toward the end of the nineteenth century. In 1877, 1.5 million women, or 17 percent of the total female population, were in employment. By 1930, this number had decreased to 1.1 million, or 9 percent of women.[11] Younger women were more likely to work than older, married women were.[12]

During the 1800s, the majority of women worked in agriculture, mainly on family farms. Many of these women, particularly in Galicia, were unpaid workers. In the south of Spain, women employed in agricultural tasks were more likely to be wage laborers, but their wages were a half to two-thirds lower than those of their male counterparts.[13] At the opening of the twentieth century, 60 percent of working women were from landless peasant families and were employed in agricultural tasks.[14] By the 1930s, industrialization had brought a change to the work patterns of many in Spain, and fewer women now worked in agriculture than in either industry or the service sector.[15]

Women were generally barred from employment in the professions, with the small exceptions of nursing and teaching (where they were limited to the primary education of girls).[16] As a result of the population shift from rural to urban areas, work was now available for poor women as servants in wealthy homes, and many women moved into domestic service.[17] Most women employed in the service sector were domestic servants, though women also worked as wet nurses and prostitutes. Prostitution was not made illegal until 1935; until then it was regulated by local governments.[18]

Large numbers of women also began to enter industry, where they were concentrated in the area of manufacturing, largely in textiles and tobacco factories. A third of all women working in industry worked in textile factories, where they accounted for 52 percent of workers and were paid half the male wage.[19] In 1930, 90,000 women were working in sweatshops, also known as the "sweated trades," which manufactured many different products such as paper and leather goods, children's products, weapons, musical instruments and clothing.[20] The working conditions in all areas of industry were abhorrent. Women regularly fell ill because of unsafe working conditions and malnourishment. Employers provided no compensation for pregnancy or childbirth, and women workers did not receive any support from trade unions. When minimal improvements to wages and working conditions were made, they were consistently more beneficial to men than to women. For example, over the years between 1919 and 1922 the male wage rose 107.1 percent while the female wage increased by only 67.9 percent. During the same period, prices rose by 93 percent.[21]

One area in which women protested against their horrendous working conditions was the tobacco industry. Throughout their history, the tobacco factories had employed women workers almost exclusively. The Seville tobacco factory in the 1840s employed 4,542 workers, of whom 4,046 were women. In 1925, the situation was much the same. A total of 14,163 women worked in the Tabacalera tobaccos factories, as opposed to only 120 men. Significantly, the majority of women employed in the tobacco industry remained in that industry throughout their lives. A high level of solidarity existed among these workers, and contributed to the level of industrial action, both organized and spontaneous.[22]

In the nineteenth century, women's protests in tobacco factories most often took the form of riots. For example, in Madrid in 1830, 3,000 women rioted for five days against a decrease in wages and working conditions in their factory. By the turn of the century, women's protests against their working conditions had gained in sophistication. In 1910, female tobacco workers began to organize themselves into unions, and a National Federation was created in 1918. One of the most significant outcomes of this unionization was an increase in wages, which doubled between the years of 1914 and 1920, and then tripled by 1930.[23]

Women's involvement in political movements was not limited to these relatively small-scale protests about their employment conditions. Earlier in the nineteenth century, women also played an important role in the resistance to Napoleon during the Spanish War of Independence from 1808 to 1814.[24] This period saw the rise of several iconic "women warriors," such as Agustina de Aragón, also known as "*La Artillera*." Aragón became famous for lighting a cannon at a critical moment during the siege of Saragossa. All of the troops protecting the position had been killed, and the story goes that Aragón took a match from the hand of a dead soldier, and lit the cannon, which pushed the French troops back.[25]

There are some examples of war heroines from this period who became legendary for participating in combat, though in reality they played a supportive role in the conflict, or in some cases no role at all. Such is the case for Manuela Malasaña, who is famous for dying on the battlefield during the *Dos de Mayo* in 1808. The legend says that she was killed while carrying cartridges to the men who were fighting in Monteleón.[26] In fact, Malasaña played no part in the resistance and merely happened to live near the artillery park where the fighting was taking place. On her way home, she was shot and killed by French troops who believed her embroidery shears to be a weapon.[27]

During the latter half of the nineteenth century and in the early twentieth century, the most significant political movements were the Republican and labor movements, from which women were noticeably absent, largely because of their position in society, which relegated them mainly to the private sphere. Consequently, it is often assumed that Spanish women around this time were apolitical.[28] However, working-class women were highly active in the area of consumer politics in Spain, particular during the years from 1875 to 1914.[29] As a result of their domestic responsibilities, one of the major concerns of women was procuring the goods and services necessary for the survival and well-being of their families. Women's political activity centered on and dominated consumer protests. Consumer activists staged protests and riots over high prices, food shortages, rents and shortages of goods and services, with the aim of influencing government policy and practice.[30] Despite the fact that the consumer politics movement was not highly organized, it nonetheless represented a significant form of collective, grassroots political action.

WOMEN AND THE SECOND REPUBLIC, 1931 – 1936

The progressive democratic Republic that was proclaimed on 14 April 1931 aimed to modernize Spain in every way: politically, economically, socially and culturally. In order to do this, the *Cortes* (Spanish parliament) extended the power of the state. The Republican government began to make changes through decrees on wages, rents and education from April to June, through a new Constitution in December 1931, and then through a series of legislative reforms. The aim was to create solid support for the new government and to foster Republicanism.[31] The results, however, were often the opposite. The broadening of state powers estranged much of the working class. Economic difficulties also limited the ability of the Republic to improve conditions for the workers, further restricting its capacity to garner support. Instead, anarchism became progressively more popular among the working class. Along with the economic crisis and the regrouping of forces on the right, this served to undermine the progressive Republic.[32] Nevertheless, the majority of the advances made for women to be discussed here occurred during these first two years of the Republic.

The situation for women began to improve from 1931, when significant advances in women's rights took place in a short period. Many legal reforms pertaining to the status of women were made, and at least under the law, women achieved equality with men. The first and perhaps most significant of the changes was declared on 1 October 1931, when Article 36 of the Republic's new constitution gave women over 23 years of age the right to vote and stand for parliament on equal terms with men.[33]

Clara Campoamor Rodríguez, Victoria Kent Siano and Margarita Nelken y Mansbergen were elected as deputies to the *Cortes* in the first Republican elections in June 1931, despite the fact that women at that point had not yet gained the vote.[34] It is interesting to note that two of these women, Nelken and Kent, argued against granting the right to vote to women, claiming that women were traditionally conservative, and that consequently their vote would weaken the Republic. Only Campoamor staunchly defended the right of women to vote.[35] In February 1936, three more women were elected to the Republican government: Matilde de la Torre, Dolores Ibárruri and Federica Montseny, who was to serve as the Minister of Health and Public Assistance from September 1936 to May 1937.[36]

Constitutional and legislative reform also ensured that all women over the age of 23 could now sign contracts, own and manage property, and act as witnesses and guardians. Women also gained legal protection against being dismissed from employment as a result of marriage.[37] The formal emancipation of women was not achieved because of a mass grassroots movement for women's rights. Rather, it came as a series of "top down" reforms intended to achieve Republican principles.[38] Another significant change for women that occurred under the Second Republic was the decriminalization of divorce in March 1932, reversing the rigid laws established by the Civil Code of 1888. [39] The reforms granted men and women equal right to seek divorce, and a civil marriage law was passed, making it possible for the first time for legal marriages to take place outside the Church.[40] Homosexuality and birth control were also decriminalized at the same time.[41]

In the general elections on 19 November 1933, the Republican center-left was defeated. The rightist bloc came to power, and Alejandro Lerroux García became Prime Minister. This conservative Republican government remained in power until 1936, during which time it began to reverse the progressive reforms made in the early years of the Republic.[42] Throughout the first year of Lerroux García's government, political pressures were rising, and the discontent of the working class increased. These tensions culminated in the October Rebellion of 1934. This revolt was precipitated by the ministers of the CEDA, who entered the *Cortes* and were given the three most significant portfolios: Agriculture, Labor and Justice. A general strike took place across Spain, but it was in Asturias that the situation became the most extreme.[43]

The October Rebellion of 1934 saw a mass political uprising that ended in the deaths of over 1,000 people and the imprisonment of 30,000 others.[44] It was an armed revolt against the Republican government in which left-wing organizations and working-class groups joined to form the *Alianza Obrera* (Workers' Alliance). The *Alianza Obrera* was successful in forming a revolutionary commune in Asturias, but was ultimately defeated.[45] Thousands of women participated in this uprising. Most of these women did not take up arms, but there were some notable exceptions. Aida Lafuente,[46] who fought and died in the revolt of October 1934, is one of the best known. Lafuente grew up in Oviedo, the capital of Asturias, the city that saw the most bitter clashes between the revolutionaries and the Regular Army during the insurrection. It was here that Lafuente took part in the fighting. She died in combat at the church of *San Pedro de los Arcos*, which stood on top of Mount Naranco.[47]

Brian Bunk has conducted extensive research into Lafuente, her involvement in the October Rebellion and her legacy in Spain.[48] He argues that propaganda that aimed to commemorate Lafuente actually transformed her "from an authentic woman warrior into a symbol of purity and motherhood. Despite her radical actions in both a political and gendered sense, memories of Lafuente served ultimately to reinforce traditional notions of proper gender behavior."[49] This was largely as a result of social conditioning and discourse surrounding women's roles at the time, which most certainly did not include a role for women in combat.

As will become evident throughout this book, the experiences of the few women who armed themselves during the October Rebellion and of the *milicianas* of the Spanish Civil War were vastly different. On the simplest level, the most crucial differences were that the numbers of women involved in combat during the October Rebellion were much smaller; the women were not specifically recruited or encouraged to take up arms; and they did so as individuals rather than alongside other women.

The involvement of women in the October Rebellion is significant because it demonstrates that while the civil war was not the first time Spanish women had participated in combat, it was the first time they had done so in an organized and collective manner, and on such a large scale. It also points to a high level of political involvement and dedication on the part of a number of women who, having participated in the October Rebellion (whether in a combat or non-combat role), went on to become militiawomen in the Spanish Civil War. This clearly demonstrates the political motivations behind their choice to bear arms during the conflict, as will be discussed further in chapter 3.

Despite the fact that the October Rebellion was defeated, it led to a sustained and organized mobilization developing from the demand for the release of political prisoners. This campaign involved an unprecedented level of involvement by women in left-wing politics. Some women were necessarily involved as they were political prisoners themselves, but thousands of others became involved in the campaign because of the imprisonment of their male relatives. In part, it was this political and social movement that led to the formation of the Popular Front, which won the general election on 16 February 1936, and formed the Republican government that went on to fight the war.[50]

POLITICAL GROUPS AND GENDER ISSUES

Helen Graham and Jo Labanyi have described the 1930s in Spain as "a period of increasing polarization."[51] However, they go on to note that many cultural issues did not correspond to political or class divisions. In particular, political and class allegiances did not determine positions on issues such as gender, religion or regional autonomy:

> There were liberal Catholics, at least to start with; bourgeois and working-class Catalan nationalists; clerical-conservative Basque nationalists who opposed Franco's "Crusade"; and the right mobilized women to protest against the Republic, while anarchist attempts to liberate women did not always question traditional definitions of femininity, and not all socialists supported giving the vote to women.[52]

Even within the left-wing political groups of the Popular Front, there were deep divisions on many questions, gender being one of the clearest examples. For this reason, it is necessary to examine the policy and practice of each of the left-wing groups, whether parliamentarian or anarchist, on the issue of women's rights and liberation. Because this book is concerned only with the communist, anarchist, dissident Marxist and socialist political tendencies (since these were the only political groups with a direct relationship to the militiawomen), it is only these groups that will be examined here.

Women in Spain prior to 1931 had developed a tradition of spontaneous political activity, which as Graham explains, "both expressed and tried to solve specific economic grievances and needs at times of acute social turmoil."[53] These protests, which included consumer riots, were generally ignored, both by the essentially male leadership of left-wing groups at the time and later by historians.[54] While the consumer riots in some ways represented an acceptance of traditionally accepted gender roles, they also reflected women's increasing political awareness and involvement in social movements. Further, women did not have a great deal of choice other than to participate in what male political leaders classified as "chaotic" and "non-political" action,[55] since they were not welcomed into organized political groups, even those that claimed to have a policy of gender equity. One proof that the needs of women were not addressed by left-wing political groups is the fact that trade unions, such as the UGT and the CNT did not agitate for improvements in such rights of women as equal pay, maternity leave and the provision of child-care.[56]

In general, the PCE did not encourage or support involvement in political activity by women within its ranks. Ibárruri recalled the condescension with which she was treated early in her career, despite the fact that she was a highly active and militant member of the party:

> The secretary of the Miners' Union, a well known Socialist [read communist], asked me one day. . . how much I knew about socialism; he asked me what works I had read. I told him, and also mentioned that I was studying *Capital*; he looked at me pityingly and asked, not without sarcasm: And have you understood any of it . . . How are you going to understand these concepts if I, who have studied them for ten years, don't understand them too well?[57]

Though her later career does make Ibárruri an extraordinary case, there is no reason why her earlier treatment in the PCE, before she rose through the ranks, cannot be taken as a general example for the treatment of female communists. It appears that while the Marxist ideology of the PCE espoused the principle of equality between men and women, this did not translate into equal treatment of women by the membership in practice.

The small amount of work that the PCE carried out during the civil war in order to improve women's rights was undertaken exclusively by women's groups (rather than the party as a whole), and was largely considered a side issue. The formation of women's groups can be seen as an attempt to win the support of women who were visibly politically active, without reforming the PCE itself or developing women's equality as a key political platform. This pattern is also evident in other political tendencies, in particular the anarchists and the resultant formation of *Mujeres Libres* (Free Women), as will be discussed shortly.

One such women's group was the AMA, founded in 1933 and commonly known as *Mujeres Antifascistas*. The formation of this group was a crucial part of a recruitment drive by the PCE, which aimed at increasing its small membership, since the AMA was popular among many middle-class women. However, the AMA followed the pattern of aiming for "top down" reform that was general for the Republican government. In early 1936, the main goal of the AMA was to influence the Popular Front government in making reforms concerning wage equality, the provision of childcare, employment opportunities for women and female representation on local councils.[58]

Given the progressive ideology promoted by the anarchists of both the FAI and CNT, it would appear that the anarchists were dedicated to ameliorating the position of women in Spain. However, there were many tensions among the anarchists over the issue of women's emancipation. Though committed in general to the creation of a classless and egalitarian society, anarchists displayed a wide variety of attitudes toward women's oppression. Anarchists did not agree on the source of women's subordination, which in turn led to varying opinions on the best way to overcome it.[59] Further, it is evident that in any case the issue of women's liberation was given little attention by most anarchists.

Although the principle of equality between the sexes had been formally recognized by the anarchists, for example at the 1918 Congress of the CNT,[60] in practice many male anarchists continued to exercise patriarchal rule over women both in public and in private.[61] Martha A. Ackelsberg,[62] an expert in the field of anarchism and women's liberation, relates that "most anarchists refused to recognize the specificity of women's subordination, and few men were willing to give up the power over women they had enjoyed for so long."[63] In 1935, the National Secretary of the CNT explained his view, clearly shared by the majority of his male comrades, that "we know it is more pleasant to give orders than to obey. . . . Between the woman and the man the same thing occurs. The male feels more satisfied having a servant to make his food, wash his clothes. . . . That is reality. And, in the face of that, to ask the men cede [their privileges] is to dream."[64]

As a result, many female anarchists were unhappy with the lack of attention paid to the issue of women's rights. These activists complained that women were often excluded or discouraged from playing an active political role. These tensions within the anarchist movement led to the creation of *Mujeres Libres*, a women's organization that focused specifically on the emancipation of women. As a result of the difficulties faced by women in attempting to overcome the "male-dominated agendas" of anarchist groups, female activists saw autonomous organization as the only possible method to achieve their goals.[65] *Mujeres Libres* was founded by Lucia Sánchez Saornil, Mercedes Comaposada and Amparo Poch y Gascón in the spring of 1936.[66] In a brochure entitled "Aims," *Mujeres Libres* explained that its first objective was "to emancipate women from the triple enslavement that they have endured and continue to endure: enslavement to ignorance, enslavement as women, and enslavement as workers."[67] Ackelsberg argues that the second aim was "to confront the dominance of men within the anarchist movement itself."[68]

While *Mujeres Libres* enjoyed a great deal of success, it also met with many obstacles. Montseny, an exceptional case as a prominent female anarchist leader in the FAI, described the lack of support that *Mujeres Libres* received from the rest of the anarchist movement:

> It is sad that this work has to be carried out by a group of female comrades fighting tooth and nail against all odds and in the midst of all sorts of economic, even moral, difficulties—because they don't feel that they are supported by the unions and the movement.[69]

The anarchist tendency might appear quite backwards by today's standards of feminism, and many criticisms can be made of both the FAI and CNT in terms of their attitudes toward women. Nonetheless, it is significant that in Spain at this time the anarchists were among the most advanced current in terms of their thinking on women's liberation, and that it was from within the anarchist rank and file that the most militant type of feminism[70] developed, in the form of *Mujeres Libres*. It is understandable that the majority of the *milicianas* came from anarchist backgrounds, as will be discussed in chapters 3 and 4.

Since its foundation in 1879, the PSOE was primarily concerned with the labor movement, and showed little to no interest in gender issues. Only a very small minority of members of the PSOE or the UGT[71] was female, and the tendency was male-dominated.[72] Women's involvement in socialism increased during the 1920s and 1930s; however, in 1932 women still accounted for only 4 percent of UGT members.[73] Mary Nash explains that, "Spanish socialism was a hostile environment to women and incapable of attracting them to the movement," and "Spanish women did not identify with the official politics of socialism."[74]

Socialist women's organizations were not formed in the same way or for the same purposes as were those in communist or anarchist circles. Instead of creating groups to deal with gender issues and carry out work among women because the central organization did not, socialist women's organizations functioned merely as an auxiliary to the PSOE. Unlike *Mujeres Libres*, which was created as a result of the belief that it was crucial to agitate for women's emancipation, groups like the Feminist Socialist Groups and Group of Feminist Socialists of Madrid were not autonomous. These groups were expected to carry out an ancillary role, and in general socialist feminists accepted this.[75] Thus, the socialists' prescribed role for women was clearly to be supportive, passive and ancillary, and this explains why so few militiawomen came from a socialist background.

The POUM placed more emphasis than other left-wing groups on the question of women's liberation, and saw the involvement of women in politics as a prerequisite for this.[76] As a relatively small organization, however, its capacity to carry out work in many areas was limited. The Female Secretariat, organized by Louise Gómez,[77] was the first women's organization set up by the POUM, though it was not established until during the civil war.

From an examination of the policies and practices of each of the left-wing political groups, it is understandable why the phrase "men are communist, socialist or anarchist from the waist up" was so popular among women throughout the 1930s.[78] It appears that while most progressive and revolutionary groups were theoretically committed to the principles of sexual equality, in practice the attitudes of the male membership toward both their female comrades and women in general demonstrated clearly that for many, this commitment was merely superficial. This fact is important for a study of the *miliciana* phenomenon, as it had an impact on the fate of the militiawomen. These attitudes underwent many changes because of the civil war, the social revolution, and women's participation in combat, as will be demonstrated throughout the book, but it is clear that ultimately traditional and conservative ideas prevailed.

NOTES

1. Adrian Shubert, *A Social History of Modern Spain*, Unwin Hyman, London, 1990, 32.

2. Geraldine Scanlon, *La Polémica Feminista en la España Contemporánea (1864–1975)*, Siglo Veintiuno Editores, Madrid, 1976, 123.

3. Shubert, *Social History*, 32–33.

4. Shubert, *Social History*, 33.

5. José Alvarez Junco, "Rural and Urban Popular Cultures," in Helen Graham, and Jo Labanyi (eds.), *Spanish Cultural Studies: An introduction*, Oxford University Press, Oxford, 1995, 86.

6. Junco, "Education and the Limits of Liberalism," in Graham and Labanyi, *Spanish Cultural Studies*, 47.

7. G. Menéndez Pidal, *La España del Siglo XIX Vista por sus Contemporáneos*, Centro de Estudios Constitucionales Madrid, 1989, 292, cited in Junco, "Education and Limits," 47.

8. Shubert, *Social History*, 36.

9. Shubert, *Social History*, 37.

10. Shubert, *Social History*, 37.

11. Shubert, *Social History*, 38.

12. In 1930, 20 percent of women between the ages of 16 and 20 were working, whereas that figure dropped to 17 percent from women aged between 21 and 25, 12 percent for those between 26 and 30, and 10 percent for women aged between 31 and 60. Shubert, *Social History*, 38.

13. Shubert, *Social History*, 38.

14. Shirley Mangini, *Memories of Resistance: Women's voices from the Spanish Civil War*, Yale University Press, New Haven, 1995, 4.

15. Shubert, *Social History*, 38.

16. Shubert, *Social History*, 41.

17. In 1877, there were 313,000 women working as domestic servants, and this number rose to 338,000 in 1930. Shubert, *Social History*, 40.

18. Shubert, *Social History*, 42.

19. Shubert, *Social History*, 39.

20. Shubert, *Social History*, 39.

21. S.G. Payne, *The Spanish Revolution*, Weidenfeld & Nicolson, London, 1970, 39.

22. Shubert, *Social History*, 40.

23. Shubert, *Social History*, 40.

24. See John Lawrence Tone, "Spanish Women in the Resistance to Napoleon, 1808–1814," in Victoria Lorée Enders and Pamela Beth Radcliff (eds.), *Constructing Spanish Womanhood: Female identity in modern Spain*, State University of New York Press, Albany, 1999, 259–282.

25. Tone, "Spanish Women," 262.

26. Tone, "Spanish Women," 260.

27. Tone, "Spanish Women," 261.

28. Junco and Shubert, *Spanish History Since 1808*, Arnold, London, 2000, 151.

29. Junco and Shubert, *Spanish History*, 151.

30. Junco and Shubert, *Spanish History*, 152.

31. Graham, "Women and Social Change," in Graham and Labanyi, *Spanish Cultural Studies*, 100.

32. Graham, "Women and Social Change," 100.

33. Judith Keene, "Into the Clear Air of the Plaza: Spanish women achieve the vote in 1931," in Enders and Radcliff, *Constructing Spanish Womanhood*, 325.

34. Keene, "Clear Air," 332.

35. Keene, "Clear Air," 335–341.

36. Frances Lannon, "Women and Images of Women in the Spanish Civil War," *Transactions of the Royal Historical Society*, Sixth Series, vol. 1, 1991, 215.

37. Graham, "Women and Social Change," 101.

38. Graham, "Women and Social Change," 101–102. In her work, Graham has established the reasons for the lack of such a grass-roots movement, and the obstacles faced by women who did attempt to enter the political sphere, for example, by joining a union such as the CNT or UGT.

39. Richard Cleminson and Efigenio Amezúa, "Spain: The political and social context of sex reform in the late nineteenth and early twentieth centuries," in Franz X. Eder, Lesley A. Hall and Gert Hekman (eds.), *Sexual Cultures in Europe: National histories*, Manchester University Press, Manchester, 1999, 187.

40. Lannon, "Women and Images," 213–215.

41. Cleminson and Amezúa, "Spain," 187.

42. Graham, "Women and Social Change," 108.

43. Graham, "Women and Social Change," 108.

44. Graham, "Women and Social Change," 108.

45. Brian D. Bunk "Your Comrades Will Not Forget," *History and Memory*, vol. 14, no. 1, Autumn 2002, 66.

46. Aida's surname is variously recorded as: Lafuente, de Lafuente or de la Fuente. This book will use the surname Lafuente, since this is the name most often used in Spanish-language primary sources.

47. Bunk, "Revolutionary Warrior and Gendered Icon: Aida Lafuente and the Spanish Revolution of 1934," *Journal of Women's History*, vol. 15, no. 2, Summer 2003, 100.

48. See for example Bunk, "Revolutionary Warrior," 99–105 and "Your Comrades," 65–94.

49. Bunk, "Revolutionary Warrior," 99.

50. Graham, "Women and Social Change," 108.

51. Graham and Labanyi, "Editors' Introduction," in Graham and Labanyi, *Spanish Cultural Studies*, 95.

52. Graham and Labanyi, "Editors' Introduction," in Graham and Labanyi, *Spanish Cultural Studies*, 95.

53. Graham, "Women and Social Change," 102.

54. Junco and Shubert argue that "it is common to assume that since most women did not join the ranks of unions or political parties they were largely apolitical. Likewise, since women were identified with the private sphere of home and family, their absence from the nineteenth century public sphere has often been taken for granted. Thus, women, especially from the working classes, are often written out of the narrative of modern politics." Junco and Shubert, *Spanish History*, 152.

55. Graham, "Women and Social Change," 102.

56. Graham, "Women and Social Change," 102.

57. Dolores Ibárruri, *They Shall Not Pass*, International Publishers, New York, 1966, 62–63, cited in Shubert, *Social History*, 141–142.

58. Graham, "Women and Social Change," 108–109.

59. Martha A. Ackelsberg, "Separate and Equal? Mujeres Libres and Anarchist Strategy for Women's Emancipation," *Feminist Studies*, vol. 11, no. 1, Spring 1985, 66.

60. Robert W. Kern, *Red Years/Black Years: A political history of Spanish anarchism, 1911–1937*, Institute for the Study of Human Issues, Philadelphia, 1978, 31.

61. Cleminson, "Beyond Tradition and 'Modernity': The cultural and sexual politics of Spanish anarchism," in Graham and Labanyi, *Spanish Cultural Studies*, 122.

62. See Ackelsberg, "Anarchist Revolution and Women's Liberation," *Society*, vol. 25, no 2, January–February 1988, 29–38, "Separate and Equal?" 63–85, and *Free Women of Spain: Anarchism and the struggle for the emancipation of women*, Indiana University Press, Bloomington, 1991.

63. Ackelsberg, "Separate and Equal?" 66.

64. Mariano R. Vazquez, "Avance: Por la elevación de la mujer," *Solidaridad Obrera*, October 1935, 4, cited in Ackelsberg, "Separate and Equal?" 66.

65. Graham, "Women and Social Change," 103.

66. Ángel Luis Rubio Moraga, "El Papel de la Mujer en la Guerra a Través de los Carteles Republicanos," *Cuadernos Republicanos*, no. 36, October 1998, 105.

67. Mary Nash (ed.), *Femmes Libres = Mujeres Libres: Espagne 1936–1939*, Pensée Sauvage, Claix, 1977, 68.

68. Ackelsberg, "Separate and Equal?" 64.

69. Cited in Nash, *Mujer y Movimiento Obrero en España*, D. L. Fontamara, Barcelona, 1983, 105.

70. Many female anarchists, particularly those of *Mujeres Libres*, did not identify with the term "feminist". In order to avoid debate over definitions, this book takes "feminism" to mean simply any ideology or movement that has at its core the aim of achieving equality between women and men. It is recognized however that the feminist movement is varied and encompasses many different ideologies and strands. Where significant, these have been identified and noted.

71. When it was founded in 1888, the UGT was dominated by the socialists. However, the communist influence over the trade union greatly increased from the beginning of the Spanish Civil War. As a result, most primary sources and contemporary historians refer to the UGT as a communist trade union for the period 1936–1939. Thus, this book refers to the UGT as a communist trade union.

72. Mary Nash, "Ideals of Redemption: Socialism and women on the left in Spain," in Helmut Gruber and Pamela Graves (eds.), *Women and Socialism, Socialism and Women: Europe between the two World Wars*, Berghahn Books, New York, 1998, 349.

73. Nash, "Ideals of Redemption," 349.

74. Nash, "Ideals of Redemption," 350.

75. Nash, "Ideals of Redemption," 351.

76. Mary Low and Juan Breà, *Red Spanish Notebook: The first six months of the revolution and the civil war*, Purnell and Sons, London, 1937, 185.

77. Keene, "No More Than Brothers and Sisters: Women in combat in the Spanish Civil War," in Peter Monteath and Fredric S. Zuckerman (eds.), *Modern Europe: Histories and identities*, Australian Humanities Press, Unley, 1998, 128.

78. Mary Nash, *Defying Male Civilisation: Women in the Spanish Civil War*, Arden Press, Denver, 1995, 116.

TWO

Women and the Social Revolution in the Republican Zone

THE OUTBREAK OF WAR AND SOCIAL REVOLUTION

The outbreak of the Spanish Civil War in July 1936 was the culmination of many years of political unrest in Spain.[1] In February 1936, a progressive Popular Front government was elected and brought the promise of sweeping reforms. Later that same month, planning began for a military overthrow of the newly elected government. The instigation for the *pronunciamiento* came from the *Unión Militar Española* (Military Union of Spain, UME).[2] The coordinated military rebellion began in Morocco on 17 July and in Spain the following day. A quick victory was anticipated. However, the instigators of the *coup d'état* did not expect the spontaneous uprising of the Spanish people to protect the Republican government. After four days, the rebels controlled only roughly a third of Spain,[3] and had failed to capture key areas, such as Madrid and Barcelona. As the Republican government maintained control over much of the navy, the Nationalists found themselves unable to transport the Army of Africa, considered their best troops, from Morocco to mainland Spain. The rebellion might have ended there, but Adolf Hitler responded to appeals from the rebel generals by sending twenty Junker Ju-52 planes to transport Franco's troops across the Straits of Gibraltar.[4] After this success, the rebellion was able to continue. Hitler later commented that "Franco ought to erect a monument to the glory of the Junkers 52. It is this aircraft that the Spanish revolution has to thank for its victory."[5]

The unexpected result of the military rebellion and of the popular uprising against it was that Spain was divided roughly in two, and a drawn-out civil war began. Both the Republican and the Nationalist camps appealed to foreign governments for assistance, with varying degrees of success. Germany and Italy provided substantial assistance to the Nationalists in the form of weapons, military equipment and troops. The Republican government, meanwhile, did not receive the aid it had been expecting from professedly democratic countries such as Britain, France and the United States. Instead, these countries signed the controversial Non-Intervention Pact. The only significant help the Republicans received was from the governments of the Soviet Union and Mexico, though approximately 42,000 volunteers from many countries traveled to Spain to fight for the Republican cause.[6] As a result of this foreign assistance, the extraordinarily large number of international volunteers, and the enormous ideological implications of the battle being fought in Spain, what normally would have been a domestic affair took on a dramatic international character.

Antony Beevor has described the Spanish Civil War as a war fought between the right and the left, centralism and regionalism, and authoritarianism and libertarianism.[7] It is significant that neither the Republican nor the Nationalist camp was homogenous, but made up of a diverse mix of political groupings whose aims did not always coincide.

Beginning at the same time as the civil war, a profound social revolution took place in what became the Republican zone of Spain.[8] The workers and peasants who had been oppressed by the church and their employers for so long rose up and overturned what they saw as an inherently unjust economic and social system. The people sought to obliterate every sign of wealth, privilege and hierarchy from society. Churches were burned or seized to be used for other purposes. Foreign observers noted that even people's attire changed as a reflection of the social revolution. In Madrid and Barcelona in particular it was observed that people no longer wore business shirts, hats, ties, or other forms of dress that were identified as bourgeois.[9] Workers seized control of their factories and began to run them collectively. Workers' control was particularly important to the social revolution in Catalonia, where approximately 70 percent of industry had been successfully collectivized by October 1936.[10] In Barcelona, all public utilities, such as electricity, gas, water and public transport, were collectivized, and wages rose approximately 10 percent.[11] This process also occurred in other areas of the Republican zone, but it was somewhat less successful. In Valencia 50 percent of industry was collectivized, whereas in Madrid only 30 percent of industry came under workers' control.[12]

The revolution that took place in the countryside of Republican Spain developed along similar collectivist lines, though the results differed from village to village. In almost all areas, property records were destroyed and peasants were no longer required to pay rent, in effect seizing possession of the land. In some areas such as New Castile, La Mancha and Aragon, village land was entirely collectivized, owned and managed equally.[13] In other areas, only partial collectivization took place, as land that had been seized from absent owners was collectivized, while land that belonged to peasants of the village remained in their possession. In yet other areas, all land was seized and distributed equally among peasants, who then managed their own plots of land. In some places, land relations remained unchanged.[14] Concurrent with this process of collectivization, the political leadership of rural villages changed. Prior to the civil war municipal governments had been in charge, but during the social revolution this system was replaced by village committees, which elected one representative for each political party in the Popular Front.[15] These committees oversaw all agricultural economic activity, such as the distribution of wages and the selling of harvests.

In general, it was the principles of anarchism and anarcho-syndicalism that drove the revolution. This political theory enjoyed overwhelming popular support in the Republican zone, and in particular in Catalonia. The FAI and the CNT both held philosophies that called for the creation of a society that was organized along egalitarian principles, and in which workers and peasants ran industry and agriculture through autonomous and democratic collectives. The *miliciana* phenomenon is closely related to the course of the social revolution.

PROGRESSIVE GAINS

Certainly, the civil war saw one of the most significant political mobilizations of women in Spanish history. Large-scale modern wars have regularly brought with them a widening of the social roles perceived to be acceptable for women. During times of total war, the work that women normally perform of caring for their families and providing food and shelter becomes a matter of public interest. Women move into the public sphere and begin to perform this work for the entire community, through organizing communal kitchens, orphanages and makeshift hospitals. In addition, women enter the paid workforce in massive numbers. As discussed in the introduction, all across Europe during WWI and WWII, women entered the industrial workforce in numbers that had previously been inconceivable, as male soldiers went to fight and die on the front lines of combat.[16]

The Spanish Civil War brought this same widening of roles, with women entering the public sphere and taking on responsibilities that had previous been out of their reach. However, the Spanish Civil War was not simply a military conflict, but was accompanied by a wide-reaching social revolution. It was this social revolution in the Republican zone and the advances in the position of women that came with it that allowed significant numbers of women to play a military role in the war, something that previously would not only have been considered unacceptable, but was in fact inconceivable.

Coupled with women's involvement in the war effort, the social revolution that followed on from the advances achieved during the Second Republic made a marked contribution toward improving the status of women in the Republican zone. The communists, anarchists, dissident Marxists and socialists all made attempts, of varying seriousness and success, to include women in their ranks and to carry out activities aimed at ameliorating the position of Spanish women in society. Though they assigned primary importance to fighting the war, these parties also endeavored to organize society in the Republican zone along the lines they hoped would spread and continue throughout all of Spain following the anticipated Republican military victory.

The Republican government and the *Generalitat de Cataluña* (Government of Catalonia) made advances for women in the areas of health and childcare. On 25 December 1936, a landmark legal reform took place in Catalonia, when for the first time in Spanish history abortion was made legal. This decree was passed by the anarchist-dominated Health Department, and was followed by legislation in March 1937 regulating the provision of abortion in hospitals and clinics.[17] The *Generalitat* also increased information on and access to birth control, as well as education about venereal disease.[18] The Republican government worked to combat prostitution.[19] In her role as Minister of Health and Public Assistance, Montseny organized refuges for women, in particular for prostitutes and single mothers. Women's agency was vastly increased, as a great number of women's magazines and newspapers were published by women's antifascist organizations that conveyed information about women's issues to the public.

Many of the gains made for women during the social revolution came as a result of the actions of anarchists, and in particular of the women's organization *Mujeres Libres*. The many activities carried out by *Mujeres Libres* during the Spanish Civil War included organizing collective kitchens and running educational classes in order to combat illiteracy and educate women about the new possibilities open to them.[20] *Mujeres Libres* was responsible for organizing parent-controlled childcare centers and educating women about prenatal and infant healthcare.[21] Emma Goldman, during a visit to Spain in 1938, saw that members of *Mujeres Libres* were also involved in "visiting the wounded in hospitals, inspecting the children's schools and the distribution of a tremendous amount of printed matter . . . [about] the purpose and importance of the anti-fascist struggle."[22] *Mujeres Libres* also devoted a great deal of energy to the fight against prostitution.[23] The training courses conducted by *Mujeres Libres* were aimed at educating women in order to provide employment opportunities that would decrease the proportion of women turning to prostitution to survive.[24] By 1938, the organization had over 20,000 members.[25]

Temma Kaplan explains that female anarchists would not stop at encouraging women to fill positions left vacant by men, only to be pushed aside again when the soldiers returned home.[26] Instead, *Mujeres Libres* went further to argue for women's liberation. They encouraged women to join the anarchist movement, to participate in decision-making and to fight for better conditions in all aspects of their lives.[27] Montseny, one of only a few leading women anarchists during the Spanish Civil War, was a fervent advocate of this view. In her role as a Republican minister, Montseny argued that before a truly egalitarian society could be created, women had to be liberated, that and this could only occur through a revolution in the attitudes of men toward women.[28] Though limited and hampered by the war, the work carried out by the anarchists to ameliorate conditions for women was in many ways successful.

The PCE can also be seen to have made efforts to improve the position of women, though once again these efforts were not made by the entire party, but through one specific section or by particular women leaders. In the case of the PCE, it was Ibárruri who carried almost the sole responsibility for the party's work among women. Through Ibárruri, the communists organized over 100,000 women into anti-fascist committees.[29] Ibárruri also organized the publishing of *Compañera*, a magazine specifically concerned with women's issues.[30] However, Ibárruri's feminism is characterized by Marie Marmo Mullaney as "routine, limited [and] subordinated to larger aims."[31] As such, Ibárruri's activities were mostly directed toward the war effort, with the concerns of women relegated to minor importance, to be dealt with only after the Republican victory.

Nevertheless, the fact that Ibárruri was one of the most prominent and popular of the communist leaders in itself had a positive effect on Spanish women. Breaking free of traditional gender stereotypes, Ibárruri was strong, confident and dominant. She was involved in all aspects of the civil war. She helped to decide party policy, gave speeches to mass meetings all over the Republican zone, visited the front to inspire troops,[32] was involved with the International Brigades,[33] and served as a deputy in the Republican Parliament.[34] Paul Preston argues that her actions "encouraged women to abandon the serene servility that was considered the proper attitude of womankind."[35]

The POUM's women's organization, the Female Secretariat, undertook a great deal of work to improve women's position in Spanish society. Its members organized a women's battalion and military training, classes for women, and centers of education and child welfare.[36] The *miliciana* and international observer Mary Low described the Female Secretariat as "a great success."[37] She wrote that 500 women joined within the first week,[38] and that it continued to grow thereafter. She also thought highly of the educational classes, relating that hundreds of women came every day to learn about "socialism, child welfare, French, hygiene, women's rights, [and] the origin of the religious and family sense."[39] Thus, the actions of the left-wing parties can be seen to have contributed to the widening of social roles for Republican women.

Despite inflation and shortages, the economic status of women in Spanish society improved dramatically because of conditions created by the war, as women entered the workforce in large numbers. The social revolution, and the left-wing groups driving it, aided this process by developing a new ideology regarding acceptable roles for women and their strength and capabilities, an ideology reflected in much of the war propaganda used at the time. In Republican Spain, women rushed to occupy the vacancies in all areas of the workforce left by men. Shirley Mangini recounts that "thousands [of women] replaced men in the factories in order to keep the country running."[40] Constancia de la Mora told of the enthusiasm with which women worked to unload ships and toiled in the fields.[41] Mullaney contends that the ability of women to enter the workforce so quickly and ably was "vital to the success of the loyalist cause."[42] The assistance offered by civilian women to the war effort also extended to the organization and distribution of food and supplies to the military;[43] providing medical aid;[44] and even traveling to the front in theater groups to entertain the troops.[45]

As well as being able to enter areas of employment from which they had previously been almost completely absent, women improved their access to vocational training during the war. *Mujeres Libres* organized many technical and professional schools for women, in both urban and rural areas.[46] Women in rural areas were also able to learn new skills. Dr. Amparo Poch y Gascon of *Mujeres Libres* traveled throughout the Republican zone to train women in advanced first aid and midwifery.[47] Rural women were also trained in viticulture and stockbreeding.[48]

The central importance of women's contribution to the Republican war effort directly affected the way women saw themselves. Having lived all their lives in a Spain that Montseny described as viewing them as nothing more than "a beast of the field or as an incubation machine for sons,"[49] many women now became more self-assured. Mullaney relates that many observers at the time saw that women "drew confidence and pride from their participation in the war effort, both on and off the front."[50]

The abovementioned changes in the status and self-image of women, coupled with the impact of the war and the social revolution, caused a substantial change in the attitudes of men toward women. Mullaney records that this was especially evident in Madrid, where hundreds of women "appeared in public unchaperoned or wearing trousers, actions that would have been unthinkable before."[51] In Barcelona, while observers such as Franz Borkenau noted that many Spanish women still appeared in public only with a chaperone, they nonetheless demonstrated a new confidence and had begun to wear what had previously been considered male clothing.[52] Rosa Vega remembered that when walking home alone at night in Madrid she felt safe, whereas before the war she would not have done so. She believed that "women were no longer objects, they were human beings, persons on the same level as men."[53] Margarita Balaguer of Barcelona also recalled the change in relationships between men and women: "It was like being brothers and sisters. It had always annoyed me that men in this country didn't consider women as beings with full human rights. But now there was this big change."[54]

Spanish women in the Republican zone certainly experienced many newly found freedoms during the tumultuous period of the civil war. Women were able to play many different roles that had previously been prohibited to them. Things had changed so much that when the war broke out women had *two* options when deciding how to participate in the anti-fascist resistance. They could do so fighting at the front, or aiding the auxiliary in the rearguard.[55] This is miraculous considering that at the beginning of WWI, for example, women across Europe would not have considered for a moment that they could play a role anywhere but on the home front, or as a nurse or other member of the auxiliary at the front. In Spain during the civil war, hundreds of thousands of women instigated and participated in a militant fight against fascism that, lamentably, was ultimately defeated.

Clearly the circumstances caused by the intersection of the Second Republic, the civil war, and the social revolution created a situation in which gender roles had begun to change for Spanish women.[56] It was this change in traditionally accepted behaviors that allowed women to play a military role in the conflict. These conditions allowed women to develop the confidence and motivation to volunteer for combat, and caused sufficient change in attitudes toward women that this new role was generally considered acceptable by Republican society. The *milicianas* were a manifestation of the new gender roles and opportunities created by the civil war and social revolution. The process of change was dynamic, however, as the existence of the militiawomen also served to challenge further accepted codes of behavior and to inspire more women to fulfill new roles in society.

THE FAILURE OF THE REVOLUTION

Unfolding amid the chaos and deprivations of the civil war, the revolution immediately faced big problems. Not only was it difficult for revolutionary social change to proceed amid the need to maintain war production, but revolutionaries had also to deal with political groups such as the communists and right-wing socialists who promoted the idea that the war must first be won before the revolution could be pursued. Another hindrance was the fact that some groupings, including the communists and socialists, were actually opposed to any social revolution taking place even after the war.

Republican military losses were often blamed on the fact that, particularly in Catalonia, a dual power existed with authority shared between the state and the revolutionary workers' committees. Pierre Broué and Emile Témime explain that:

> In fighting a war a single authority is essential. The duality between the power of the Committees and the state was an obstacle to the conduct of war. In autumn 1936, the only problem was to know which of the two powers, Republican or revolutionary, would prevail.[57]

During the latter half of 1936 the PCE, which at the outbreak of the civil war held only sixteen seats in the *Cortes* and had a membership of only 40,000,[58] rose to a position of dominance within the Republican government. The communists achieved this as a result of a number of factors, one of the most important of which was their intimate connection to the Communist Party of the USSR, and their control over much of the foreign aid flowing to the Republic. Another factor, elucidated by Leon Trotsky in his "Lessons of Spain: The last warning,"[59] was that the communists' anti-revolutionary stance won them support not only from the middle class, but also from most of the other parties within the Republican government, including the socialists and elements of the anarchists who feared losing the support of the bourgeoisie. Many historians, particularly those of a Trotskyist persuasion, have cited the rise to power of the communists, and their anti-revolutionary policies, as the decisive reason for the failure of the social revolution.[60] The issue of the failure of the revolutionary leadership must also be considered in relation to the failure of the revolution. Of particular importance is the anarchists' decision not to create an overarching political structure that would have been capable of both advancing the social revolution and fighting the war more effectively.[61]

The policy of the PCE and PSUC in Spain was dictated by the resolutions of the Communist International, which unswervingly served the interests of the USSR. In 1936, the foreign policy of the USSR was not to pursue international working-class revolution, but to endeavor to maintain good relations with Britain and France. The communists themselves had no qualms about expressing their anti-revolutionary policy. André Marty, a member of the Executive Committee of the Communist International, wrote in a widely published article:

> The working-class parties of Spain, and especially the Communist Party, have on several occasions clearly indicated what they are striving for. Our brother party has repeatedly proved that the present struggle in Spain is not between capitalism and socialism, but between fascism and democracy. In a country like Spain, where feudal institutions and roots are still very deep, the working-class and the entire people have the immediate and urgent task, *the only possible task*—and all recent appeals of the Communist Party repeat it and prove it—not to bring

about the socialist revolution, but to defend, consolidate, and develop the bourgeois democratic revolution. The only slogan of our party which was spread right across *Mundo Obrero*, its daily paper, on July 18, was "Long Live the Democratic Republic!"[62]

In a bid to end the situation of dual power and bring the workers' committees under their control, the communists invited the anarchists and the POUM to join the Republican government, which they did. A process then began to dissolve the workers' committees in Catalonia, under the slogan "All power to the *Generalitat!*"

The Trotskyists Mary Low and Juan Breà named December as the crucial month for the failure of the revolution, which is why their *Red Spanish Notebook* documents only the first six months of the war. Low and Breà state in their introduction that they were interested only in recording and participating in the social revolution, and in December, when they believed it had ended, they left Spain. Others view the events of the May Days in Barcelona as the decisive moment for the failure of the social revolution. If it is possible to date the failure of the revolution, one might argue that the revolution floundered for several months, beginning perhaps as early as September 1936, before it failed in May 1937 (though some, such as Low and Breà, may have felt that the course of the revolution was sealed prior to this date).

The culmination of these tensions came in May 1937, when the communists sent troops and tanks to take control of the telephone exchange that had been seized by the anarchists during the insurrection in July. The anarchists resisted, refusing to give up the exchange. In what became known as the "civil war within the civil war,"[63] a violent conflict took place between two factions within the Republican zone, the anarchists and POUM on one side, and the communists on the other. Over a period of three or four days, an estimated 400 people were killed. The defeat of the anarchists and POUM in the May Day events unleashed a fierce repression against them. Anarchists and POUMists were "disappeared," arrested and assassinated. The POUM was outlawed entirely, under the pretext that it had been collaborating with the Nationalists.

The Prime Minister Francisco Largo Caballero, while refusing to intervene for fear of breaching Catalan autonomy, did protest against the activities of the communists in Catalonia. Unfortunately, this served only to steel communist opposition against him. Burnett Bolloten describes the overthrow by the communists of the Largo Caballero government in May 1937 as their "greatest triumph in their rise to power."[64] Largo Caballero was replaced with the right-wing socialist Juan Negrín. Under this new government, the left-wing socialists and anarchists were systematically removed from all positions of responsibility within the Republic. Though a member of the PSOE, Negrín worked closely with the PCE from the time of his appointment as Prime Minister. Indeed, Bolloten states that

Negrín "was more responsible than any one Spaniard for the later success of the Communist Party."[65]

As a result of the defeat of the social revolution, many progressive gains that had been won for the working class and women were rescinded. These included the reversal of much of the workers' control of industry and factories, and the cessation of agricultural reforms such as collectivization. More traditional gender roles began to be reestablished, hence women's military participation in the war was no longer seen as acceptable. Women did continue to play more of a role in the public sphere than they had done prior to the war; however, they mainly did so in employment (where it was economically necessary) and in volunteer roles that were seen to be an extension of their caring, nurturing nature, such as nursing, and running kitchens and orphanages. It was in this context that the *milicianas* were removed from their combat roles and returned to take up "acceptable" roles on the home front. An understanding of the historical and political context that gave rise to the *miliciana* phenomenon, and ultimately caused its end, is necessary both in order to understand the significance of the experience of the militiawomen, and to draw from it broader conclusions in relation to gender issues in Spain, and the role of women in war and revolution more generally.

NOTES

1. The causation of the Spanish Civil War is a complex issue and will not be dealt with here. For detailed accounts, see Hugh Thomas, *The Spanish Civil War*, 4th Edition, Penguin, London, 2003; Burnett Bolloten, *The Spanish Civil War: Revolution and counter-revolution*, University of North Carolina Press, Chapel Hill, 1991; and Antony Beevor, *The Spanish Civil War*, Orbis Publishing, London, 1982.

2. Beevor, *Spanish Civil War*, 48.

3. Thomas, *Spanish Civil War*, 244.

4. Gabriel Jackson, *A Concise History of the Spanish Civil War*, Thames and Hudson, London, 1974, 50.

5. Thomas, *Spanish Civil War*, 357.

6. Thomas, *Spanish Civil War*, 944.

7. Beevor, *Spanish Civil War*, 7.

8. For a detailed discussion of the social revolution, see for example Gerald Brenan, *The Spanish Labyrinth: An account of the social and political background of the Spanish Civil War*, Cambridge University Press, Cambridge, 1960; Felix Morrow, *Revolution and Counter-Revolution in Spain, Including the Civil War in Spain*, Pathfinder Press, New York, 1974; and Paul Preston, *The Spanish Civil War, 1936–1939*, Harper Perennial, London, 2006.

9. George Orwell, *Homage to Catalonia*, 3rd edition, Secker & Warburg, London, 1954, 3; and Franz Borkenau, *The Spanish Cockpit: An eyewitness account of the political and social conflicts of the Spanish Civil War*, Pluto Press, London, 1937, 70.

10. Jackson, *Concise History*, 67.

11. Jackson, *Concise History*, 67.

12. Jackson, *Concise History*, 68.

13. Jackson, *Concise History*, 69.

14. Jackson, *Concise History*, 69.

15. Jackson, *Concise History*, 69.

16. See for example Maurine Weiner Greenwald, *Women, War and Work: The impact of World War I on women workers in the United States*, Cornell University Press, Ithaca, 1990, x; and Chester W. Gregory, *Women in Defense Work during World War II: An analysis of the labor problem and women's rights*, Exposition Press, New York, 1974, xvi.

1᷄. Cleminson, "Beyond Tradition," 121.

1᷄. Temma Kaplan, "Spanish Anarchists and Women's Liberation," *Journal of Contemporary History*, vol. 6, 1971, 108.

1᷄. A great deal more could have been done to combat prostitution had the political leadership of the social revolution been sufficiently dedicated to the cause. Chris Ealham argues that in Barcelona at least the anarchist movement could have easily closed down all the brothels in the city had the male-dominated leadership not been ambivalent on the importance of the eradication of prostitution. Chris Ealham, "The Myth of the Maddened Crowd: Class, culture and space in the revolutionary urbanist project in Barcelona, 1936–1937," in Ealham and Michael Richards (eds.), *The Splintering of Spain: Cultural history and the Spanish Civil War, 1936–1939*, Cambridge University Press, Cambridge, 2005, 130.

20. Nash, *Femmes Libres*, 66.

21. Kaplan, "Other Scenarios: Women and Spanish anarchism" in Renate Bridenthal and Claudia Koonz (eds.), *Becoming Visible: Women in European history*, Houghton Mifflin, Boston, 1977, 416.

22. David Porter (ed.), *Vision on Fire: Emma Goldman on the Spanish Revolution*, Common Ground Press, New York, 1983, 258.

23. Beevor, *Spanish Civil War*, 89.

24. Kaplan, "Spanish Anarchists," 109.

25. Kaplan, "Other Scenarios," 415.

26. Kaplan, "Other Scenarios," 415.

27. Kaplan, "Other Scenarios," 415.

28. Shirley Fredricks, "Feminism: The essential ingredient in Federica Montseny's anarchist theory," in Jane Slaughter and Robert Kern (eds.), *European Women on the Left: Socialism, feminism and the problems faced by political women, 1880 to the present*, Greenwood Press, Westport, 1981, 126.

29. Marie Marmo Mullaney, *Revolutionary Women: Gender and the socialist revolutionary role*, Praeger, New York, 1983, 214.

30. Mullaney, *Revolutionary Women*, 214.

31. Mullaney, *Revolutionary Women*, 216.

32. Preston, *Comrades! Portraits from The Spanish Civil War*, HarperCollins, London, 1999, 294.

33. Mangini, *Memories of Resistance*, 40.

34. Mangini, "Memories of Resistance: Women activists from the Spanish Civil War," *Signs*, vol. 17, no. 1, 1997, 172.

35. Preston, *Comrades*, 277.

36. Jim Fyrth and Sally Alexander (eds.), *Women's Voices from the Spanish Civil War*, Lawrence & Wishart, London, 1991, 258.

37. Fyrth and Alexander, *Women's Voices*, 261.

38. Fyrth and Alexander, *Women's Voices*, 258.

39. Fyrth and Alexander, *Women's Voices*, 261.

40. Mangini, "Memories of Resistance," 172.

41. Constancia de la Mora, *In Place of Splendour: The autobiography of a Spanish woman*, M. Joseph, London, 1940, 420.

42. Mullaney, *Revolutionary Women*, 214.

43. Mangini, "Memories of Resistance," 172.

44. Mullaney, *Revolutionary Women*, 214.

45. Mangini, "Memories of Resistance," 180.

46. Kaplan, "Spanish Anarchism," 107.

47. Kaplan, "Spanish Anarchism," 107.

48. Kaplan, "Spanish Anarchism," 107.

49. Fredricks, "Feminism," 128.

50. Mullaney, *Revolutionary Women*, 214.

51. Mullaney, *Revolutionary Women*, 214.

52. Borkenau, *Spanish Cockpit*, 72.

53. Quoted in Ronald Fraser, *Blood of Spain: The experience of Civil War 1936–1939*, Allen Lane, London, 1981, 286.

54. Quoted in Fraser, *Blood of Spain*, 287.

55. Mónica Carabias Álvaro, *Rosario Sánchez Mora (1919)*, Ediciones del Orto, Madrid, 2001, 14.

56. Scanlon, *Polémica*, 291.

57. Pierre Broué and Emile Témime, *The Revolution and the Civil War in Spain*, Faber and Faber, London, 1972, 188.

58. Burnett Bolloten, *The Grand Camouflage: The Spanish Civil War and Revolution, 1936–1939*, Pall Mall Publishers, London, 1968, 81. Bolloten cites the figure given by Manuel Delicado, a member of the Central Committee, as the 18 July 1936 membership.

59. Leon Trotsky, "The Lessons of Spain: The last warning," in Nick Soudakoff (ed.), *Marxism versus Anarchism*, Resistance Books, Chippendale, 2001, 171–188.

60. See Bolloten, *Grand Camouflage* and *The Spanish Civil War: Revolution and counter-revolution*, University of North Carolina Press, Chapel Hill, 1991, Broué and Témime, *Revolution and the Civil War*, and Morrow, *Revolution and Counter-Revolution*.

61. Nick Soudakoff, "Introduction," in Soudakoff (ed.), *Marxism versus Anarchism*, Resistance Books, Chippendale, 2001, 20–21.

62. *L'Humanité*, 4 August 1936; *Communist International*, October 1936, *International Press Correspondence*, 8 August 1936; *Daily Worker*, London, 5 August 1936. Cited in Bolloten, *Grand Camouflage*, 101.

63. For Orwell's account of the May Day events, see his chapters X and XI. Orwell, *Homage*, 129–192.

64. Bolloten, *Grand Camouflage*, 17.

65. Bolloten, *Grand Camouflage*, 121.

THREE

The Initial Reaction: Street Fighting and Formation of the Militias

The sudden outbreak of the Spanish Civil War provoked the spontaneous involvement of many civilians in the military defense of Republican Spain. When the Nationalist insurrection began in Spain on 18 July 1936, it was met immediately with an uprising of Republican supporters and anti-fascists who fought in the streets against the Nationalists to put down the rebellion. As the Republican government hesitated to arm the population, people in many cities besieged armories and requisitioned weapons in order to fight the Nationalist rebels. The participation of women in this struggle was crucial to the anti-Nationalist resistance. Women were immediately active in the social, economic and military spheres in the fight against fascism. In the early days of the civil war, women joined in storming barracks to obtain weapons. Having armed themselves, women built barricades and participated in street fighting that put down the Nationalist uprising in many areas. Women's involvement in the anti-Nationalist movement had a significant impact. For the first time in their lives, women were participating in events on equal terms with men. Their actions were considered heroic, and their impromptu involvement was an integral factor in the initial Republican victories. This chapter will demonstrate the military significance of women's participation in the initial uprising against fascism, an issue that has previously not been reflected in much of the historical literature regarding the Spanish Civil War.[1]

The spontaneous armed participation of women in the hastily organized resistance to the Nationalist uprising in July presented a serious challenge to the conservative gender roles of Catholic Spain. But the challenge these women presented became more serious when close to a thousand of them went on to join the militias who fought at the front lines.

49

Women volunteered for combat and fought in Aragon, Guadalajara, the Basque country, the Sierra of Madrid, Andalusia, Majorca and the Maestranza as well as in many other areas.[2] Further, thousands of women also joined militias in the Republican zone that were armed and trained to protect their towns and cities. Though the majority of these women were never stationed at what was traditionally considered the "front," many of them nonetheless participated in combat as the Nationalist army advanced through Spain.

This chapter will examine the methods by which women were recruited and enlisted in the militias. While no one was conscripted into the Republican or anarchist militias, leftist political parties did specifically encourage women to enlist for active combat duty. This demonstrates that women's participation in combat was indeed seen to be valuable by the Republican leadership in 1936, as will be evidenced below.

The significance of the militia women is undermined by the widespread notion that there were never very many of them. Underestimating their numbers allows some historians to ignore or misunderstand both the military importance of the *milicianas* and the impact that these militiawomen had on Spanish society. Included in this chapter will be a researched estimate of how many women actually took part in armed combat in the front lines and in the rearguard. Thus far, historians have varied widely in their opinions on how many women fought at the war fronts. Mary Nash claims fewer than 200 women were *milicianas*,[3] while Anthony Beevor cites almost 1,000.[4] Beevor also estimates that several thousand armed women fought in the rearguard.[5] This book will argue that Beevor's is the more accurate figure.

This chapter will discuss why these women volunteered so readily for active combat, and show how their self-motivation and dedication to the Republican cause and social revolution served to heighten the historical significance of the *miliciana* phenomenon. These women did not go unthinkingly into combat. Rather, they were motivated by a range of complex political and social factors.

THE INITIAL RESISTANCE: FIGHTING IN THE STREETS

In those first few days after the insurrection, women were integral to the anti-Nationalist resistance. They ran hospitals and cared for the wounded, requisitioned supplies and distributed food, medicine, guns and ammunition, built barricades and defenses for buildings and streets, sewed uniforms, formed committees, made decisions and relayed information. For the first time, masses of Spanish women entered the public sphere, and their contribution was not only welcomed—it was vital.

While women's active and crucial performance of auxiliary functions in the anti-Nationalist resistance was clearly an advance for Spanish women, it is also true that in some ways this was an extension of the roles women were already playing in their homes. Running hospitals and orphanages can be seen as a public, and larger scale, fulfillment of women's traditional responsibility for caring for the young, old and sick. The social significance of women's participation in the early stages of the Spanish Civil War lies in the fact that, for the first time, women entered the hitherto exclusively male sphere of warfare and claimed their right to bear arms.

The most noteworthy examples of women's military participation in the initial resistance occurred in Madrid and Barcelona. In both cities, women took part in the storming of the barracks and armed themselves. They helped seize the *Cuartel de la Montaña* (Montaña Barracks) in Madrid, and the Atarazanas Barracks in Barcelona.[6] Having obtained weapons, women fought in the streets alongside the men against the Nationalists. Ingrid Strobl points out that some women had more difficulty than men did in obtaining a weapon since they were in short supply, but once they had succeeded in doing so, they took those arms and climbed onto the trucks and buses that were driving toward the zones of the city where the fighting was taking place.[7]

The presence of significant numbers of women among the anti-Nationalist fighters in both cities was highly visible and was remarked upon both by the press and by foreign observers. The communist newspaper *Muchachas* and the anarchist *Mujeres Libres* both reported later that women took part in the defense of the Somosierra Bridge in Madrid, as well as in many other places around the city.[8] In *The Spanish Cockpit*, Franz Borkenau noted the presence of armed women in the streets of Barcelona.[9] He commented that many of the women wore pants and demonstrated a new confidence in public, both of which had previously been inconceivable for women in Spain.

Early in the morning, trade unions had sounded sirens to indicate that the Nationalist uprising had begun, and to call the people to arm themselves and join the resistance. Cristina Piera awoke to the sound of these sirens. Like many other anarchist women, Piera left her house to participate in the people's fight against the military rebellion: "I woke up in the morning and heard that people were in the armory. . . . So I went there. Everybody went . . . I took a pistol and two ramrods [for rifles]. What I could carry. They had gunpowder there, too. . . . Even me, with the little I knew, and could do, I was there. People took arms and ammunition, and I took what I could."[10] Her account conveys a sense that many anarchist women were immediately willing to aid in the military defense of their city.

The experience of Concha Pérez Collado, an anarchist from Barcelona and a member of the FAI, can be seen in many ways as representative of the experiences of many anarchist women at the outbreak of the war. Pérez Collado was armed and ready when the Nationalist insurrection began. In fact, Pérez Collado and her comrades had been prepared for several days before the uprising, aware that it would begin at any moment. In my interview with Pérez Collado in Barcelona in 2005, she explained that members of the FAI were ready and waiting, but that they took the precaution of staying in groups in comrades' houses rather than at the union headquarters.[11] It was in these pre-formed political groups that Pérez Collado and other anarchists took part in the fighting against the Nationalists during the first days of the civil war.

Immediately on receiving the news that the Nationalist uprising had begun, Pérez Collado and her comrades left for one of their rendezvous points, the *Els Federals* bar in the *Les Corts* district. At the bar, the anarchists met up with members of the POUM and the *Catalan Esquerra*, some Republicans and a few communists.[12] That night they began commandeering mattresses and overalls, and the next morning the anarchists took the truck belonging to the bar and set off to join the fight.[13]

One of the first actions Pérez Collado participated in was the attack on the Model Prison to liberate the political prisoners held there.[14] She also remembers being involved in the requisitioning of a convent, and building barricades around her neighborhood.[15] Pérez Collado's group was spontaneously transformed into a militia. In the back of a truck covered with a mattress, and with only four weapons, Pérez Collado and her comrades went to the Pedralbes Barracks and took part in the fighting there, where they managed to obtain more weapons.[16] It was after this that the group decided they could best aid the cause by going to the Aragon front. Pérez Collado and her comrades went to the committee headquarters of the FAI, received military equipment, waited for enough volunteers so that their unit would form part of a group of 100, and from there traveled to the front.[17]

Many communist women also participated in the street fighting against the Nationalists that took place in Barcelona. Caridad Mercader is reported as having taken part in the assault on the Military Headquarters, before joining the Durruti Column and leaving to fight on the Aragon front.[18] A foreign volunteer from Holland, identified only as Fanny, was a member of the Communist Party and had been in Barcelona at the time the war broke out. She immediately armed herself and joined a group that participated in the street fighting at the most dangerous places, near the statue of Columbus, in front of the Military Headquarters, and at the Atarazanas Barracks.[19]

Though fewer in numbers, female members of the POUM took part enthusiastically in the uprising. Mary Low, an Australian volunteer, and several of her female comrades armed themselves with Mauser rifles and defended the besieged POUM headquarters from behind makeshift parapets.[20]

The importance of women's participation in the initial fighting can be seen from the military significance of their contribution. The participation of Angelina Martínez in the assault on the *Cuartel de la Montaña* is a poignant example of women participating in battle on equal terms with men from the very first days of the war. Martínez was a young communist woman from Madrid and member of the JSU. On 1 August, the independent Republican newspaper *Estampa* printed a two-page article, which featured an interview with Martínez, and large photographs of her and several other *milicianas*.[21] The article was a tribute to her bravery during the attack on the Montana Barracks, during which Martínez fought alongside the men in her group that would become a militia, just as she continued to do in every battle afterward. Martínez fought with a handgun, which she believed "is the best weapon."[22] She related that she kept fighting even after the men of her unit had been shot. "Comrades were falling on all sides of me and I realized that, after every shot, my weapon was still working . . . Boom! Boom! I shot to kill. I assure you. I couldn't hurt a fly. But what pleasure to crush a fascist!"[23]

While the insurgents had gained control of several cities and roughly one third of Spanish territory, mostly in the northwest of Spain and a small section in the south, they had failed to seize control of the two most important cities: Madrid and Barcelona. The Nationalist rising was considered a failure, and might have ended there, had General Francisco Franco not managed to enlist the support of Nazi Germany in transporting his troops from Morocco into Spain. This was the turning point that transformed the failed uprising into a full-scale civil war. It was then that the militias were formed and the battle lines were drawn. The country was divided roughly in two, and militias traveled to the front lines across Spain to defend the Republic.

RECRUITMENT AND ENLISTMENT: FORMATION OF THE MILITIAS

Recruitment and enlistment took place for women in much the same manner as for men. Some pre-existing groups within political parties and trade unions were transformed into militias at the outbreak of the war, either through official registration or simply by obtaining weapons and traveling to the fronts.[24] This was especially true of the FAI and the CNT. When it was time to leave for the front, Pérez Collado went with her group in the FAI, which had already been fighting in the initial resistance to the Nationalists in Barcelona.[25] Other militias were formed spontaneously, with groups of people simply jumping in trucks and traveling to the fronts to fight, as was the case in Madrid. Many volunteers traveled north to the Guadarrama Mountains in order to stop the progress of the Nationalists toward the city.[26] As the days went by and it became clear that the Nationalist rebellion would not be defeated overnight, the popular militias became more organized in their recruitment and enlistment of members.

The majority of *milicianas* joined anarchist or POUM militias, and it is generally believed that this was because the revolutionary left supported the "unmilitarised military."[27] This meant that there was no hierarchy or saluting, officers were elected and the units functioned using democratic decision-making. This environment was more inclusive of women.[28] The fact that many militias were formed out of pre-existing political groups from within the CNT, FAI and POUM also aided women's ability to participate in combat.[29] Since women already belonged to these organizations, this made it easier for them to participate in combat alongside the men of their groups. It is also significant that the anarchists and the POUM were more advanced in their thinking on the subject of women's liberation, and as a result implemented more overtly egalitarian policies within their groups and militias. However, women also joined communist and socialist militias, and fought in battalions organized by the JSU.[30]

Political parties and trade unions set up makeshift enlistment centers in the plazas of towns and cities, or in front of their headquarters. Volunteers made their way there to be assigned a unit, and in most cases to be issued with a weapon and supplies. Militiamen and women then traveled to the front lines, usually in cars and trucks or sometimes on buses. Many photographs of these enlistment centers were published in newspapers in the Republican zone, showing plazas and courtyards filled with people in militia uniform. The independent newspaper *ABC* printed photographs of groups of armed and uniformed women who had just enlisted and been assigned to a battalion organized in the *Cuartel de Francos Rodrigues*.[31] Another independent newspaper *Crónica* often featured the enlistment office organized in the courtyard of the *Cuartel General del 5 th Regimiento de las Milicias Populares* (General Headquarters of the 5th Regiment of the Popular Militias). These photographs depicted newly joined *milicianas* receiving weapons training before leaving for the front.[32]

While women's military participation in the Spanish Civil War was self-motivated and driven by their dedication to the Republican cause and the social revolution, women were also encouraged to enlist by various political groups. Women were encouraged to enlist in much the same way as men were, which demonstrates that the contribution of the militiawomen was considered important by the Republican political leadership at the time. Republican Spain was beginning to succeed in changing attitudes about gender roles and about what was acceptable behavior for women.

For at least several months at the beginning of the war, there was a coordinated and consistent effort on the part of the anarchist and dissident Marxist political groups to recruit women to play a combat role in the war. Other parties and trade unions also made several calls to combat aimed at women, though it is true that these were less organized and consistent. For example, one front-page article published in *L'Instant* provides evidence that the MFAC in Barcelona did organize with the specific purpose of recruiting women for combat at the front, and moreover that they were highly successful in doing so, sending over 500 militiawomen to the front between July and September 1936.[33] The MFAC also publicized their campaign to recruit women for combat, producing propaganda posters for this precise purpose. One such poster was affixed above the entrance to the MFAC offices.[34]

Teófila Madroñal was a member of the UGT. She fought as a member of the 5th Regiment of the Popular Militias, and later became a sergeant in her unit.[35] Madroñal recalled in an interview with Antonina Rodrigo the specific calls to combat that were directed at women in July 1936: "Women, heroes of the nation! Remember the heroism of the Asturian women in 1934; you must fight as well, beside the men, to defend the life and liberty of your children who are threatened by fascism!"[36] Madroñal also remembered the enthusiasm with which she and other women answered these calls. The Republican recruitment posters that featured uniformed and armed *milicianas* could also be considered proof that efforts were made to recruit women as well as men into combat positions.

Several notable historians agree that a campaign was organized with the specific purpose of recruiting women to combat positions. Carmen Alcalde argues decisively that the anarchist CNT in Madrid did indeed organize a coherent campaign to recruit women specifically for combat positions at the front. She relates that the anarchists used their newspaper *Frente Libertario* to carry out this campaign, as well as using various propaganda posters and slogans that were plastered in the streets.[37] Ángel Rubio Moraga also agrees that the streets were covered in propaganda posters that called for the enlistment of both "men and women" in the militias to defend the Second Republic.[38] Inmaculada Julián is another proponent of the view that the propaganda posters that were visible everywhere in Spanish cities such as Madrid and Barcelona, were not aimed solely at men in an effort to encourage them to enlist. Rather, Julián argues that these posters "were a call to fight for men and women indiscriminately."[39]

Further, the fact that many women's battalions were organized and provided with military training in the rearguard (most often with the assumption that the members of these units would participate in some form of combat) is another example of a concerted campaign to recruit women to combat positions. While these women may not have been shipped off to the fronts immediately, or in some cases ever, that does not negate the fact that political parties and unions such as the PCE, JSU, POUM and others did recruit these women to play a military role in the anti-Nationalist resistance.[40]

A common misconception about the *milicianas*, undoubtedly caused by the media coverage they received, is that the women who volunteered for combat were all very young. Paloma Fernández Quintanilla, in her book *Mujeres de Madrid*, relates that at the beginning of the war, "the youngest and most determined women incorporated themselves at the first moment into the Voluntary Militias, with whom they fought in the fronts of the Madrid Sierra and the Casa de Campo."[41] This is misleading. While many *milicianas* were between the ages of sixteen and twenty-five, there were also older women who joined the militias. The communists Teófila Madroñal and Trinidad Revolto Cervello were both thirty-one years old when the war began and they joined the militia to fight.[42] Every so often older *milicianas* were pictured in the press, though they were not featured as often as their younger and more conventionally beautiful counterparts were.[43] There were also a small number of *milicianas* who were even younger, as young as fourteen.[44]

The initial response of outspoken members of the public in the Republican zone to the incorporation of women into combat positions within the militias was positive. There exists a plethora of evidence including newspaper articles, oral testimonies and memoirs of foreign volunteers and observers that all indicates that, at least initially, there was not a great deal of controversy or apprehension over the idea of women fighting in the front lines. The figure of the *miliciana* was glorified, especially in the press and propaganda, to such an extent that she came to symbolize the people's fight against fascism.[45]

QUANTITATIVE SIGNIFICANCE: NUMBERS OF WOMEN IN COMBAT

Debate continues over the number of women who participated in armed combat during the Spanish Civil War. Estimates of the number of *milicianas* are usually divided into two figures: the number of women who fought at the front and the number who participated in combat (or combat training) in the rearguard.[46] However, it is the *milicianas* who fought in the front lines that have received the most attention, because they demonstrated a more radical change to traditional gender roles.

An abundance of primary evidence suggests that the number of women who fought in the front lines was around 1,000, and reputable historians, such as Beevor, Coleman and Shirley Mangini support this estimate. *Milicianas* were present in the fighting forces in many areas and on many fronts in Spain. Claude Cockburn reported in *The Daily Worker* on 13 August 1936 the presence of women fighters in the Mangada Column, fighting at Novalperal (west of the Sierra front).[47] Syd Quinn witnessed armed women in combat at Lopera, in Andalusia.[48] Tom Clarke related stories of the bravery of women he saw fighting at the Battle of Jarama in February 1937.[49] Borkenau reported a "considerable number" of foreign militiawomen in Barcelona.[50] He also witnessed the bravery of Spanish militiawomen under bombardment in the town of Cerro Muriano, in Andalusia.[51] On 28 July 1936, the *ABC* reported that a group of women joined a battalion organized in the *Cuartel de Francos Rodrigues* and left to fight on the front in the Somosierra.[52] *El Diluvio* also published an article and photograph of *milicianas* after they had participated in the winning battle at Navacerrada in August of 1936.[53] Women were also reported to have fought at Madrid,[54] Toledo,[55] Oviedo,[56] Valencia[57] and Huesca.[58] These are just a few examples of the many reports that confirmed the presence of fighting women in numerous locations around Spain.

Clara Thalmann, a Swiss volunteer and anarchist who fought with the Durruti Column on the Aragon front[59] and later published her memoirs of the war, estimated during an interview in 1976 that women constituted 2 percent of the members of the militias fighting on the front lines.[60] An approximate figure of 150,000 has been calculated for members of anarchist militias,[61] and there were roughly 5,000 foreign volunteers who fought in militias.[62] A smaller number of combatants also fought with militias organized by the POUM, the Republican Left, the *Catalan Esquerra* and the communists, but historians do not seem to have provided any estimates of the size of these forces.[63] Not taking into account these other militias, 2 percent of the figure 155,000 is 3,100. It is not noted in the interview how many militia members Thalmann believed there were, but it is clear that she was knowledgeable on the subject, being not only a member of a militia herself but also someone who deliberately observed and wrote about the war. Thus, it is not unreasonable to assume that the figure she had in mind was roughly accurate. Strobl, while commenting that "it is difficult to speak of an exact number," gives Thalmann's estimate of 2 percent as being the most accurate estimate of the number of *milicianas*.[64] Strobl also notes that no one has accounted for the number of women who fought in the Republican Army, as opposed to the militias, which would indicate that the number of women who participated in combat was in fact even higher.

Further, on 9 September 1936, the Barcelona newspaper *L'Instant* featured on its front cover the article "*Les Nostres Dones També Lluiten*" ("Our Women Also Fight").[65] This source states that one organization alone in Barcelona recruited more than 500 women specifically for combat and sent them to the front to fight. The two-page article features an interview with an unnamed militiawoman from the Offices of Control and Enlistment of the MFAC, in Barcelona. It is written by an author identified only as J.P. The militiawoman explains that all the recruits were given weapons training before being placed in a column and sent to the front. Questioning the number of women enlisted by the organization, the reporter asked, "how many *milicianas* have been sent to the front, since the beginning of the revolution?" The woman answered, "certainly I cannot say exactly, but I believe the number is over 500."[66] Since this woman worked in the Office of Control and Enlistment for the MFAC, and since the interviewer was asking her to recall information from the last three months rather than from years ago, this source can be seen as reliable.

Since this article provides evidence that one organization in Barcelona alone sent over 500 women to the front to fight, and since there is a plethora of evidence to show that *milicianas* belonged to many different organizations, political parties and trade unions, and came from many Spanish cities and towns other than Barcelona, there may have been well over 1,000 women participating in combat at the front.

There is also evidence that more women would have enlisted in the militias and volunteered for combat positions had they been given the opportunity. In 1936, it was highly unusual for women to move around Spain unchaperoned, and many women who could not obtain the permission of their parents were unable to volunteer. There is also evidence that toward the end of 1936, women who tried to enlist in the militias were turned away, as attitudes toward the *milicianas* had begun to change.[67] Thus, it is possible that had women not been removed from combat, the number of *milicianas* would have grown as the war progressed.

The estimated number of women who participated in combat in defense of the rearguard is discussed less often. Beevor refers to "several thousand [women] under arms in the rear areas and a woman's battalion [that] took part in the defense of Madrid,"[68] and Mangini supports this assessment.[69] However, many historians do not comment on this issue. This may be the case because it is more difficult to estimate the number of armed women who played a combat role in the rearguard since these militias were often less regimented, and members lived in their homes, not in barracks or trenches. Clearly, it is easier to maintain records of the size of a militia when all its members are stationed in one place. This book argues that the number of women who were armed and ready to defend their cities in the rearguard (whether or not they eventually participated in actual combat) was approximately 5,000. This is based on the number of women members of the *Unión de Muchachas* who fought in the Battle for Madrid, the women's militia organized by the PSUC in Barcelona[70] and the Rosa Luxemburg Battalion[71] that both took part in the battle to defend Majorca, the women's militia organized by the POUM in Barcelona,[72] the communist battalion in Madrid named after Lina Odena,[73] and the women's unit of the Madrid battalion *Avanti*,[74] among others.

The *miliciana* phenomenon is highly important, regardless of whether it was 200 or 2,000 women who took up arms in the front lines. The existence of a substantial number of uniformed and armed women participating in modern warfare was something never before seen in Spain.

MOTIVATIONS: VOLUNTEERING FOR COMBAT

For the first time in Spanish history, women stepped outside their traditionally defined gender roles in large numbers to volunteer for combat and defend the Republic. Alongside the men, both Spanish and foreign, who have been routinely discussed by historians, women too lined up outside the *cuarteles* to enlist in the militias, be issued their weapons and jump into the back of a truck and travel to the front. Their reasons for enlisting in combat were varied, and an examination of these motives can reveal a great deal about the women involved in the conflict.

The vast majority of women appear to have had, or at least claim to have had, political reasons for volunteering for combat. These women can be divided into two groups. First, there are those who held firm political convictions and most often were already active members of political parties or trade unions prior to the outbreak of the war. Frequently, these women had already played a role in other social movements prior to the civil war. A second group of women consists of those who at the outbreak of the war appear to have been spontaneously moved to defend the advance achieved during the Second Republic, or were reacting to their instinctive anti-fascism.

For those who had previously been members of left-wing political parties or trade unions, their decision to take up arms to defend the Republic can be seen as an extension of their participation in previous social movements, such as the October Rebellion of 1934 or the fight against the dictatorship of Miguel Primo de Rivera (1923–1930). Herrmann confirms that the social and political background of women was highly important in their decision to become involved in combat. When the eight militiawomen that she interviewed were asked what motivated them to take up arms, all answered that they "had been born into proletarian communities variously inspired by one or another faction of the Russian Revolution."[75] She states that "to join a militia group as a consequence of their syndicalism or party association was an integral part of their microculture."[76]

Pérez Collado relates that when she armed herself and began fighting in Barcelona, she did so with a full knowledge of the implications of the Nationalist rebellion, and the urgency of stopping it in its tracks. In 1936, Pérez Collado was already a militant anarchist, and had been since her youth.[77] Following in the footsteps of her father Juan Pérez Buey, Pérez Collado was a member of the FAI, the CNT and the FIJL. Both Pérez Collado and her father had participated in the resistance during the dictatorship of Primo de Rivera.[78] During the strikes of the October Rebellion in 1934, Pérez Collado had been caught hiding a pistol for one of her comrades from the CNT, and had been sent to jail for five months.[79]

During my interview with her, Pérez Collado declared proudly, "I have always lived the life of an activist."[80] As a result of her previous militancy and political activism, there is little need for skepticism when Pérez Collado relates that her reasons for volunteering for combat were solely political. The situation in which Pérez Collado found herself was common for anarchist women, many of whom had been active in the FAI, CNT or FIJL prior to the outbreak of the war.

The ideological convictions of many communist women had also been formed before the outbreak of the war, and the historian can be confident that their motivations for volunteering for combat were based on political ideas. One example is Fidela Fernández de Velasco Pérez (known as Fifí). When the Spanish Civil War began in 1936, Fernández de Velasco Pérez had a strong political background and was already trained in the use of arms.[81] She had joined the youth organization of the PCE at only thirteen years of age, and had been given military instruction as well as an education in communist literature as part of her training. Fernández de Velasco Pérez noted that the youth organization did not differentiate between its female and male members in terms of training.[82]

At the time she received news of the Nationalist insurrection, she was already armed and standing guard in her local party office. When Fernández de Velasco Pérez enlisted in the militia and volunteered for front-line combat, she did so with unmistakable political motivations and was under no illusions about the nature or seriousness of the conflict. Fernández de Velasco Pérez was only sixteen when she went off to the front to fight. Her determination and courage were clear from the moment she said good-bye to her parents, telling them, "come, give me a kiss because I am going to war, I have to go to war."[83]

Rosario Sánchez de la Mora serves as a further example of a communist woman who was clearly motivated by political conviction to volunteer for the militia. When the war broke out, Sánchez de la Mora was seventeen years old, living in Madrid with relatives and attending sewing and remedial education classes at the Aida Lafuente School.[84] She was already a member of the JSU.[85] In an interview with Pilar Panes in December 1987,[86] Sánchez de la Mora told the story of how she came to volunteer for the militia. On 20 July 1936, a group of young communist men visited her school to make a speech about the importance and urgency of opposing the fascists and to ask for volunteers. When the young activist asked for volunteers, he used the masculine form of the word as opposed to the feminine, even though there were only women present in the class. Sánchez de la Mora recounted that she stood up and shyly asked if women could volunteer, to which the young man replied, "of course."

The next day at eight in the morning, Sánchez de la Mora climbed on a truck that took her to the front.[87] In another interview with Maite Goicoechea, Sánchez de la Mora revealed that when she heard this speech, she immediately understood the importance of quelling the Nationalist rebellion. She knew that "if the rebels were not stopped we would have a dictatorship and we workers would have a bad time."[88] When Sánchez de la Mora volunteered for the militia, she did so understanding that she would be required to participate in combat.

International women volunteers also possessed deeply held political beliefs that moved them to travel to Spain and fight against fascism as members of militias. The Argentinean Mika Etchebéhère and her husband Hipólito had both been part of the anti-Stalinist opposition and were associated with the founding members of the Trotskyist Fourth International.[89] In Germany in 1933, they witnessed the horrific impact of fascism on left-wing politics, which served to cement their anti-fascism.[90] Immediately after the Nationalist rebellion began in Spain, Etchebéhère and her husband traveled there to join the resistance. Initially, it was only Hipólito who served in armed combat as the commander of a POUM column that fought in the Sigüenza sector. Etchebéhère worked as an administrative assistant[91] and ambulance officer for the unit until her husband was killed on 16 August.[92] After his death, Etchebéhère took up arms in his place and was later promoted to the position of captain of her unit.[93]

Another example of an international volunteer who took up arms to defend the Republic as a result of her political convictions is Felicia Browne, a young British woman, who was already in Barcelona when the civil war began. She had been visiting Spain with the intention of attending the Workers' Olympics (an alternative to the 1936 Olympics to be held in Nazi Germany).[94] Browne had been a member of the British Community Party since 1933, and had participated in the armed street fighting that took place in Berlin when Hitler came to power.[95] Upon the outbreak of the Nationalist insurrection, Browne immediately volunteered to join a militia, spurred on by her communist principles and fervent anti-fascism. She was reported in the British *Daily Express* to have left for the front with the words, "I am not afraid at all, I am fighting for a different country but the same cause."[96]

In July of 1936, due to the advances in women's rights introduced by the progressive Second Republic, many women from all political backgrounds did not consider their gender to be an issue when they volunteered for combat positions in the militias. It did not cross the mind of Pérez Collado that it was inappropriate or unacceptable for her to join the militia. In an interview with Nash in 1981, she recalled that:

> The group that went, we went as a man. We went, not as soldiers, because we did not consider ourselves to be soldiers, but as a group. And I tell you, there were ten of us, as we considered that there were ten of us, nine men and a woman![97]

Similarly, the communist Lena Imbert told Teresa Pàmies that she volunteered for combat because she believed that only the wounded or children should fulfill roles on the home front.[98] Elisa Garcia, a *miliciana* killed on the Aragon front in September 1936, wrote a letter to her parents shortly before her death that demonstrated her vehement belief that women should be able to participate fully in the anti-fascist resistance, including in combat roles. She wrote:

> My heart cannot remain impassive seeing the struggle my brothers are carrying out. . . . And if anyone says to you that fighting is not for women, tell them that discharging revolutionary duty is the obligation of all who are not cowards.[99]

When examining the second group of women, those who claimed to have volunteered for political reasons but who had not previously been active or involved in a political group or social movement, it is necessary to exercise caution. Here the possibility of a slight revision of history on the part of interview subjects is more likely. Prior to the war, these women had not acted on, or fully developed, their political convictions. The political reasons of these women for volunteering are said to have been born out of a spontaneous or instinctive anti-fascism, or out of a loyalty to the Republic.

It is possible some women simply found it appealing to play a military role that had previously been considered unacceptable for them, and wished to break with conservative traditions that had dictated their behavior for so long.[100] These women may have rejected a role in the rearguard on the grounds that they believed it was a supportive and thus less important role, and because they wanted to participate in the struggle against fascism in a more direct and decisive way. Margarita Fuente, a 21-year-old woman from Madrid, had never been a member of a political party or trade union. However, at the outbreak of the war she immediately enlisted in the militia, explaining to a journalist shortly afterward, "what I wanted was to serve the Republic!"[101]

The independent press in the Republican zone reported that many women's reasons for volunteering for combat were based on patriotism and on this instinctive anti-fascism. An article printed in *ABC* on 7 August 1936 observed that "each day that passes, women identify more and more with men in their patriotic anti-fascist ardor. And like the men, they come constantly to enroll in the militias, which crush the rebels in all the fronts of combat."[102]

Dolores Ibárruri, in her speech "Women at the Front," which was printed in *Defence* on 4 September 1936,[103] spoke of a woman who took up arms against the Nationalists. When asked by Ibárruri why she had joined the militia, the unnamed *miliciana* from Toledo answered, "to fight fascism, to crush the enemies of the working people and . . . to avenge the death of my brother." She continued, "I have come here to join the ranks, to take the place he would have occupied, and to avenge his death, to show the fascist scoundrels that when men die, women take their place." The militiawoman was adamant that she, and the other militiawomen in her unit, were "fighting with the same enthusiasm and courage as the men." Ibárruri's questioning of the militiamen in the unit revealed that the young *miliciana* had shown a great deal of bravery and heroism in battle.[104]

The above example also demonstrates another reason many women gave for their decision to join the militia: in order to avenge the deaths of family members or loved ones. Asunción Herrera was one of these women.[105] She was a nineteen-year-old from Villamiel, where her father had been president of a trade union and had tried to organize the defense of the town against the Nationalists in the early days of the civil war. Herrera's father and her two brothers, one a militiaman and the other a soldier loyal to the Republic, had all been shot and killed by the fascist rebels. Moreover, Herrera's boyfriend had been taken prisoner by the Nationalists and she knew nothing of the whereabouts of her mother. Herrera related that it was for these reasons that she had taken up arms—to avenge the deaths of her family members and to take their place among the anti-fascist fighters. Several months later, she explained to a reporter from the *ABC*, "I want to bring an end to all the fascists, to all of them, so that their families know what it is to suffer."[106]

In a minority of cases, however, the motivations of women who became *milicianas* appear not to have been political or based on a natural loyalty to the Republic or a desire for revenge. For some it was romanticism, or the appeal of an adventure, that motivated them to join the militias. While these apparently trivial motivations existed, they should not overshadow the fact that most women did volunteer, wholly or partly, for political reasons. In the past, some historians have used these "frivolous" motivations to subtly discount or discredit the majority of the *milicianas*.[107]

It is also noteworthy that while some women may have had what might be considered trivial reasons for volunteering for combat initially, this does not render their military role any less significant. Women who went to the front out of a sense of adventure most likely would not have stayed there long had they not developed a deeper dedication to the cause. In addition, many young men may have gone to the front out of a similar sense of adventure, or for other foolish reasons, but this fact is never used to discredit the majority of militiamen.

The anonymous *miliciana* whose diary was published by Josep Massot i Muntaner criticized several women of the thirty in her unit in Majorca. She referred to them as "girls who think they have come on holidays," and wrote specifically of one named Teresa who often left her post because "she prefers better company and spends the day chatting, going for walks or bathing on the beach."[108] The communist newspaper *Treball* published an article on 1 September 1936 that differentiated the Catalan *miliciana* Caridad Mercader from those who joined for frivolous reasons, stating that "Mercader is as far removed from the rowdy girl who wears 'overalls' for reasons nobody can figure out, as she is from the girl who

appears today in illustrated pages of a certain press that is always sensa-
tionalist and even at times yellow."[109]

The anarchist sexologist Dr. Félix Martí Ibáñez in his text *Tres Mensajes
a la Mujer* (*Three Messages to Women*)[110] divided the militiawomen into
three groups. The first was women whom he considered genuine revolutionaries with valid reasons for volunteering, who understood the cause
for which they may be sacrificing their lives. Ibáñez argued that this first
group was the smallest. The second and largest group, according to
Ibáñez, was comprised of women whose motivations were solely roman-
tic, who based their decision on having read romance novels about war
and dreamed about being like Joan Crawford, and then "fainted in front
of the body of a militian or a soldier mutilated by shrapnel."[111] Thus,
Ibáñez employs the common stereotype that women's actions are most
often irrational and emotionally motivated. Nash points out that Ibáñez
fails to see the possibility of this argument also being applicable for
young men who volunteered for the front, in the hopes of becoming
heroes like Gary Cooper.[112] The third group described by Ibáñez was
made up of prostitutes.

Some historians cite instances of women following their brothers,
fathers or partners to the front, and use these cases as examples of wom-
en who did not have political reasons for volunteering. There are many
examples of this occurring. *ABC* published a photograph of a mother,
father and daughter who had all enlisted in the militia together and went
to fight on the front at Sigüenza.[113] On 6 August 1936 a similar photograph was printed that featured Eugenia Sánchez and her father Matías
marching toward the front, both armed. The caption suggested that this
was a common example of a "family united in the fight against fascism."[114] In an article published on 2 August 1936, *Crónica* told the story
of a sixteen-year-old woman who was told she was too young to enlist, to
which she replied adamantly that she had already fought on the front in
Somosierra, in the same unit as her father and her four brothers.[115]

However, it is entirely possible that these women nonetheless had
their own reasons for volunteering. The fact that a woman joined a militia
alongside a man is not necessarily proof that her motivations were frivolous. One such example is the anarchist Sara Berenguer who joined the
same militia as her father, but who in her memoirs wrote adamantly of
her loyalty to the Republic as her sole motivation for joining the battle.
She wrote, "only one thing moved me to action . . . a yearning to serve the
cause."[116] Her continued involvement in politics during and after the war
would suggest that this was indeed the case. In 1936, Flor Méndez, her
father and her brother were all members of the CNT. As a dedicated and
experienced anarchist, Méndez had her own reasons for volunteering for
combat, as did her brother. They both joined the same militia and were
sent to fight on the Huesca front.[117] There are also examples of this occurring among communist women. One example is Adelina Vázquez, who

immediately volunteered for combat with the Victoria Battalion at the outbreak of the war and was astonished to discover that her father had also volunteered with the same militia. Both father and daughter traveled with their battalion to the Guadarrama mountains outside Madrid to fight.[118]

If some women had not gone to the front accompanied by a family member or a partner, they might not have had the opportunity to go at all. Mangini relates that until July 1936, women in Spain were not able to move freely about the country unaccompanied and that normally only prostitutes and teachers were able to move without their families. It was considered socially acceptable for a woman to live only with her parents until she was married.[119] In many cases, it was not even considered "proper" for a woman to be seen in public unaccompanied. Strobl argues that "the biggest obstacle that girls and young women had to defeat [in order to volunteer for combat] in the first phase of the war was their own parents."[120] This possibility does not seem to have been considered by historians who use examples of women following their family or partners to the front as proof that these women did not hold their own serious reasons for volunteering.[121]

Some international women volunteers were also known to have enlisted along with their partners or husbands. Some notable examples are Low and Juan Breà, Mika and Hipólito Etchebéhère and Clara and Paul Thalmann. What is not known is whether these women would have volunteered for combat had their partners not done so. The three women cited as examples above were each dedicated political activists in their own right, so it is highly likely that their desire to volunteer would have remained the same without the influence of their partners. In the case of lesser known international volunteers, there is less evidence (and in many cases none) upon which to judge whether the woman would have volunteered regardless of the presence of her male partner. Only in a few instances does this evidence seem conclusive. Edith Shawcross, a 24-year-old British woman, wrote in 1938 about a female friend and the friend's fiancé who had both been killed while participating in combat in Spain. Shawcross is adamant that her friend would never have volunteered had it not been for her fiancé, whom she followed to Spain.[122]

An analysis of women's reasons for joining the militias and playing a military role in the conflict, as related by the women themselves, indicates that the majority of them volunteered with deeply held political, anti-fascist and loyalist convictions.[123] In any case, the majority of women gave these as their reasons for volunteering. Many women related that they felt a sense of duty and obligation that drove them to volunteer, and others explained that they felt compelled to protect the Republic that had offered them so much. A small number of women (and indeed men) enlisted on a frivolous impulse, inspired by romanticism or adventure. Nevertheless, even these women may have found more compelling reasons to fight once at the front. Otherwise, they would probably have returned home before long.

It was a diverse group of women with varied motivations who went to fight in the front lines. They were communists, anarchists, dissident Marxists and socialists, or not members of a political party or trade union at all. They were young women and old. They were students, seamstresses, writers, factory workers, typists, poets, mothers and housewives.[124] These women were not an ideological elite. It was not only these initial volunteers, who had gained experience during the street fighting after the outbreak of the war, who enlisted and went off to fight. More women, other women, were compelled to take up arms and did so from the beginning of the war right up until the time when they were no longer allowed to enroll in the militias or Republican Army. What occurred was a phenomenon that affected a large number of Spanish women, not just an exceptional few. It is possible that there would have been a constant influx of women fighters into the Republican forces, had they been allowed, until the end of the war.

An examination of this period immediately after the outbreak of the war provides a fascinating insight into the revolutionary enthusiasm of these women, and their dedication to the Republican cause and social revolution. When the political, economic and social position that women held in society prior to the Second Republic is considered, the military role played by women during the war was clearly groundbreaking.

NOTES

1. The *miliciana* phenomenon is considered to be militarily significant in terms of the numbers in which women fought, the crucial time at which they participated in combat, and by the fact that by all accounts they fought passionately even if the end result was not militarily favorable.

2. Mary Nash, *Defying Male Civilization: Women in the Spanish Civil War*, Arden Press, Denver, 1995, 105.

3. Mary Nash, "Women in War: *Milicianas* and armed combat in revolutionary Spain 1936–1939," *The International History Review*, vol. 15, no. 2, May 1993, 275.

4. Anthony Beevor, *The Spanish Civil War*, Orbis Publishing, London, 1982, 89.

5. Beevor, *Spanish Civil War*, 89.

6. Frances Lannon, "Women and Images of Women in the Spanish Civil War," *Transactions of the Royal Historical Society*, Sixth Series, vol. 1, 1991, 217.

7. Ingrid Strobl, *Partisanas: La mujer en la resistencia armada contra el fascismo y la ocupación alemana (1936–45)*, Virus, Barcelona, 1996, 44.

8. *Muchachas*, 24 July 1937, 1 and *Mujeres Libres*, no. 13, 1938.

9. Franz Borkenau, *The Spanish Cockpit: An eyewitness account of the political and social conflicts of the Spanish Civil War*, Pluto Press, London, 1937, 72.

10. Martha A. Ackelsberg, "Interview with Cristina Piera," Barcelona, August 6, 1981, in Ackelsberg, *Free Women of Spain: Anarchism and the struggle for the emancipation of women*, Indiana University Press, Bloomington, 1991, 69.

11. Lines, "Interview with Concha Pérez."

12. Mateo Rello, "Concha Pérez and Anarchy," *Solidaridad Obrera*, 17 July 2006.

13. Lines, "Interview with Concha Pérez."

14. Dolors Marín, "Las Libertarias," in Strobl, 354.

15. Lines, "Interview with Concha Pérez."

16. Marín, "Libertarias," 354.

17. Marín, "Libertarias," 354.

18. Marín, "Libertarias," 358.

19. Margarita Nelken, "De las Jornadas Trágicas de Barcelona: Fanny, la heroína de Casal Carlos Marx," *Estampa*, 22 May 1937, 16.

20. Mary Low and Juan Breà, *Red Spanish Notebook: The first six months of the revolution and the civil war*, Purnell and Sons, London, 1937, 38.

21. Francisco Coves, "Angelina Martínez, la Miliciana que Tomó Parte en el Asalto en Cuartel de la Montaña," *Estampa*, 1 August 1936, 18–19.

22. Coves, "Angelina Martínez," 18.

23. Coves, "Angelina Martínez," 18.

24. Geraldine Scanlon, *La Polémica Feminista en la España Contemporánea (1864–1975)*, Veintiuno Editores, Madrid, 1976, 292.

25. Marín, "Libertarias," 353.

26. Lannon, "Women and Images," 217.

27. See *Estampa*, 1 August 1936, 18; Judith Keene, "No More than Brothers and Sisters: Women in combat in the Spanish Civil War," in Peter Monteath and Fredric S. Zuckerman (eds.), *Modern Europe: Histories and Identities*, Australian Humanities Press, Unley, 1998, 122; and Mary Nash, "Ideals of Redemption: Socialism and women on the left in Spain," in Helmut Gruber and Pamela Graves (eds.), *Women and Socialism, Socialism and Women: Europe between the two World Wars*, Berghahn Books, New York, 1998, 367.

28. Keene, "Brothers and Sisters," 122.

29. Scanlon, *Polémica*, 292.

30. Strobl, *Partisanas*, 44.

31. *ABC*, 28 July 1936, 10; 2 August 1936, 3; and 21 August 1936, 1.

32. *Crónica*, 2 August 1936, 2; 2 August 1936, 5–6; and 30 August 1936, 2.

33. J.P., "Les Nostres Dones Tambe Lluiten," *L'Instant*, 9 September 1936, 1.

34. J.P., "Dones Tambe Lluiten," 1.

35. Antonina Rodrigo, *Mujer y Exilio 1939*, Compañía Literaria, Madrid, 1999, 61.

36. Rodrigo, *Mujer y Exilio*, 67.

37. Carmen Alcalde, *La Mujer en la Guerra Civil Española*, Editorial Cambio 16, Madrid, 1976, 123.

38. Ángel Luis Rubio Moraga, "El papel de la mujer en la guerra a través de los carteles republicanos," *Cuadernos Republicanos*, no. 36, October 1998, 108.

39. Inmaculada Julián, "Dona i Guerra Civil a Espanya (1936–1938): Representació gràfica," in Mercedes Vilanova (ed.), *Pensar las Diferencias*, PPU, Barcelona, 1994, 354.

40. For more detail on these battalions and the issue of whether or not they were organized with the intention that they would participate in combat, see chapter 3.

41. Paloma Fernández Quintanilla, *Mujeres de Madrid*, Avapies Madrid, Madrid, 1984, 167.

42. Rodrigo, *Mujer y Exilio*, 62 and 75.

43. *Ahora*, 2 October 1936, 8; and *Sydney Morning Herald*, 14 September 1936, 10.

44. See Catherine Coleman, "Women in the Spanish Civil War," in Juan P. Fusi Aizpurau, Richard Whelan, et al. (eds.), *Heart of Spain: Robert Capa's photographs of the Spanish Civil War*, Aperture, New York, 1999, 48; and *Sydney Morning Herald*, 19 August 1936, 18.

45. These initial positive attitudes toward the *milicianas* will be discussed in Chapter 4. The representation of *milicianas* in the press and propaganda in the Republican zone in many ways reflects the positive attitude held by the public toward these fighting women, and this will be discussed in detail in chapter 6.

46. The definition of what is the "front" and what it the "rearguard" is a complex issue. Some historians seem to classify those who participated in combat in Madrid as

the rearguard, though as the war progressed and the Nationalists advanced, it is clear that Madrid became the front, both during the Battle for Madrid in November 1936 and then again toward the end of the war. In fact it could be said that all those combatants in the rearguard who fought in defense of their cities could at one point be considered to be fighting at the front, as the battle front advanced across the country until every city and town had been captured by the Nationalists.

47. Claude Cockburn, "With Men and Women Fighters in the Front Line," *The Daily Worker*, 13 August 1936, in James Pettifer (ed.), *Cockburn in Spain: Dispatches from the Spanish Civil War*, Lawrence and Wishart, London, 1986, 52.

48. James K. Hopkins, *Into the Heart of the Fire: The British in the Spanish Civil War*, Stanford University Press, Stanford, 1998, 221.

49. Ian MacDougall (ed.), *Voices from the Spanish Civil War: Personal recollections of Scottish volunteers in Republican Spain 1936–1939*, Polygon, Edinburgh, 1986, 62.

50. Borkenau, *Spanish Cockpit*, 73.

51. Borkenau, *Spanish Cockpit*, 164.

52. *ABC* 28 July 1936, 10.

53. *El Diluvio*, 11 August 1936, 9.

54. Beevor, *Spanish Civil War*, 136.

55. *ABC*, 29 July 1936, 6.

56. *ABC*, 11 November 1936, 8.

57. *Tierra y Libertad*, 5 November 1936.

58. *Crónica*, 11 October 1936, 1.

59. Francis Morris (ed.), *No Pasarán: Photographs and posters of the Spanish Civil War*, Arnolfini Gallery, London, 1986, 12.

60. Clara Thalmann and Karin Buselmeier, "Entrevista sobre el Papel de la Mujer en la Revolución Española 1936–1939," in Cornelio Krasser and Jochen Schmuck (eds.), *Frauen in der Spanischen Revolution 1936–1939*, Libertad Verlag, Berlin, 1984, 68.

61. Eddie Conlon, *The Spanish Civil War: Anarchism in action*, WSM Publications, Dublin, 1986, 12.

62. These are the volunteers classified as "other" by Hugh Thomas, and referred to as those "who fought for the Spanish Republic outside the International Brigades" by Beevor. Hugh Thomas, *The Spanish Civil War*, 4th edition, London, 2003, 944 and Beevor, *Spanish Civil War*, 124–125.

63. Beevor, *Spanish Civil War*, 105. Indeed it is difficult for historians to give an accurate estimate of the size of the Republican forces in 1936. This is because the majority of militias were non-governmental, decentralized, non-conscripted, locally recruited units. No central government recruiting or conscripting agency existed to leave written records, until the professionalization of the militias and the creation of the Republican Army.

64. Strobl, *Partisanas*, 46.

65. J.P., "Dones Tambe Lluiten," 1–2.

66. J.P., "Dones Tambe Lluiten," 2.

67. Nash, *Defying*, 108.

68. Beevor, *Spanish Civil War*, 89.

69. Mangini, *Memories of Resistance*, 80.

70. Nash, *Defying*, 107.

71. Nash, *Defying*, 107 and Keene, "Brothers and Sisters," 123.

72. Low and Breà, *Notebook*, 185.

73. Coleman, "Women in the Spanish Civil War," 49.

74. *ABC*, 4 November 1936, 2.

75. Herrmann, "Voices of the Vanquished," 18.

76. Herrmann, "Voices of the Vanquished," 18.

77. Marín, "Libertarias," 354.

78. Marín, "Libertarias," 354.

79. "Entrevista a la Anarquista Concha Pérez, CNT," *El País*, 4 August 2004.

80. Lines, "Interview with Concha Pérez."

81. Strobl, *Partisanas*, 52.
82. Strobl, *Partisanas*, 52.
83. Strobl, *Partisanas*, 52.
84. Mangini, *Memories of Resistance*, 82.
85. Álvaro, *Rosario Sánchez*, 93.
86. Interview of Pilar Panes with Rosario Sánchez Mora, December 1987 in Madrid, cited in Strobl, *Partisanas*, 39.
87. Panes in Strobl, *Partisanas*, 39.
88. Maite Goicoechea, "Mujer y Guerra Civil: La historia que no se contó. Milicianas del 36: Las olvidadas," *Vindicación Feminista*, vol. 26–27, September 1978, 52.
89. Keene, "Brothers and Sisters," 126.
90. Keene, "Brothers and Sisters," 126.
91. Keene, "Brothers and Sisters," 126.
92. Low and Breà, *Notebook*, 170.
93. Low and Breà, *Notebook*, 170.
94. Tom Buchanan, *Britain and the Spanish Civil War*, Cambridge University Press, Cambridge, 1997, 123.
95. Angela Jackson, *British Women and the Spanish Civil War*, Routledge, London, 2002, 219.
96. Sydney Smith, "London Girl Off to Fight," *Daily Express*, 4 August 1936, 1.
97. Interview with Concha Pérez Collado, Barcelona, 16 June, 1981, in Nash, *Defying*, 105.
98. Teresa Pàmies, *Cuando Éramos Capitanes: (Memorias de aquella guerra)*, Dopesa, Barcelona, 1975, 48–49.
99. J. Balius, "Elisa García ha Muerto en el Frente de Aragón," *Solidaridad Obrera*, 3 September 1936.
100. Nash, *Defying*, 106.
101. Claudio Lain, "Historias de Milicianas," *Estampa*, 29 August 1936, 26.
102. *ABC*, 7 August 1936, 3.
103. Ibárruri, "Women at the Front," in Ibárruri, *Speeches and Articles*, 22.
104. Ibárruri, "Women at the Front," 22.
105. "Una Muchacha que Quiere Vengar a su Familia," *ABC*, 9 November 1936, 11.
106. "Una Muchacha," 11.
107. Nash, *Defying*, 105–107, Mangini; *Memories of Resistance*, 83–84; and Coleman, "Women in the Spanish Civil War," 48.
108. "Diario de la Miliciana," in Josep Massot i Muntaner, *El Desembarcament de Bayo a Mallorca, Agosto-Septiembre de 1936*, Publicacions de l'Abadia de Montserrat, Barcelona, 1987, 396.
109. Amadeu Bernado, "La Dona i la Revolució. Caritat Mercader, nervi de la frustrada Olimpiada Popular de Barcelona, parla als sues companys del P.S.U. i als lectors de Treball," *Treball*, 1 September 1936.
110. Felix Martí Ibáñez, *Tres Mensajes a la Mujer*, Barcelona, 1937.
111. Ibáñez, *Tres Mensajes*.
112. Nash, *Defying*, 113.
113. *ABC*, 30 July 1936, 5.
114. *ABC*, 6 August 1936, 5.
115. Rafael Martínez Gandia, "Las Mujeres en la Lucha," *Crónica*, 2 August 1936, 6.
116. Sara Berenguer, *Entre el Sol y la Tormenta*, Seuba Ediciones, Barcelona, 1988, 53.
117. Herrmann, "Voices of the Vanquished," 21.
118. Herrmann, "Voices of the Vanquished," 20.
119. Mangini, *Memories of Resistance*, 83.
120. Strobl, *Partisanas*, 44.
121. Had these family and social hindrances not existed, it is possible that more women would have volunteered for combat to defend the Republic.
122. Edith Shawcross, "The Hand that Rocks the Cradle," in Keith Briant and Lyall Wilkes (eds.), *Would I Fight?*, Basil Blackwell, Oxford, 1938, 93.

123. It is necessary to note, however, that women with a political background were more likely to write their memoirs or participate in interviews than were other women, so the sample is somewhat biased toward *milicianas* with political motivations.

124. Lain, "Historias de Milicianas," 26.

FOUR

Milicianas in Combat

An understanding of militiawomen's participation in combat and of their activities in the front lines and in the rearguard is necessary to gain an appreciation of the significance of the *miliciana* phenomenon. The absence of such an understanding allows the misconceptions to continue concerning the women who took up arms against the Nationalists in Spain. The historical significance of the *miliciana* phenomenon lies not only in the extent to which these women aided the war effort. The combat role played by militiawomen signified a change in gender roles that was occurring in the Republican zone as a result both of the war and of the social revolution. Part of the significance of the *miliciana* phenomenon also lies in its uniqueness in Spanish history. While a limited number of Spanish women had participated in combat prior to the Spanish Civil War, this was the first instance in which a large number of women not only took up arms to fight, but were integrated into the fighting force as combatants on equal terms with men.

There are several important distinctions between the *milicianas* who fought in the front lines and those stationed in the rearguard, and it is for this reason that these two subjects have been discussed separately in this chapter. Front-line *milicianas* were with few exceptions integrated into the Republican fighting force as members of mixed-gender battalions. In contrast, the *milicianas* in the rearguard were organized into women-only battalions. A further difference is that front-line combatants moved around Spain depending on the needs of the conflict, whereas *milicianas* of the rearguard remained living in their homes. Women's battalions in the rearguard played a defensive role and participated in combat only when the battle came to their cities and towns. There is little evidence of movement of women between the front lines and rearguard. Thus, front-line and rearguard *milicianas* can be seen as two separate and distinct groups of women.

This chapter will demonstrate the scope of women's military participation through a systematic examination of their military activities. A comprehensive picture of what life was like for women who fought on the front lines will be provided, outlining the combat roles that they played on a daily basis. Contrary to what has been previously thought, it will be demonstrated that the great majority of *milicianas* did actually participate in combat on equal terms with men, though they were also responsible in many cases for fulfilling an auxiliary role.

Further, it will be demonstrated that the *milicianas* played a more extensive and sophisticated combat role than has previously been shown. This chapter will present a detailed discussion of the many military activities women undertook in the front lines, including participation in battles and advances, standing guard, taking prisoners, fabricating bombs and firing upon the enemy. The aim of this chapter is to analyze the actions of the *milicianas* and the many ways they participated in the armed resistance to fascism, rather than to emphasize the auxiliary roles that militia women often played at the front, as has been the case in previous historical discussions about the *milicianas'* front-line actions.

Such a comprehensive examination of the military roles played by *milicianas* as the one that will follow has not previously been undertaken. In the past, historical accounts of the militia-women have focused on the actions of several individual women, or have included merely a brief mention of women's participation in combat (often providing only a handful of examples), and have then continued by emphasizing the non-combat duties fulfilled by women in the front lines. A broad discussion of all the military roles played by women, using the evidence available that concerns many women, has not yet been published.

Most often, articles or chapters dedicated to the *milicianas* have been based on the oral histories or memoirs of one or several militia-women, and have thus examined only the roles played by these individuals at the front. However, these accounts frequently do not take into consideration the roles played by many other women, nor do they attempt to establish what the norm was for militia-women at the front. The account provided here will take into consideration primary evidence from oral testimonies, memoirs, newspaper articles and observer commentaries, and will provide a clearer picture of what daily life at the front was like for most women, rather than for only a few individuals.

This chapter will also include a discussion on the auxiliary tasks *milicianas* carried out when not in combat. In many cases, women suffered a double burden at the front, as they were expected to carry out both combat and supportive tasks. This demonstrates that while gender roles were changing, they had not been completely revolutionized. Women in the Republican zone had not been liberated, and true equality had not been achieved. Rather, certain traditional and sexist attitudes prevailed, even among some members of the Republican militias and left-wing political groups.

Though not often included in a discussion about the militiawomen, an important aspect of the *miliciana* phenomenon was the presence of thousands of armed and trained women in the rearguard, who were organized into women's battalions and were prepared to participate in combat if needed, whether it be in the front lines or in defense of their cities and towns. This book takes as its definition of a *miliciana* any armed woman who participated in combat, or who was trained and prepared to do so, in defense of the Republic during the Spanish Civil War. While these rearguard *milicianas* are not often discussed in many other books, it is clear that these women played a significant role not only in military terms, but also in terms of demonstrating to Spanish society the change in gender roles and accepted codes of behavior that was occurring concurrently with the war. This chapter includes a discussion of the rearguard *milicianas*, the battalions into which they were organized, their arms training, their military role in the Republican defense, battles in which they took part, and the debate surrounding their purpose.

Notwithstanding the positive achievements for women brought about by the social revolution, it is also necessary to consider its limits, as is demonstrated by the treatment of the *milicianas* by the militiamen. The final section of this chapter will consider these limits. For the most part, *milicianas* reported that they did not suffer from any form of discrimination or harassment while fighting as part of the militias. However, there is evidence that this did at times occur. The existence of discrimination against women in the Republican militias underlines the strength of tradition and continuity with the past even among revolutionary elements in matters of gender equity, in much the same way, as does the double burden suffered by the *milicianas*. It is important to examine the presence of such discrimination, as in some ways it is the continuation of these sexist attitudes that allowed the removal of women from combat, a change that began in March 1937.

MILICIANAS *IN FRONT-LINE COMBAT*

During the first eight months of the Spanish Civil War, *milicianas* played an important role in the Republic's war efforts. This section aims to correct three misconceptions surrounding women's military participation in the civil war: first, that women did not participate in combat equally with men; second, that they played a limited and unsophisticated role in combat; and third, that their participation was not as dangerous or as life-threatening as that of their male comrades.

The vast majority of *milicianas* in communist, anarchist, POUM and even Republican Army units participated in combat on equal terms with their male counterparts. This was the case despite the fact that they also suffered a double burden, as they were often expected to undertake tasks traditionally considered "women's work," such as cooking, cleaning, sewing and laundry. In an interview with Dolors Marín, Concha Pérez Collado related adamantly that anarchist *milicianas* participated in combat equally with the men:

> Look, exactly what the men did, well that's what we women did. At any rate, look, because we were women we always took on some extra work, like cleaning more or cooking or something. But then we stood guard equally with the men. When there was the attack at Belchite, we went into the attack equally with the men. We did what we humanly could, some of us [women] were stronger than others, same as the men.[1]

Pérez Collado reiterated this opinion during my interview with her in 2005, asserting that men and women acted equally in combat.[2] The testimony of Pérez Collado is significant because, at the very least, it demonstrates that the *milicianas* themselves felt that they were making the same military contribution to the war effort as were the militiamen.

In the POUM column captained by Mika Etchebéhère, women and men most certainly participated in combat equally. In fact, as will be discussed below, in this column all tasks, both combat and supportive, were undertaken equally and there was no gendered division of labor.[3] Evidence suggests that even female combatants in the Republican Army participated in combat on equal terms with their male comrades. Captain Fernando Saavedra of the Sargento Vázquez Battalion reported on the military activity of three female combatants in his unit, Ángeles, Nati and Paca. In an interview that was printed in the independent newspaper *Crónica* in December 1936, he stated, "[they are] three comrades who, rifle in arms, have come to fight with us. I have to say that they are brave, and that, like the men, they carry out their mission. They stand guard, go to the trenches, and, finally, they fight like any one of us."[4] Further evidence that the military contribution of individual women was as significant as that of individual men can be found below in the discussion of the various combat duties undertaken by *milicianas* at the front.

The combat experiences of militiawomen do not differ widely, regardless of the political group (if any) to which they belonged. The evidence below has nonetheless been presented according to political group, in order to demonstrate this point. There appears to be only one exception, which is that according to the stories of the *milicianas* that have been examined here, anarchist and POUM militiawomen changed units or left the front and returned later according to their own will, while communist women spoke of being "transferred" or else of remaining with the same unit.

Similarly, there is no evidence of communist *milicianas* leaving the front to play a non-military role in the rearguard and later returning, unless they had been wounded. This may have been the result of lower levels of discipline and military authority within anarchist and POUM militias. However, not enough evidence on this subject is available to show whether this was a widespread trend. It was only later, after the political dynamics of the war and revolution had changed in December 1936 that the experience and treatment of *milicianas* belonging to various political groups began to vary significantly. The evidence provided here demonstrates that communist, anarchist, POUMist, socialist and unaffiliated *milicianas* played a sophisticated and extensive military role in the conflict.[5]

Lina Odena was perhaps the best-known *miliciana*, becoming famous after she died in combat early in the Spanish Civil War. Odena was a young communist activist, and a member of the *Dirección Nacional* (national leadership body) of the JSU.[6] From the first day of the Nationalist insurrection, Odena was a leader of the anti-fascist resistance. In July, she helped to organize the militias in Almería, on the southern coast of Spain, and fought in the front lines there. From there she went to Guadix and led the militias into battle.[7] Odena traveled to various sectors of the Granada front, in command of a militia unit,[8] and achieved the post of commandant.[9]

On 13 September 1936, Odena died on the Granada front, in the Guadix sector. Odena and a comrade were on a reconnaissance mission that night, past the most advanced post of the sector and behind enemy lines. They became lost, and were discovered by the Nationalists who began to fire upon them. They both returned fire, but were outnumbered. Almost out of ammunition and fearing being taken prisoner, Odena used her last bullet to shoot herself in the head. Clearly, she was aware of the horrors of rape and mutilation that almost certainly awaited her upon her capture. Shortly after her death, Odena's unit was successful in the attack that she had planned.[10] Her suicide was reported widely in the communist, socialist and independent press as a brave and noble act, and she became a Republican war legend.[11]

Another prominent *miliciana* who rose to the status of a legend during the war was the communist Rosario Sánchez de la Mora. The example of Sánchez de la Mora, though unique in some ways as a result of her later notoriety, can be seen as representative of the experience of communist women who were stationed in the front lines during the Spanish Civil War. Sánchez de la Mora volunteered for combat very soon after the war began, and was stationed at Buitrago, south of the Ebro River. When she arrived at the front, Sánchez de la Mora joined the first shock group of the 46th Division, and received a short weapons training course.[12] She explained, "in all cases, we had to shoot continually in order that the fascists would note that we were presenting a strong resistance. Our carbines had a range of less than 30 meters. They were very old rifles."[13] Sánchez de la Mora fought in the front line of what was a very important sector, since the Ebro River provided water to Madrid and it was imperative to safeguard this water supply. She related that her position was always "the same hell. We shot day and night, of course thanks to this I learnt very quickly how to fight."[14] Sánchez de la Mora fought for two months without a break, before she was given her first 48-hour pass to visit her village.[15]

Sánchez de la Mora considered standing guard to be the worst of all her duties at the front, because of the grave responsibility that came with the task. "You were scared of failing, of perhaps falling asleep, scared that through your failing the war might be lost, that [the enemy] might attack your comrades and kill them. It's incredible what one can imagine might happen in two hours. In my case it was made worse by the fact that I was a woman, and for this reason I tried even harder not to let myself fail."[16] Despite her feelings about the difficulty of standing guard, Sánchez de la Mora always remained at her post for a few minutes longer than the men, even though this meant losing precious time for sleep that she desperately needed. She explained later that she felt strongly the need to prove herself because she was a woman at the front.[17]

After several months in the trenches at Buitrago, Sánchez de la Mora was transferred into the dynamite section of a mobile shock troop. Her captain was Emilio González.[18] Upon her arrival, Sánchez de la Mora received training in the construction of bombs, and learned how to use them in various methods of attack. Even during her training, Sánchez de la Mora made bombs for use in combat, and shortly she became an expert. In September 1936, an accident took place in which she lost her hand. The group was training in a new method of attack, standing in a diagonal line taking turns to light and throw their grenades. Sánchez de la Mora was standing at the end of the line, so close to the militiaman next to her that their arms were touching. She had already lit her grenade when someone yelled, "throw!" but immediately afterward another person screamed, "don't throw!" Sánchez de la Mora realized that if she threw her grenade it would injure or possibly kill one of her comrades, so she turned around in an effort to get rid of it safely. Before she could do so, the grenade exploded in her hand. It was after this heroic action that left her without a hand that Sánchez de la Mora became a war legend, celebrated throughout the Republic in the communist and independent press, in poems, and in speeches.

A member of the communist youth from the age of thirteen, Fidela Fernández de Velasco Pérez had already been politically active and trained in the use of arms long before the civil war broke out.[19] She fought in the front lines against the Nationalists from the very beginning of the war. Very soon after being sent to the front outside Madrid, she participated in an attack that successfully captured a cannon from the defeated Nationalists. She later fought in Toledo, and then returned to the Madrid front where she was transferred into the same unit as Sánchez de la Mora. Strobl notes that Fernández de Velasco Pérez was always involved in the most dangerous actions. Not only did she fight in the front lines, but she also took part in many missions behind enemy lines as part of a group of shock troops.

For years afterward Fernández de Velasco Pérez could remember exactly how to construct a bomb. She recalled, "we boiled cans of condensed milk and filled them with bits of crystal, rocks and nails, and we added dynamite. The fuse came out the top and we had to throw them very fast because the fuse was quite short."[20] Fernández de Velasco Pérez remembered that life in the trenches was difficult, as it was necessary to sleep in the mud, in the snow, and standing up. Often there was no food. After a year and a half of fighting on the front, Fernández de Velasco Pérez was injured and unable to continue fighting. Instead, she became a secret agent and took on many dangerous missions behind enemy lines. She remained in this role until the end of the war.[21]

The stories of lesser known communist militiawomen also emphasize their participation in battle and their dedication to the Republican cause. Consuelo Martín, a member of the PCE, suffered a bullet wound to the leg while fighting in the Somosierra.[22] When a reporter from the independent newspaper *Estampa* asked how long she had been fighting there, Martín replied, "since the first day! I left with the first battalion that went to the Somosierra, the Galán [battalion], and I was there for twenty days until I was made to leave because I was wounded, but it is already healing. . . . Wednesday I want to leave with the *Intendencia* column!"[23]

Margarita Ribalta was interviewed by the same reporter, since she was also wounded and recuperating at the communist militia headquarters. She told him that she was a member of the JSU, and had enlisted in the militia with a male companion at the beginning of the war. He was sent to the front, but Ribalta was assigned to work at headquarters, about which she was not pleased.[24] After a few days, she was enrolled in a column and left for the front. Once there, she volunteered immediately to go out with an advance party. She explained that the group climbed to the top of a hill, and saw a group of Nationalists shooting a machine gun in the distance. The Republicans opened fire at the Nationalists. They shot and killed the man who had been handling the weapon. The rest of the group of Nationalists were either shot or fled.[25]

Ribalta ran into the field between the two posts, the whole advance party following her, and seized the machine gun. The group dismantled the weapon and was returning to the Republican line, with Ribalta carrying the machine gun on her back, when a Republican airplane appeared. Unfortunately, upon seeing the group advancing toward the loyalist lines in possession of a machine gun, the plane mistook the group for Nationalists and dropped a bomb just as they had reached the top of the hill. Ribalta dropped to the ground and began to roll down the hill, but was wounded in the face and arms. When she returned to the communist militia headquarters to recover, Ribalta discovered that her male friend was also convalescing there. Ribalta explained that it was for this reason that she stayed on to recover: "I am here because he is also. If not, with bandages and all, I would have already returned to the front." [26]

Caridad Mercader was a Catalan communist and member of the PSUC. After taking part in the assault on the Military Headquarters in Barcelona during the first few days of the war, she went on to fight on the front in the Maestranza. Later she fought on the Aragon front in a column under the command of Pérez Farras and Durruti. [27] She was wounded by a shell while fighting in the town of Tardienta, [28] and died in a Nationalist prison after the war. [29]

Trinidad Revolto Cervello joined the JSU in 1933. [30] Having participated in battle in front of the Military Headquarters and at the Atarazanas Barracks in Barcelona during the first few days of the uprising, Revolto Cervello then joined the Popular Militias and took part in the attack on Majorca. [31] At the beginning of the war, Teófila Madroñal enlisted in the Leningrad Battalion and underwent arms training. [32] When the Siege of Madrid began on 7 November 1936, Madroñal fought in the sector near the Estremadura highway. At the age of only seventeen, Julia Manzanal became the Political Commissar for the *Batallón Municipal de Madrid* (Municipal Battalion of Madrid). Despite the fact that her primary role was to provide a political educational to her comrades, Manzanal related that she was armed with a rifle and a .38 Messerschmitt revolver, participated in combat during battles, took her turn standing guard, and on several occasions even worked as a spy. Such was Manzanal's dedication to her military participation, upon discovering that she was pregnant in the early stages of the war, Manzanal decided to have an abortion so she could continue to fight in the front lines. [33]

It is significant that several communist women held leadership positions within militias and in the Regular Army. Aurora Arnáiz at twenty-two years of age was in command of the first column of the JSU, and led them into battle on the Madrid front against General Mola's troops. [34] Odena, as previously mentioned, also served as a commandant and led her troops into battle in Granada. [35]

The experiences of communist international volunteers do not appear to have been notably different to those of Spanish communist *milicianas*. A volunteer from Holland identified only as Fanny was dubbed the "hero of *Casal Carlos Marx*" (the headquarters of the PSUC in Barcelona). [36] She had participated in the street fighting at the outbreak of the war, and once the insurrection had been put down in Barcelona, Fanny caught the first train leaving for the Saragossa front where she fought using a machine gun. In her youth in Holland, Fanny had practiced shooting as a sport, and was already highly trained in the use of arms.[37] Fanny fought on various fronts from Grañén to Tardienta, until she suffered a form of paralysis in her legs due to the harsh conditions of trench warfare in the extreme weather conditions of Tardienta. Once she was released from hospital, the PSUC sent her to the *Escuela de Comisarios* (Commissary School) and later she was appointed as a teacher to the Regular Army.[38]

Another communist international volunteer, Felicia Browne, became well known for her participation in combat, since she was the first British volunteer to die in the Spanish Civil War.[39] Claude Cockburn reported in *The Daily Worker* that Browne had volunteered for the militia immediately upon hearing that they were accepting women, and was readily accepted. He related that for a short time Browne was stationed in Barcelona on patrol duty, but after receiving a weapons training course she was sent to the front.[40] Browne was stationed in the Tardienta sector on the Saragossa front, and was involved in various battles and dangerous missions. It was during one such night mission to rig explosives to blow up a munitions train that Browne was killed.[41]

George Brinkman, a German volunteer who was another of the ten in the group, wrote a detailed report on the mission and the specifics of Browne's death.[42] He related that the group traveled by car to the furthest point of the front, after which they walked twelve kilometers to reach the railway line. Browne and two of her comrades stood guard while the rest of the group rigged explosives on the railway tracks, to blow up a munitions train that passed soon afterward. The group was delayed on their way back to Tardienta when they came across the wreckage of a Republican airplane and the corpse of its pilot. While burying the pilot, the group was discovered by a section of nearly forty Nationalists who began to fire upon them. An Italian member of the militia was shot, and Browne went to his aid. It was at this point that Browne was shot and killed.[43]

The stories of anarchist militiawomen do not differ significantly from those of communist *milicianas*. Once the Nationalist uprising in Barcelona had been quelled, Pérez Collado traveled to Caspe on the Aragon front where she joined the Ortíz Column.[44] Her unit then moved on to Azaida, where they remained until the attack on Belchite, in which Pérez Collado and her militia took part, began on 24 August.[45] While stationed in Azaida, Pérez Collado met other anarchist militiawomen who had come to the front to fight, including Carmen Crespo, a member of the Sur-Ebro Column. Crespo was later killed by a grenade in a battle at the Sierra de la Serna in December 1936.[46]

In my interview with her, Pérez Collado related how her militia moved around the front lines, advancing and retreating. Sometimes her unit would be stationed in a town, where they would stay in houses and spend their time in weapons training and standing guard, waiting for an attack. At others, Pérez Collado's unit would be stationed in the trenches at the front lines and would be involved in battle consistently.[47] In December, after fighting for more than four months on the Aragon front, Pérez Collado returned to Barcelona for a short period of leave.[48] However, it was not long before she rejoined the militia and traveled to Huesca to fight.[49] Pérez Collado spent only several more months fighting in the Tardienta sector before she returned once again to Barcelona. She believed she would be more useful in the rearguard, where she worked in a collectivized munitions factory.[50]

The Basque anarchist Casilda Méndez fought on many fronts and in several different militias during the war. Initially, Méndez fought as a member of the Likiniano Group in the street fighting, and then traveled with this group to the San Marcial front, where she fought until the fall of Irun.[51] While Méndez reveals that she did the cooking for her unit, she emphasizes that she was not merely the cook. She participated in combat along with the men in her militia, and was equally involved in other military tasks such as erecting parapets and digging trenches.[52]

Later she fought with the Hilario-Zamora Column on the Aragon front, and took part in the attack on Almudévar.[53] She notes that on the Aragon front women enjoyed a greater equality, and their identity changed from "'woman' to 'combatant.'"[54] For a short time, she fought with Maria Ruis, an anarchist from Barcelona, who was also a member of the Hilario-Zamora Column. Méndez fought in the battle to capture Quinto and Monte Carmelo.[55] After a short period working in a factory in the rearguard, she again returned to the front in the Ebro sector with the 153rd Division, where she relates that conditions were continually unfavorable for the Republicans, and fought in the Battle for the Ebro River.[56] Méndez believed that the battle "bled us dry without doing us any good," except that "perhaps it delayed the end of the war a little."[57]

The stories of the *milicianas*, while most often emphasizing their confidence and capability in combat, also include information on the difficulties they faced in the front lines. The old weapons used by the Republicans were often very heavy and cumbersome, and this is one problem that was often discussed. However, having described the initial problems caused by these weapons, most women's stories end with an emphasis on how strong and capable they felt once they were able to use and carry these weapons effectively.

Sofia Blasco interviewed an anarchist *miliciana* named Carmen whom she met on the Sierra front. Carmen had been a seamstress's assistant in Madrid before the war, and had joined the militia planning to do laundry and sew for the militiamen. Once at the front, having witnessed the severity of the conflict and having seen comrades killed, she took up a weapon and joined the armed resistance against fascism.[58] Blasco met Carmen again several months later and noted that she had been transformed. Carmen herself had been shocked by her transformation: "fancy me, a weak woman, and now I can manage a gun with the ease that I used to wield a needle."[59] Carmen had become an expert in the use of her weapon and now, far from having difficulty carrying the heavy rifle, as she "tramped up hill and down she had the sense that it was the gun that was carrying her along."[60]

Many of the stories of *milicianas* do not end with their forced removal from the front in 1937, but with their deaths in battle. A group of anarchist *milicianas* from the International Group of the Durruti Column were killed in the fighting at Perdiguera in October 1936. Among them were Suzanne Girbe and Augusta Marx who were killed on 16 October. Augusta was a member of the German Socialist Workers' Party and was a qualified nurse, but joined the militia as a combatant.[61] Juliette Baudard, Eugenie Casteu and Georgette Kokoczinski were killed in action the following day. Kokoczinski had served as a nurse in the column, but regularly took part in nocturnal raids behind the Nationalist lines with the *Hijos de la Noche* (Sons of the Night) group. She was captured by the Nationalists and executed.[62] Suzanne Hans, also from the International Group of the Durruti Column, was killed in a battle in Farlete in November 1936, at the age of twenty-two. Her partner Louis Recoulis was killed in the same attack.[63] Leopoldine Kokes was one of the few *milicianas* from the International Group of the Durruti Column left alive to be expelled from the militia several months later.[64]

While there were fewer POUMist *milicianas* than communist and anarchist, their stories are nonetheless well known as a result of Etchebéhère's widely published memoirs, *Mi Guerra de España*, and also the memoirs of Mary Low and Juan Breà, *Red Spanish Notebook*. In *The Spanish Cockpit* Franz Borkenau relates an incident during which he met and spoke with a group of POUM militiawomen outside the Hotel Falcon in Barcelona, which the POUM was using as its headquarters, but he does not give any specific information on their actions in battle.[65] One of the *milicianas* is said to be a foreign volunteer, married to a Swiss newspaper correspondent. Later Borkenau refers to an English woman whom he also met in Barcelona, and who had volunteered for the POUM militia.[66]

Etchebéhère became a combatant after the death of her husband Hipólito, taking his place in the militia. In October 1936, Etchebéhère was stationed in Sigüenza during the Nationalist siege, in which soldiers, militiamen and women, and civilians were trapped and hid in the cathedral while they were bombarded by the Nationalists.[67] Later, Etchebéhère met Low and Breà in Barcelona, and related to them the story of what had happened at Sigüenza. This conversation was recorded in *Red Spanish Notebook*, which was written only months later:

> I was there till the last. . . . We barricaded ourselves in the cathedral —
> those of us who had been trapped in the town — and determined to put

up a good show for our money. We were there for four days, without food or anything, firing out into the town, and dying like flies. They kept on shooting cannon balls into the cathedral. It stood up pretty well, but in the end the walls began to fall down on us, and we had no ammunition left at all, so those of us who were still left decided to make a run for it after dark as we couldn't fight anymore. . . . It was awful. There was a thick fog in the night we made the get-away, and some of the comrades got lost and ran straight into the Fascists and were shot to pieces. They began firing on us at once, of course, and we scattered and reached the woods through a rain of machine-gun bullets. I wandered about for twenty-four hours, hiding among the trees and undergrowth, while they hunted me, before I could reach our lines. They shot lots of us, of course. About a third of us who set out from the cathedral reached home. I was almost delirious from exhaustion and want of food.[68]

As a result of her bravery and decisiveness in action at the siege of Sigüenza, Etchebéhère was promoted to the position of Captain of Second Company of the POUM's Lenin Battalion.[69] She was then transferred to the front in Moncloa, where she led a special brigade of shock troops that undertook the most dangerous operations.[70]

Low, the Australian *miliciana* who joined the POUM in Barcelona, tells in her memoirs the story of another foreign volunteer, Simone. She had wanted to bring weapons with her when she came to fight with the POUM, but had been unable to enter the country with the weapons through normal channels. She took a small airplane to Spain, but it refused to land in the war-torn country. Such was her determination that Simone strapped the machine guns to her body and jumped out of the airplane over Catalonia. Later Simone demonstrated this same resolve in battle in the front lines. Low spoke with a young militiaman who had fought alongside Simone in the trenches. He told Low of the first time their unit came under attack. "We hadn't been under fire before, and when the Fascists made the first big attack and came right over at us, Pepe and I really thought that everything was up with us and we had better run for it. But not she! She knocked our heads together—how it hurt—yes, she really had time to think of everybody in a moment like that—and pushed us back by the scruff of our necks." Low asked the man if they had held their position after this. "Oh yes, we held it. We kept on holding it, you know."[71]

Low also included in her memoirs the story of a young German militiawoman named Margaret Zimbal, whose nickname was Putz. Concerned for her safety, Low had tried desperately at the beginning of the war to persuade her to volunteer as an ambulance driver rather than as a militiawoman, but Zimbal refused to do anything but fight at the front as a member of a POUM militia. Low met her again later at the POUM party headquarters in Barcelona, after her unit had returned from the failed attack on Majorca. Zimbal's lover, a young German volunteer, had been killed in the fighting at Porto Cristo. Zimbal had been devastated and depressed, but despite her hardship, she had lost none of her determination. "Well, I shall go to another front as soon as possible, that's all."[72]

Two days later Zimbal left for the Aragon front with four young Spanish men. They had gone away singing. Soon afterward, Low received a report that the group had only been at the front for six hours when all four men were shot and killed on either side of Zimbal. Nonetheless, she remained at the front and was assigned to act as a scout, going on dangerous solitary night missions into the territory between the Republican and enemy lines, all the time unaware of how close to the fascists' advanced positions she might have been.[73]

Low met up with Zimbal later, when the latter had returned to Barcelona to work for the International Bureau. At that time, Zimbal's lover was an older German man, who refused to allow her to rejoin the militia. One afternoon Low and Breà were eating in a café with Zimbal when the *Bandera Puig* militia, the first that Zimbal had joined, marched down the street past them after having been recalled to the front. Low reported that "suddenly Putz jumped up and threw away her chair and ran after then all down the street, crying 'Wait for me, wait for me, I'm coming too! I'm coming.'"[74] That was the last time that they saw her alive. Zimbal was killed in October 1936[75] at the Huesca front, shot in the back by a Nationalist sniper.[76]

Red Spanish Notebook is rich with stories and observations of the militiawomen that Low and Breà met during their time in Spain. Some of the women they met are only mentioned briefly, but despite the little information available regarding these women, what we do know of them is fascinating. Early in the war, Low met a "short, broad woman in blue overalls and a red tie, with frizzy hair standing out round her head." All that is related about the conversation they had is the following:

> [She] leaned over and said to me eagerly: "I was at the front, too. I got shot in the foot." She had a very deep, husky voice and spoke softly, and it seemed as if the words were coming out from behind a velvet curtain. "What did you do before you joined the militias?" "I helped in my aunt's shop," she said, "but I like it better at the front, it's more exciting."

Breà reported a conversation he had with a Swiss militiawoman identified only as Clara, who recalled her experiences on the Aragon front in a POUM militia. She related that her sector was relatively quiet, and that the worst of her duties was standing guard: "most of the time it would have been all right, if it wasn't for the dust. Standing guard outside was frightful, when the wind blew, and we all had to take our turn. One daren't turn away and cover one's head even for a moment because we were always expecting a surprise attack, and your eyes got so full of sand

and bloodshot and it was heck."[77] Clara also showed Breà a large dark blue bruise on her shoulder that she had received from firing her musqueton. She explained, "they're so much lighter to carry than a rifle when you're springing about, but what a kick they've got to them!" She then concluded positively that "you get used to it in time . . . [and] I'm not a bad shot at all now."[78]

Despite styling itself as a revolutionary party, the PSOE rejected the notion of the radical militiawoman from the very beginning. For the PSOE, the only acceptable role for a woman to play in the anti-fascist resistance was as a "home front heroine," undertaking tasks in the vein of civil resistance, ensuring the everyday survival of the population, and carrying out voluntary relief work.[79] This is not surprising, given the PSOE's historical lack of attention to gender issues. Though some *milicianas* had been members of the PSOE, they were relatively few in number. The JSU, the communist and socialist youth organization, had recruited some of its female members into front-line combat positions, so it was mainly in this way that socialist women became militarily involved in the civil war.[80]

María Elisa García is one of the few women identified specifically as socialist who is known to have participated in combat. García escaped from Oviedo with her father and her brothers on 18 July 1936, to join the Popular Militias. She fought with her father as a member of the *Somoza* company, the third company of the Asturias Battalion.[81] She first participated in battle on the Lugones front (north of Oviedo), where her father was killed. From there, García went on with her battalion to fight in the Basque mountains. An article in the communist newspaper *Mujeres* relates an incident during a particularly cold night, when the men of her company, concerned for her, assured her that she did not need to take her turn, and should return inside their temporary quarters to warm herself. García refused adamantly: "no, no, I'm staying here, with you. Yes. I will stay right here. I have to avenge someone. I have to avenge my father."[82] On the night of 9 May 1937, while García was at her post in the mountains of Múgica, the enemy attacked. García went into battle, alongside her male comrades, just as she had during every other attack. During the clash, she was shot in the head and died instantly.[83]

Not all of the primary evidence pertaining to women in combat specifies the political background of the *miliciana* in question. Further, not all *milicianas* identified themselves in political terms, since not all were members of political groups. Below is a selection of evidence demonstrating the military involvement of these women.

Jacinta Pérez Alvarez was one of the ten *milicianas* of the sixth company of the Acero Brigade.[84] Pérez Alvarez had never considered the idea of women participating in combat to be unusual. In fact, when asked what she planned to do after the war, Pérez Alvarez had replied that if there were a women's army, she would enroll in it.[85] She was killed in

August 1936 during a battle in which she had fought for five consecutive days, in the first advance party on the front outside Madrid.[86] A newspaper article printed in the independent *El Sol* reported that after being shot, Pérez Alvarez bravely shouted to her comrades: "advance, keep going forward, it's only a nuisance, I will follow you at once."[87]

The first company of the Largo Caballero Battalion contained roughly ten *milicianas*, of whom Josefina Vara was one.[88] The battalion fought on the Sierra front, and in an article published in *Crónica* on 13 September 1936, Vara received a special mention due to her actions in battle on 4 August. She supplied ammunition to the advance party as well as firing her own weapon, and later helped her captain to capture and disarm several prisoners.[89] It was reported that Vara knew no fear, and only worried that she would be made to leave the front for the rearguard.[90]

The communist press reported on women who were promoted to leadership positions. Argentina García was the captain of the machine gun company of the second Asturias Battalion.[91] Three months before being promoted to the position of captain, García had been wounded and left for dead while fighting at Oviedo. She had sustained four wounds in her stomach and arm, and remained unconscious for hours on the battleground. That night the cold woke her, and she managed to reach the Republican lines without being discovered by the enemy. As soon as she had healed, García returned to fight on the front at San Esteban de las Cruces, and was promoted to captain for her bravery in battle.[92] Consuelo Rodríguez was ranked as a sergeant in October 1936, and led her troops into battle at the Madrid front.[93]

Francisca Solano, a member of the *Circulo Socialista del Oeste* unit, took part in the capture of El Espinar in July 1936 alongside two other *milicianas* in her unit.[94] These women and many others from their area had been involved in the armed resistance to fascism since the insurrection.[95] Upon the outbreak of the civil war, Solano's uncle encouraged her to go to the front as a nurse, since she had worked previously in that capacity. However, Solano refused to do so, preferring to join the militia as a combatant: "No. No I won't be a nurse. I want to go and fight the fascists!"[96] Despite the objections of her family, Solano enlisted in the *Circulo del Oeste*, received her uniform and gun, and left for the front that day. It was this determination that led her to take part in battle alongside her male comrades.

Early on a Saturday morning in August, Solano's unit advanced into El Espinar, without firing a single shot. They headed to the town hall and raised the flag of their column.[97] On their way to the central plaza they met with several Civil Guards who assured them that the town was quiet, but shortly afterward the unit learned that a battalion of Nationalists were advancing along the road toward the town. Preparations were made to defend El Espinar against the Nationalists, but the attack came unexpectedly from in front and behind. Solano and her group began to retreat, fighting as they went. During the battle, one of Solano's comrades was injured and she took him to the hospital to be treated.

The rest of the unit did not discover this fact until they had safely retreated and the fighting had stopped. They realized that Solano and her comrade were missing, and they never saw them again. There were rumors about what happened to Solano, but no one knew the truth. Some believed that she had been taken prisoner at the hospital, while others had heard that when she was apprehended she had shot and killed a Nationalist lieutenant. Still others believed that she had been shot by a firing squad. The members of Solano's unit remembered her as their heroine, "who had always been in the lead, the most enthusiastic and courageous of all."[98]

Though the majority of women fought as members of a militia, some women did enter the Republican Army. Esperanza Rodríguez was one of them. Rodríguez not only fought alongside her male comrades against the Nationalists, but her captain described her as the bravest fighter in the unit. In an article printed in *Estampa* on 10 October 1936, Rodríguez's captain said of her: "how brave! Seriously! Look, it's eight years that I've been in the Regular Army, and I know this is a serious thing." He described her as "the best in combat, always the most lively, the first to shoot, the most tireless. In one battle she spent eleven hours on her feet, shooting."[99]

As shown earlier, the majority of *milicianas* fought as members of mixed-gender battalions. One of the few women-only battalions in the front lines was the Women's Battalion stationed outside Madrid. At the end of July 1936, the PCE decided it was necessary to organize a Fifth Regiment in Madrid, though there had only ever been four stationed in the city.[100] Nash indicates that "the Fifth Regiment did have a number of women present in the early months."[101] She is careful to emphasize, however, that these women performed auxiliary tasks such as "culinary, laundry, sanitary, postal, liaison, and administrative assignments."[102] She also gives the example of two *milicianas* who left the Fifth Regiment to join Etchebéhère's unit, where they would have the same rights as men, and would not be obliged to carry out all the domestic work on their own.[103] These are the only references to the Fifth Regiment that Nash makes in relation to militiawomen.

In reality, there were more than a few women members of the Fifth Regiment. An entire battalion of women, the *Batallón Femenino del 5th Regimiento de Milicias Populares* (Women's Battalion of the Fifth Regiment of Popular Militias), was organized. This battalion specifically recruited and trained women for combat, and sent them to the front outside Madrid. A three-page article printed in the independent newspaper *Crónica* on 2 August 1936[104] provides evidence about this battalion and the military actions of its members. It should be noted that women also joined and took part in combat in sections of the Fifth Regiment other than the women's battalion.[105]

The *Crónica* article begins by describing a large group of women amassing in the courtyard of the Fifth Regiment headquarters in order to enlist, receive their uniform and weapon, and be organized in their units ready to leave for the front. The article makes special mention of a group of women who had already been to the Sierra front working as nurses, but who had returned in order to enlist as militiawomen. They explained, "we want to fight. For this reason, we have enlisted in the Women's Battalion."[106] The article speaks of a student who was adamant she must be sent to the Somosierra, in order to be reunited with her two brothers fighting there. A widow explained that the day before her husband was killed fighting in the Sierra, and she had promised him she would keep fighting. A sixteen year old, already training with her weapon, related that her father and four brothers were already at the front. The article included several photographs of women undergoing weapons training, and relates that the training they receive is "exactly equal to that of the men."[107] It finishes by describing the large group of women climbing aboard trucks and leaving for the front.

Once recruited and trained, the members of the Women's Battalion of the Fifth Regiment were stationed in the front lines outside Madrid. Walter Gregory, in his memoirs *The Shallow Grave*, recalls the regular sight of members of the battalion coming on and off duty. He explains that they marched up and down Gran Vía in twos and threes, since it was so often shelled that it was too dangerous for them to march in proper formation.[108] He remarked that "they looked very like women the world over and only their disheveled khaki uniforms after several nights in the trenches marked them out as something special."[109]

While it is certain that the *milicianas* of the Women's Battalion of the Fifth Regiment did indeed undertake auxiliary tasks such as cooking and cleaning, while the militiamen in other battalions of the regiment were not expected to do so, it remains clear that these women were armed and had been trained in the use of their weapons, and that they did in fact participate in battle at the front. The fact that these women also fulfilled an auxiliary role should not diminish the reality that they took part in combat.

Many testimonies from foreign observers highlight the courage displayed by the *milicianas* in battle, demonstrating that in some cases they exhibited even more valor than the militiamen did. Borkenau, in his entry of 5 September 1936, wrote of the bombardment of the village of Cerro Muriano. While he was shocked to witness troops from Jaén and Valencia who "ran away before our eyes," Borkenau noted a small militia from Alcoy (south-east of Valencia), including two *milicianas*, who "stood the bombardment . . . with the proudest gallantry and unconcernedness."[110]

He emphasized that the two women were "more courageous even than the men."[111]

Similarly, in his oral testimony the Scottish volunteer Tom Clarke related that during the Battle of Jarama in January 1937, it was the bravery of three Spanish militiawomen that stopped their battalion from retreating:

> I remember there was a bit of a retreat. There was a rumour went round, can't remember what it was, and they started retreating. We'd gone back a bit, and some of them were actually running. And here we came across three women sitting behind a machine gun just past where we were, Spanish women. I saw them looking at us. You know, I don't know whether it shamed us or what. But these women they stayed there.[112]

The bravery of the *milicianas* is also demonstrated by the fact that they risked injury and death to defend the Republic. When caught, the militiawomen were not protected from execution by the mere fact that they were women. Antony Beevor relates that the German ambassador was alarmed during a visit with General Francisco Franco when he ordered the execution of a group of *milicianas* who were being held prisoner, and then continued to eat his lunch.[113] Breà reported having met a man in Sigüenza named Casimir who told him that even pregnant militiawomen were executed by the Nationalists:

> He had been telling me about some prisoners that had been taken by the Fascists while he was still serving in their army and looking for a way of escape. "They were three men, and a woman." . . . "I know what happened to those prisoners because I had to wait on the officers that day at their lunch and they talked in front of me. 'Well, have you had those four prisoners shot yet?', one of the officers inquired. You should have heard the casual way they talked about it, as though it had been so many heads of cattle. And the doctor guffawed, and winked at the captain. 'Four? You meant the five prisoners, surely? . . . You forget that the woman was . . . well. . .'"[114]

NON-COMBAT ROLES IN THE FRONT LINES

As shown earlier, the vast majority of *milicianas* participated in combat on equal terms with their male comrades. Clearly, gender roles were changing in the Republican zone during the Spanish Civil War, and accepted codes of behavior were becoming more progressive. However, gender roles had not been completely revolutionized, and equality had not yet been achieved. Sexism remained prevalent in Spanish society, even among revolutionary elements. This is clear because *milicianas* largely suffered a double burden in the front lines, carrying the responsibility for the bulk of the domestic tasks in addition to their combat duties.

It is the combat role played by *milicianas* that is most important, however, in order to give a complete picture of what life was like for the *milicianas* in the front lines, it is important to discuss the non-combat roles they played in addition to their military activities. Women performed many auxiliary tasks at the front, regardless of whether they were fighting with militias controlled by the communists, anarchists, POUM, socialists or the Republican government. Once again, the day-to-day experiences of women in the front lines did not vary significantly according to the political group to which they belonged. These tasks included cooking, cleaning, laundry, sanitary, medical and political work. In some cases, these tasks were carried out by men and women equally, but in most cases, it is true that women suffered a double burden, since it was expected that they would complete these chores as well as fulfilling the same combat duties as the men.

Blasco reports that the five militiawomen she met, Maria, Rosario, Anita, Julia and Margarita,[115] were always working. They would be cooking, cleaning, doing laundry and repairing clothes well into the night after their male comrades had long since completed their combat duties for the day. The women told Blasco that they were constantly exhausted. Despite taking their turn standing guard and participating in combat just as the men did, they were also responsible for the "irksome duties that always fall to women."[116] Leonor Benito also explained that even though she stood guard and undertook other combat duties equally with the men in her unit, she was still expected to do the washing for the men.[117]

The two *milicianas* Manuela and Nati who asked to join Etchebéhère's column described the domestic duties that they were required to undertake in the Pasionaria Column of the Fifth Regiment of the Popular Militias, and gave this as the reason why they wanted to join a different column. Theirs is a notable example because it is one of the few in which *milicianas* report being prevented from fulfilling a combat role: "My name's Manuela . . . I'm from the Pasionaria Column, but I'd rather stay here with you all. They never wanted to give guns to the girls. We were only good for washing dishes and clothes. Our quarter is empty. Most of the militia fight elsewhere. The others are helping Martínez de Aragon to defend the cathedral, they say. The captain wants all the girls to leave Sigüenza." To this, one of Etchebéhère's militiamen responded, "then why haven't you left?" Manuela explained, "because we want to help." She also declared, "my friend whose name is Nati also wants to stay with you. She used to have long pigtails. Now she's cut them off, because you know, if we fall into the hands of the fascists they'll shave our heads, so it's better to have short hair. So can we stay?"[118]

Initially, the two women were refused by an old militiaman who claimed they would not know how to use a gun. Nati quickly responded, "yes we do, we can even dismantle it, grease it, everything. . . . We can also fill the cartridges with dynamite. But if you won't give us a gun, let us at least stay to cook and clean; this floor is very dirty." However, Manuela interjected indignantly, "that, we won't do. I have heard it said that in your column the *milicianas* have the same rights as the men, and they don't [just] wash clothes or dishes." In what has become a renowned statement, Manuela proclaimed, "I did not come to the front to die for the revolution with a dish cloth in my hand."[119] At this, the militia applauded, and the two women were allowed to join Etchebéhère's column.

Milicianas were often also responsible for caring for the wounded. Breà reported having met a *miliciana* from the POUM who was directed by her captain to aid the nurses in a hospital while her unit was stationed in a town.[120] The communist Browne was shot while providing first aid to a fallen comrade.[121] The anarchist Kokoczinski, a member of the International Group of the Durruti Column, served as both a *miliciana* and a nurse.[122] This is a complex issue as many women who served in the front lines primarily as nurses were also armed and undertook limited combat duties. At times, it is unclear who can be classified as a *miliciana* who also took care of the wounded, and who was a nurse who also participated in combat. The communist Josefa Rionda is an example of this. She served as a nurse in the front lines at Colloto, and she routinely fired upon the enemy while in the trenches aiding the wounded. Rionda is referred to as both a nurse and a *miliciana* in an article printed in *Mujeres*.[123]

Descriptions given by the *milicianas* themselves of non-combat activities tend to focus on inequity and the women's dislike of what they considered a discriminatory situation. However, instances in which the independent Republican press highlighted the domestic activities of the *milicianas* tend to present this role in a very different manner. The independent press, demonstrating continuing sexist attitudes despite the advances made toward equality, appeared to view the domestic role of *milicianas* in the front lines in positive terms. Newspapers such as *La Voz* and *ABC* published numerous photographs depicting women fighters cooking, cleaning, washing and sewing, and presented them in a way that clearly demonstrated that the journalists and editors believed this was the natural role for women to be playing in the front lines.

A photograph published in *La Voz* on 9 September 1936 showed three *milicianas* on the Somosierra front, washing clothes. The caption read, "these brave women who after shooting bullets, now wash in a stream the clothes of their male combatant comrades."[124] A photograph with a similar theme was printed in the independent *ABC* on 3 November 1936. It depicts a *miliciana* who fought as part of the advance party on the front lines. The photograph shows her in uniform and with her rifle beside her, sewing the uniform of a militiaman. The caption reads, "this girl . . . has just left her combat post in order to sew the clothes of her male comrades."[125] In late 1936, the number of photographs and references to *milicianas* completing supportive tasks in the front lines increased sharply.

This issue of the media's representation of *milicianas* undertaking auxiliary tasks in the front lines will be discussed at length in chapter 6.

Not all the non-combat duties performed by *milicianas* at the front could be considered traditional "women's work." The communist Manzanal performed an abundance of tasks at the front as well as her combat duties. She worked as a political commissar, which required that she keep her comrades informed of news from other fronts and political developments, give courses in reading and writing, conduct political education, and also keep the spirits of her unit up.[126]

However, it was not the case in every militia that men were excused from domestic duties. In some units, such as the POUM unit captained by Etchebéhère, auxiliary tasks were distributed equally between the male and female fighters. These instances are important because they demonstrate that inroads were being made into the traditionally sexist attitudes held by Spanish society. Soon after Etchebéhère had been promoted to captain, the men in her unit refused to make beds, sweep or carry out other domestic tasks, as they claimed that this was "women's work," and that the four *milicianas* of the unit should do it. Very calmly, Etchebéhère asked if they expected her to wash their socks. "Not you, of course not,"[127] one of the men replied. "Neither the other women, comrade," Etchebéhère declared. Addressing herself to the entire unit, the captain announced, "the girls who are among us are militians, not domestics. We are all fighting for the revolution, men and women, equal to equal, never forget it. And now, quickly, two volunteers to do the cleaning."[128]

The division of labor was also equal in Fernández de Velasco Pérez's communist column. In her interview with Strobl, Fernández de Velasco Pérez confirmed that when it was meal time, everyone took turns to cook, including the men. "There was no difference, everyone did everything. And sometimes I too took my turn to peel potatoes, although not very often. . . . We were treated like men in all respects, and we acted like men as well."[129] It is interesting to note that in order for women to be treated as equals, they had not merely to be treated like men, but to act like them too.

Historical accounts that emphasize the auxiliary role played by *milicianas* at the front and either ignore or play down the fact that militia-women also participated in combat on equal terms with men implicitly disparage the military contribution made by women during the civil war. In addition, these accounts deny the courage of *milicianas* like García, Browne, Solano, Odena and many others who died under enemy fire while carrying out their normal duty as a militiawoman.

WOMEN'S BATTALIONS IN THE REARGUARD

Women's military participation during the Spanish Civil War was not limited to the front lines. A great many more women were involved in the armed defense of their cities and towns, or were training in preparation for such a defense. Thousands of women in the Republican zone were organized into militias and trained in the use of arms from July 1936, with a view to their being sent to the front (though there is no evidence of this having occurred) or so that they could contribute to the military defense of their homes should this become necessary.

The *milicianas* of the rearguard are not often discussed in the history of the Spanish Civil War, and in the few cases in which they are, they are not categorized as combatants. Most historians do not include the women's battalions of the rearguard in their discussions of the *milicianas*, and in some cases do not discuss them at all. However, these women did play an important military role. The *milicianas* of the rearguard were armed, trained and prepared for combat. Some, though not all, of these women did participate in some form of combat during the civil war.

The women combatants in the rearguard were significant because they played an important military role in the defense of cities, even if ultimately they were not required for combat. Further, these *milicianas* were far more numerous and more visible to the rest of Spanish society than were the militiawomen stationed at the front. As a result, it could be argued that they played an even larger role as models of the changing gender roles and new codes of behavior for women that were developing during the social revolution. The female combatants of the rearguard prove that during the Spanish Civil War, women's military participation was accepted and formed a part of everyday life in the Republican zone.

There is evidence that several women's battalions took part in battles to defend their cities. These units include the women's militia organized by the PSUC in Barcelona, the Rosa Luxemburg Battalion that took part in the battle to defend Majorca,[130] and the *Union de Muchachas* that fought in the Battle for Madrid in November 1936.[131]

While the Battle for Madrid in November 1936 can clearly be considered front-line combat, the example is discussed here because the majority of women who participated in this battle were members of rearguard women's battalions. The defense of Madrid is probably the most prominent example of rearguard *milicianas* participating in combat. The battle began on 8 November 1936, when the Nationalists attacked with three main assault forces at the Casa de Campo, while also attacking Carabanchel Alto as a diversion.[132] Having received a warning about the diversionary tactic, General José Miaja had stationed only 12,000 of his force in Carabanchel and organized 28,000 of his troops to be prepared at the Casa de Campo (twice the number of Nationalist troops assembled there). The fighting force at the Casa de Campo is described by Beevor as a "heterogeneous mass of militia," which included regular soldiers, militiamen and -women, untrained volunteers, and a women's battalion stationed at the *Puente de Segovia* (Segovia Bridge).[133]

Catherine Coleman reports that thousands of women took an active part in the battle to defend Madrid. Among these were the *Unión de Muchachas* (Girls' Union), a communist youth group of 2,000 women aged fourteen to twenty-five who had been undergoing arms training and target practice since the outbreak of the war. This group of women participated in combat in the area around the Segovia Bridge as well as on the Carabanchel front near Gestafe.[134] These women fought bravely, and were reported to be the last to retreat.[135] Despite the fact that women comprised a significant percentage of the fighting force in Carabanchel, and despite the large part played by these and other women in the Battle of Madrid, it is very rare to find information about them included in general histories of the siege.

During the war, there were various schools of thought on the need for women in the rearguard to receive military training and to form women's battalions. Some felt that the military training of women was necessary in case they were needed at the front. Carlos Rodríguez, for example, argued in an article printed in *Estampa* that women's battalions "constituted a rearguard so organized it could present itself as the actual front of combat. Militarization does not have to be only for men."[136] An examination of these different perspectives will show that the *milicianas* of the rearguard contributed militarily to the Republican war effort, and played a significant role in the fighting.

An article by Etheria Artay published in *Crónica* detailed the military training that various women's battalions were receiving, and explained, "the women of Barcelona are preparing, in case the moment arrives when they, too, must fight."[137] Several hours each week, beginning at 8 a.m. on Sunday mornings, these women underwent military training. Mostly factory workers, they were referred to as "future *milicianas*," as it was believed that the military situation might become so dire that it was necessary to send these women into combat in the front lines to aid the Republican defenders.[138] The article explained that it was not only in Barcelona that women in the rearguard were undergoing military training, but that the same was taking place in Madrid, Valencia, Vizcaya, Santander and Asturias.[139]

The majority of women's battalions were not formed for the purpose of being transferred to the front, but rather with the intention that the women be militarily prepared to defend their own towns or cities.[140] The Lina Odena Battalion in Madrid was formed soon after the war began, with the purpose of providing military training for women in the rearguard. The battalion was not meant to be used at the front, except as an emergency if the rearguard ever became the front line of combat.[141] An article published in *ABC* declared, "women, determined to defend the Republic with arms, prepare for the war. These girls, enlisted in the Lina Odena Battalion, learn military instruction."[142] The photograph shows a group of women marching in formation down a street, but they do not wear uniforms or carry weapons. Another rearguard battalion in Madrid, *¡Avanti!* was formed for a similar purpose. It included both young women and men, and photographs of their military training show the recruits marching through the streets, though at times they are shown without any uniforms or weapons.[143]

Louise Gómez, the organizer of the Women's Secretariat of the POUM in Barcelona, decided it was necessary to form a women's battalion soon after the war began. Low became a member shortly after her arrival in Spain, and wrote of her experiences in her memoirs.[144] She reported that the regiment met and trained daily, participating in drills, practicing marching, receiving weapons training and performing target practice.[145] Low wrote in detail about the weapons training that her battalion received. She reported that after target practice and drills, the women received specialized training in the use of machine guns:

> It was the only thing which was really difficult. We had no mechanical turn, and spent a long time learning to take all the parts of the machine to pieces and put them back correctly together again, and besides, the machine was so hard and heavy for us. But we did learn. In the end, I think that we could have assembled the parts of a machine-gun in the dark, without a clank to show the enemy where we were hidden, and fired it off as a surprise.[146]

Such was Low's appreciation for weaponry that later, when she and Breà were leaving Spain and crossing the border into France, she "couldn't bear parting" with her revolver.[147]

Some argued that women should receive military training in order to defend themselves individually if necessary, rather than to participate in battle. A male French volunteer at the POUM barracks in Barcelona asked some women from the women's battalion why they bothered undergoing military training, when they explained that they did not believe in principle that all women should go to the front. "How dense you are," one of the women replied. "Because all human beings should be properly equipped for defence when they are liable to be attacked."[148]

There were also proponents of the view that women in the rearguard should not receive any military training at all. Ramon Martorell, for example, wrote an article for *Crónica* that argued that it was pointless for women to receive military training in order to fight on the front when it became necessary, since he believed that this moment would never arrive.[149] He argued that "there are legions of men waiting impatiently and eagerly for the arrival of a rifle and the urgent order to go to fight."[150] Even this would not be necessary, he argued, since entire columns from other areas could come to reinforce Madrid if necessary. Having said all this, Martorell then went on to argue that even if the moment of desperation did arrive when *all* forces became necessary, the women of Madrid were already prepared and sufficiently trained to take up their posts in combat alongside their male comrades. He even admitted that they would fight with "equal or greater courage" than the men.[151] Overall, Martorell provided a positive view of the dedication and military readiness of these rearguard *milicianas*, describing them as "perfectly organized" and "brave."[152]

The Republican government was constantly battling the problem of a severe weapons shortage, and at times there was debate over the usefulness of providing guns to women's battalions in the rearguard, particularly when some people did not expect they would ever participate in combat. However, despite the difficulty in obtaining weapons, all these women's battalions received training in the use of arms. These rearguard militiawomen may not have been armed at all times, but they did receive consistent weapons training and target practice.

WAR AND THE LIMITS OF THE REVOLUTION

The cultural and social significance of the *miliciana* phenomenon lies in the dynamic relationship between these women and the changing gender roles in the Republic. The change in accepted gendered behaviors brought on by the Second Republic, civil war and social revolution created a situation in which women were able to take up arms and defend the Republic militarily. Then, once the *milicianas* had armed themselves and entered the purportedly male sphere of combat, the very existence and actions of these fighting women further strengthened and perhaps hastened the process of change. This occurred in part because the *milicianas* served as models of a "New Woman." Their example demonstrated to other women the new roles and opportunities now available to them. Thus, the *milicianas* were both the product and the cause of changing gender roles. Despite the persistence of sexism in both Spanish society and left-wing groups, and the fact that full equality had not been achieved, the advancements made for women during this time were nonetheless significant, especially given the position that women had occupied in Spanish society prior to the formation of the Second Republic.

The question of whether or not the militiawomen were treated as equals by their male counterparts can serve as a litmus test for how much gender roles had changed in Spanish society in the Republican zone. If they truly suffered no discrimination, then equality had been achieved. If they were consistently harassed and subjected to mistreatment, then clearly gender roles had not changed sufficiently to allow Spanish society to accept the idea of a female soldier or militiawoman. The reality appears to have been a mix of the two. Evidence supports the argument that women were most often treated as equals by the men in their militias, and that as a result they did not in general suffer from sexual harassment or discrimination. However, even in the climate of social revolution men in some cases still saw women as sexual objects and treated them as such. As a result, militiawomen did suffer a limited amount of discrimination and harassment while in the front lines. This suggests that though gender roles had begun to change and the women's liberation was moving forward, equality had not yet been achieved and certain problems still existed.

The attitudes of a great many men changed, and so did the everyday tenor of relations between men and women at the front. *Milicianas* were treated with a great deal more respect than they could have expected in Spain before the civil war, even under the Second Republic. An episode that Low and Breà relate in *Red Spanish Notebook* serves as an example of how everyday relations between men and women had changed during the civil war. Upon their arrival at the village of Tierz, the authors met two women international volunteers, one a Swiss militiawoman and the other a French nurse. They invited Low and Breà, and the two doctors and driver of their group, to go swimming with them, and though they had to decline because they needed to report their presence to the People's Committee in the town, they agreed to come down to the river to have a quick look.[153] Once at the river, Low and Breà were slightly astonished to discover that all the group, men and women, were swimming together naked. After a pause, the driver of the group laughed and said, "ha, ha, comrade, there's the revolution for you."[154]

Breà questioned the Swiss woman if she felt embarrassed, "bathing like this in your skin with all those naked chaps."[155] The *miliciana* replied, "why, whatever for? They're quite harmless. Of course sometimes one or other of them does a little masturbation, but so respectfully that one has really nothing to say."[156] The fact that these women felt so comfortable and uninhibited with the militiamen is a solid indication that they did not suffer from any kind of discrimination or harassment.

Another Swiss *miliciana* that Breà met later told him what it was like for her being the only woman in her unit on the Aragon front. She provides another example of a woman who suffered no particular harassment or discrimination during the civil war: "the men are all right. They try it on a bit at first, just to see what you're like, but they soon fall in if you're the right sort. Half of them are only kids, anyway. We got along famously."[157]

A foreign volunteer from Holland in a letter home wrote of an experience he had when a militiawoman boarded the train that his unit was traveling on: "space was made for her on our bench, there was laughing and joking, but no one was fresh or too free at any time."[158] It is significant that these militiamen, as well as those from Clara's unit, did not sexually harass these women, regardless of the fact that they were alone and could have been seen as vulnerable for this reason. Etchebéhère in her memoirs also indicated that she never experienced any form of discrimination of harassment. She felt that this was partially because she was cautious never to become sexually involved with any of the men in her unit, and because she immediately rejected any sexual propositions that she received from them. [159]

In her interview with Carmen Alcalde, Fernández de Velasco Pérez testified that for the entire time that she served as a combatant during the civil war, she was always treated as an equal by all of the militiamen she met and fought with. Fernández de Velasco Pérez asserted that she could not remember even one occasion on which a joke was made about her. [160]

Borkenau also reported the respect with which the sole *miliciana* of Grossi's column was treated. He met her on the Saragossa front on 14 August 1936, and wrote at length about her relationship with her male comrades: "she was very good-looking but no special attention was given her by the militia-men, for all of them knew that she was bound to her lover." [161] He mentioned that she was respected for her courage in battle, and that "there was nothing awkward about her position among the men." Indeed, she was "just a comrade among them." [162]

Low and Breà also recalled in their memoirs an incident that showed that while progress was being made toward equality between Spanish men and women, problems were met along the way. Breà's militia unit had begun making sexist jokes comparing women to chickens, but had stopped themselves. "It would be more revolutionary to stop all the ragging and treat the women as though they were our equals," one militiaman had said. [163] Another answered, "yes, he's quite right. We must just treat them as real comrades, and nothing more." A young militiawoman named Remedios took offense at the idea that in order to be treated as an equal, she had to be treated as if she were a man. "I don't want to be treated as if I wasn't a woman. I took a man before I took a gun," she protested. [164] Despite the progression toward equality that occurred during the civil war, many rigid conventions and traditional ideas remained in force. According to the backward thinking of some Spanish men, equality meant treating women as though they were men, and raising them to the status of men, rather than accepting the idea that women and men were equal.

The *milicianas'* stories also relate the times when they did suffer from sexual harassment or some other form of discrimination. Though fewer in number, these serve as a demonstration that sexist ideas and practices had not left the left-wing ranks completely. The unidentified militiawoman who fought in Majorca, and whose diary has been published by Josep Massot i Muntaner, wrote on two occasions about the sexual propositions and harassment that occurred in her unit, and the problems suffered by women who did not accede to these sexual advances.[165]

Blasco makes an indirect reference to sexual harassment in her published observations of the civil war, when she writes of the hardships faced by *milicianas* who remained fighting in the front lines as late as 1938. She writes of the difficulties caused by fatigue and harsh conditions, and of the fact that "despite themselves they tended to become a disturbing element for men who have been torn away from their normal lives."[166]

Manzanal was the only woman in her unit, and insisted in her interview with Strobl that the militiamen she knew respected her and treated her as if she were their equal. However, she admitted that she was not able to avoid discrimination completely. She reported a humiliating experience in which she went with some of the men of her unit into town, and was required to wait outside for them while they went into a brothel.[167]

While female combatants did suffer from some forms of discrimination, such as the expectation that they would carry out the domestic work of their militia, and while they were at times victims of sexual harassment, for the most part the newfound equality enjoyed by the *milicianas* demonstrated the successes of the social revolution and the new opportunities for women created by the war. The military role played by women during the Spanish Civil War was sophisticated and extensive. Militiawomen in units stationed on the front lines were not limited in the combat roles they could play in defense of the Republic and social revolution. Members of women's battalions in the rearguard also performed a valuable military role, and served as examples to the wider public of the gender roles for women that now existed in the Republican zone. However, despite these positive steps toward women's liberation and the achievement of complete equality, and despite the value of the military contribution of the *milicianas* to the Republic, public and political attitudes toward the militiawomen began to change drastically as little as six months after the war began.

NOTES

1. Dolors Marín, "Las Libertarias," in Ingrid Strobl, *Partisanas: La mujer en la resistencia armada contra el fascismo y la ocupación alemana (1936–45)*, Virus, Barcelona, 1996, 356.

2. Lines, "Interview with Concha Pérez."

3. Mika Etchebéhère, *Mi Guerra de España*, Alikornio, Barcelona, 2003, 39–40.

4. Antonio García Vidal, "Entre los Héroes que Defienden a Madrid," *Crónica*, 6 December 1936, 5.

5. The *miliciana* phenomenon is considered to be militarily significant in terms of the numbers in which women fought, the crucial time at which they participated in

combat and by the fact that by all accounts they fought passionately even if the end result was not militarily favorable.

6. "Los Dirigentes de la Juventud en Primera Fila: Lina Odena en el frente de Granada.," *Mundo Obrero,* Wednesday 2 August 1936, 2.

7. "Dirigentes," *Mundo Obrero,* 2.

8. *Mundo Obrero,* 26 August 1936, 3.

9. Ángel Luis Rubio Moraga, "El Papel de la Mujer en la Guerra a Través de los Carteles Republicanos," *Cuadernos Republicanos,* no. 36, October 1998, 104.

10. Dolores Ibárruri, Aurora Arnáiz et al, *Lina Odena: Heroína del pueblo,* Ediciones Europa América, Madrid, 1936, 4.

11. *ABC,* 6 October 1936, 15; *Ahora,* 26 September 1936, 2; *Claridad,* 23 September 1936, 8; *Crónica,* 4 October 1936, 1; *El Mono Azul,* 15 October 1936, 4; *Estampa,* 3 October 1936, 19; and *Mundo Obrero,* 22 September 1936, 4.

12. Mónica Carabias Álvaro, *Rosario Sánchez Mora (1919),* Ediciones del Orto, Madrid, 2001, 25–28.

13. Strobl, *Partisanas,* 70.

14. Strobl, *Partisanas,* 70.

15. Strobl, *Partisanas,* 71.

16. Strobl, *Partisanas,* 70.

17. Strobl, *Partisanas,* 71.

18. Álvaro, *Rosario Sánchez,* 34.

19. Strobl, *Partisanas,* 52.

20. Strobl, *Partisanas,* 53.

21. Strobl, *Partisanas,* 53–55.

22. Claudio Lain, "Historias de Milicianas," *Estampa,* 29 August 1936, 25.

23. Lain, "Historias de Milicianas," 25.

24. Lain, "Historias de Milicianas," 25.

25. Lain, "Historias de Milicianas," 26.

26. Lain, "Historias de Milicianas," 26.

27. Carmen Alcalde, *La Mujer en la Guerra Civil Española,* Editorial Cambio 16, Madrid, 1976, 140.

28. Teresa Pàmies, *Cuando Éramos Capitanes: (Memorias de aquella guerra),* Dopesa, Barcelona, 1975, 43.

29. Nash, *Defying,* 50.

30. Antonina Rodrigo, *Mujer y Exilio 1939,* Compañía Literaria, Madrid, 1999, 76.

31. Rodrigo, *Mujer y Exilio,* 80.

32. Rodrigo, *Mujer y Exilio,* 62.

33. Strobl, *Partisanas,* 63–66.

34. Scanlon, *Polémica,* 292.

35. Rubio Moraga, "Papel de la Mujer," 104.

36. Margarita Nelken, "De las Jornadas Trágicas de Barcelona: Fanny, la heroína de Casal Carlos Marx," *Estampa,* 22 May 1937, 16.

37. Nelken, "Jornadas Trágicas," 17.

38. Nelken, "Jornadas Trágicas," 17.

39. Walter Gregory, *The Shallow Grave: A memoir of the Spanish Civil War,* Victor Gollancz, London, 1986, 73.

40. Claude Cockburn, "English Sculptress Killed in Spain," *The Daily Worker,* 4 September 1936, in James Pettifer (ed.), *Cockburn in Spain: Dispatches from the Spanish Civil War,* Lawrence and Wishart, London, 1986, 63.

41. Angela Jackson, *British Women and the Spanish Civil War,* Routledge, London, 2002, 103.

42. "Report by George Brinkman, Barcelona, 30.8.36. MML, Box 21/B/1a," in James K. Hopkins, *Into the Heart of the Fire: The British in the Spanish Civil War,* Stanford University Press, Stanford, 1998, 130.

43. Hopkins, *Into the Heart,* 130.

44. Mateo Rello, "Concha Pérez and Anarchy," *Solidaridad Obrera,* 17 July 2006.

45. Hugh Thomas, *The Spanish Civil War*, 4th edition, Penguin, London, 2003, 704.

46. Marín, "Libertarias," 354–355. Antoine Giménez and Les Gimenologues, *Les Fils de la Nuit: Souvenirs de la guerre d'Espagne*, L'Insomniaque and Les Giménologues, Montreuil, 2006, 239.

47. Lines, "Interview with Concha Pérez."

48. Lines, "Interview with Concha Pérez."

49. Marín, "Libertarias," 355.

50. Marín, "Libertarias," 356.

51. Luis Maria Jiménez de Aberasturi, *Casilda, Miliciana: Historia de un sentimiento*, Editorial Txertoa, San Sebastian, 1985, x.

52. Jiménez de Aberasturi, *Casilda*, 42.

53. Jiménez de Aberasturi, *Casilda*, x.

54. Jiménez de Aberasturi, *Casilda*, 49.

55. Miguel Iñiguez, *Cuadernos para una Enciclopedia Biográfica del Anarquismo Español*, Vitoria, no. 31, January 1985, entry no. 488.

56. Jiménez de Aberasturi, *Casilda*, 65.

57. Jiménez de Aberasturi, *Casilda*, 65.

58. Sofia Blasco, *Peuple d'Espagne. Journal de guerre de la madrecita*, translated by Henrietta Sauret, Nouvelle Revue Critique, Paris, 89–91.

59. Blasco, *Peuple d' Espagne*, 89.

60. Blasco, *Peuple d' Espagne*, 90.

61. Giménez, *Fils de la Nuit*, 293 and 535.

62. Giménez, *Fils de la Nuit*, 241–242 and 533.

63. Giménez, *Fils de la Nuit*, 276 and 535.

64. Giménez, *Fils de la Nuit*, 536.

65. Franz Borkenau, *The Spanish Cockpit: An eyewitness account of the political and social conflicts of the Spanish Civil War*, Pluto Press, London, 1937, 72.

66. Borkenau, *Spanish Cockpit*, 113.

67. Etchebéhère details the entire incident. Etchebéhère, *Mi Guerra*, 84–95.

68. Mary Low and Juan Breà, *Red Spanish Notebook: The first six months of the revolution and the civil war*, Purnell and Sons, London, 1937, 171–172.

69. Andy Durgan, "International Volunteers in the POUM Militias," Fundación Andréu Nin. Expanded version of a paper originally presented to the Conference on the International Brigades organized by the University of Lausanne, 19–20 December 1997. http://www.fundanin.org/durgan1.htm . Accessed on Monday 19 April 2004.

70. Low and Breà, *Notebook*, 169 and 172.

71. Low and Breà, *Notebook*, 191–192.

72. Low and Breà, *Notebook*, 175–176.

73. Low and Breà, *Notebook*, 177–178.

74. Low and Breà, *Notebook*, 178.

75. Durgan, "International Volunteers," 7.

76. Low and Breà, *Notebook*, 179.

77. Low and Breà, *Notebook*, 144.

78. Low and Breà, *Notebook*, 144.

79. Mary Nash, "Ideals of Redemption: Socialism and women on the left in Spain," in Helmut Gruber and Pamela Graves (eds), *Women and Socialism, Socialism and Women: Europe between the two World Wars*, Berghahn Books, New York, 1998, 374.

80. Alcalde, *Mujer en la Guerra*, 123.

81. Olga Zubizaola, "Nuestras Heroínas," *Mujeres*, 5 June 1937, 9.

82. Zubizaola, "Nuestras Heroínas," 9.

83. Zubizaola, "Nuestras Heroínas," 9.

84. *ABC*, 30 July 1936, 23.

85. Alcalde, *Mujer en la Guerra*, 133.

86. "Entierro de una Miliciana de la Brigada de Acero," *El Sol*, 19 August 1936, 2.

87. "Entierro," *El Sol*, 2.

88. "Héroes del Pueblo: La primera compañía del batallón Largo Caballero," *Crónica*, 13 September 1936, 5.

89. "Héroes del Pueblo," *Crónica*, 5.

90. "Héroes del Pueblo," *Crónica*, 5.

91. "Estampas de Oviedo: Nuestras milicianas," *Mujeres*, 6 March 1937, 6.

92. "Estampas de Oviedo," *Mujeres*, 6.

93. "Las Heroínas de la Causa Popular," *Ahora*, 24 October 1936, 1.

94. *ABC*, 29 July 1936, 3.

95. "La Heroína de El Espinar," *Claridad*, 27 July 1936, 3; and Lazaro, "El Circulo Socialista del Oeste, Modelo para todas las Organizaciones de Retaguardia," *Claridad*, 28 July 1936, 6.

96. Eduardo de Ontañon, "Francisca Solano, Heroína de las Milicias," *Estampa*, 8 August 1936, no. 447, 10–12.

97. Ontañon, "Francisca Solano," 11.

98. Ontañon, "Francisca Solano," 11.

99. "Cada Region, Su Milicia," *Estampa*, 10 October 1936, 15.

100. Gabriel Jackson, *A Concise History of the Spanish Civil War*, Thames and Hudson, London, 1974, 87.

101. Nash, *Defying*, 108.

102. Nash, *Defying*, 108.

103. Nash, *Defying*, 108.

104. Rafael Martínez Gandia, "Las Mujeres en la Lucha," *Crónica*, 2 August 1926, 5–7.

105. See *ABC*, 13 August 1936, 4; and 6 October 1936, 4.

106. Gandia, "Mujeres en la Lucha," 5.

107. Gandia, "Mujeres en la Lucha," 6.

108. Gregory, *Shallow Grave*, 73.

109. Gregory, *Shallow Grave*, 73.

110. Borkenau, *Spanish Cockpit*, 164.

111. Borkenau, *Spanish Cockpit*, 164.

112. Ian MacDougall (ed.), *Voices from the Spanish Civil War: Personal recollections of Scottish volunteers in Republican Spain 1936–1939*, Polygon, Edinburgh, 1986, 62.

113. Antony Beevor, *The Spanish Civil War*, Orbis Publishing, London, 1982, 89.

114. Low and Breà, *Notebook*, 165–166.

115. Blasco, *Peuple d' Espagne*, 125–126.

116. Blasco, *Peuple d' Espagne*, 125–126.

117. Julio Arostegui (ed.), *Historia y Memoria de la Guerra Civil: Encuentro en Castilla y León*, Consejería de Cultura y Bienestar Social, Valladolid, 1988, 159.

118. Etchebéhère, *Mi Guerra*, 73.

119. Etchebéhère, *Mi Guerra*, 74.

120. Low and Breà, *Notebook*, 105.

121. Jackson, *British Women*, 103.

122. Giménez, *Fils de la Nuit*, 241–242 and 533.

123. *Mujeres*, 6 March 1937, 6.

124. *La Voz*, 9 September 1936, 2.

125. *ABC*, 3 November 1936, 5.

126. Strobl, *Partisanas*, 63.

127. Etchebéhère, *Mi Guerra*, 39.

128. Etchebéhère, *Mi Guerra*, 39–40.

129. Strobl, *Partisanas*, 53–54.

130. Nash, *Defying*, 107 and Keene, "Brothers and Sisters," 123.

131. Catherine Coleman, "Women in the Spanish Civil War," in Juan P. Fusi Aizpurau, Richard Whelan et al., *Heart of Spain: Robert Capa's photographs of the Spanish Civil War*, Aperture, New York, 1999, 48.

132. Beevor, *Spanish Civil War*, 136.

133. Beevor, *Spanish Civil War*, 136–137.

134. Coleman, "Women in the Spanish Civil War," 48.

135. Liz Willis, *Women in the Spanish Revolution*, Solidarity, New York, Solidarity Pamphlet Number 40, October 1975, 4.

136. Carlos Rodríguez, "Las Mujeres Formaran Nuestra Retaguardia," *Estampa*, 13 February 1937, 3.

137. Etheria Artay, "Las Mujeres de Barcelona se Preparan," *Crónica*, 20 December 1936, 7–8.

138. Artay, "Mujeres de Barcelona," 7.

139. Artay, "Mujeres de Barcelona," 8.

140. Gina Herrmann, "Voices of the Vanquished: Leftist women and the Spanish Civil War," *Journal of Spanish Cultural Studies*, vol. 4, no. 1, 2003, 18.

141. Scanlon, *Polémica*, 295.

142. *ABC*, 31 October 1936, 4.

143. *ABC*, 4 November 1936, 2.

144. Low and Breà, *Notebook*, 185–190.

145. Low and Breà, *Notebook*, 186–187.

146. Low and Breà, *Notebook*, 190.

147. Low and Breà, *Notebook*, 238.

148. Low and Breà, *Notebook*, 189.

149. Ramón Martorell, "Batallones de Mujeres," *Crónica*, 22 November, 1936, 14.

150. Martorell, "Batallones de Mujeres," 14.

151. Martorell, "Batallones de Mujeres," 14.

152. Martorell, "Batallones de Mujeres," 14.

153. Low and Breà, *Notebook*, 95–96.

154. Low and Breà, *Notebook*, 97.

155. Low and Breà, *Notebook*, 98.

156. Low and Breà *Notebook*, 98.

157. Low and Breà, *Notebook*, 145.

158. Marcel Acier (ed.), *From Spanish Trenches: Recent letters from Spain*, Cresset Press, London, 1939, 36.

159. Keene, "Brothers and Sisters," 127.

160. Alcalde, *La Mujer en la Guerra*, 169–173.

161. Borkenau, *Spanish Cockpit*, 106.

162. Borkenau, *Spanish Cockpit*, 106.

163. Low and Breà, *Notebook*, 87.

164. Low and Breà, *Notebook*, 87.

165. "Diario de la Miliciana," in Josep Massot i Muntaner, *El Desembarcament de Bayo a Malloraca, Agosto-Setiembre de 1936*, Publicacions de l'Abadia de Montserrat, Barcelona, 1987, 396 and 404.

166. Blasco, *Peuple d'Espagne*, 47.

167. Strobl, *Partisanas*, 64.

FIVE

Changing Attitudes and the Decision to Remove *Milicianas* from Combat

PART ONE: FROM HEROINES TO "WHORES"

From the outbreak of the Spanish Civil War and during the six months that followed, *milicianas* were celebrated in Republican Spain as heroic figures, and came to symbolize the Republic's fight against fascism. The majority of the left-wing political groups in the Republican zone expressed support for women's military contribution. In general, the attitude of the press and the public toward the militiawomen was positive. However, toward the end of 1936 those attitudes began to change.

Beginning in the period between late November and early December, a noticeable shift began to take place in the attitudes of both left-wing political groups and the press toward the *milicianas*. The precise moment at which this change occurred is impossible to pinpoint, since it was a complex transformation rather than a decisive shift. What is clear is that the change in attitudes toward women's military contribution took place in the context of a wider reversal of progressive attitudes and policies that coincided with the failure of the social revolution. Most historians have examined the change in attitudes toward the *milicianas* and their removal from combat in isolation, without reference to the political setting. This book aims to consider the banishing of the *milicianas* from the front within the political and historical context in which it occurred.

After being celebrated as courageous war heroines from July to November, militiawomen by December were often seen as nothing more than prostitutes spreading venereal disease. Propaganda in the Republican zone shifted. Images of militant armed women wearing blue *monos* began to fade from public memory as they were replaced with pictures of women carrying out domestic tasks such as cooking, cleaning or sewing for Republican troops. The slogan "Men to the Front, Women to the Home Front" first appeared in early November, and by late December had become widespread.[1] The message was clear that women should not consider themselves equal to men, and that men and women had very different roles to play in the anti-fascist resistance. *Milicianas* began to be openly discredited and ridiculed.

By late 1936, all political parties and groups in the Republican zone stood united on the grounds that a woman's "proper place" was in the home and not in the trenches. However, it is not entirely correct to discuss all the attitudes and policies of left-wing political groups toward *milicianas* in late 1936 in terms of a "change." In some ways, the support of a few political groups for the recruitment and enlistment of women into the militias was not wholehearted or genuine to begin with. However, a shift did occur, both in how these groups presented their views of women's military contribution to the public, and in how their policies supported the existence of militiawomen.

This chapter will address the changing attitudes and policies of the communists, anarchists, dissident Marxists and socialists through a systematic examination of primary sources, in particular newspapers. It was mainly through the press that the general population and militiawomen in the Republican zone learned of these changes, and it was here that these attitudes were most noticeable. For each of the major left-wing political tendencies, key newspapers have been systematically examined in their entirety for the first year of the Spanish Civil War. This comprehensive examination of newspapers has made it possible to trace the changes over time, and has allowed for a comparison between the attitudes and policies of various political tendencies toward the militiawomen.

This chapter will also discuss the changing attitudes of the militiamen and of foreign observers. The reversal of the favorable view of the *milicianas* will be examined using firsthand accounts, memoirs and the independent Republican press. It is important to consider the changing attitudes of the population in the framework of what occurred within political groups, since it was this shift in the political climate that helped to shape the public viewpoint.

As the armed contribution of the *milicianas* began to be viewed negatively by both the public and political groups, various arguments were developed that alleged that women were ineffective militarily, and called for their removal from combat roles. These arguments came from all sectors of Republican society, but were largely propounded by political parties. One argument put forward was that as the initial urgency of the civil war had passed, women's military involvement was simply no longer necessary. Supporters of this argument also suggested that women had only volunteered for combat in the spirit of adventure and excitement that existed in the early days of the war, and that since that phase had now passed, women themselves no longer wished to remain militarily involved.

Another argument that was widely supported held that due to a lack of military training, women were of limited use to the military effort. The biological nature of women was also a significant issue, and it was widely believed that their "natural skills" would be better suited to the home front. An anarchist sexologist, Dr. Félix Martí Ibáñez, even went so far as to argue that the removal of women from the front was necessary as the militiamen needed to preserve their sexual energy for warfare.[2] It was also suggested that due to the ingrained chivalry of Spanish men, the presence of women in the militias was dangerous, as it would provoke men to take unnecessary risks to save their lives.[3] Another significant argument that was widely discussed and believed was that militiawomen were in fact mostly prostitutes, who were responsible for spreading venereal disease and weakening the Republican forces.[4] Finally, when the popular militias began to be organized into a regular army, it was argued that women had no place in a conventional military force.[5]

Sexist underpinnings can be detected in each of the reasons given for the need to remove women from combat positions in the front lines. Each of these arguments were nothing more than pretexts.[6] The example of Republican war nurses will be discussed, and it will be shown that the presence of nurses stationed at the front was never considered inappropriate or unacceptable, precisely because these women were performing tasks traditionally considered suitable for their gender, such as caring for the sick and wounded.

While the male political leadership in the Republican zone clearly came to a common, negative view of women's armed contribution to the anti-fascist resistance, the *milicianas* themselves perceived this issue quite differently. Militiawomen did not welcome or agree with this change in attitudes, most notably on the question of prostitution in the front lines. As it was so difficult for some *milicianas* to accept that they were no longer viewed with the respect and enthusiasm that they had once enjoyed, there is evidence that some women refused to believe that such a change ever took place. A minority of *milicianas* appear to have been convinced by the argument that their proper place was in the home front, and returned there to make their contribution to the Republican cause in a different way. However, the majority of the *milicianas* remained resistant to the ideas about them that developed beginning in late 1936, and did not voluntarily leave the front. The question of how the militiawomen viewed these changing attitudes will be examined primarily using oral testimonies.

It is important to place the change in attitudes toward the *milicianas* in its political and historical context. It is highly significant that these changes took place against the backdrop of the failure of the social revolution, and a conservative push from within the Republican government that reversed the many progressive achievements that had been made. The negative attitudes that developed toward women in combat in late 1936 did not occur in isolation, but arose in the context of a general decline of progressive ideas, values and social movements. The end of the revolution came as a result of the regressive policies and practices of the PCE, which came to dominate the Republican government. However, this book does not aim to give a detailed account of the course of the social revolution or the reasons for its failure. This subject has been dealt with by historians on many other occasions in political and social histories of the war.[7]

Part 1 of this chapter limits itself to a discussion of the changing attitudes of both political groups and the press that saw the continued military contribution of the *milicianas* to the Spanish Civil War lose support, as well as of the arguments that were developed for the removal of women from combat. The formal decision(s) to withdraw women from combat are discussed separately in part 2.

THE CHANGING ATTITUDES OF LEFT-WING POLITICAL PARTIES

The transformation in political opinion toward the *milicianas* was a complex process that took place over a period of months, rather than a decisive, instantaneous shift. The change in attitudes began around late November or early December 1936, intensified throughout the period between December and February, and reached its peak in March 1937. This process of transformation was complex, because it was not driven by any single organization or political force. Coming from a variety of sources, it displayed varying characteristics. In some sectors, there was outright denigration of *milicianas*, and in other sectors, the process seems to have involved simply replacing discourse and images of *milicianas* with references and representations of women undertaking purely auxiliary tasks. In these sectors, the figure of the *miliciana* was slowly phased out, but when references appeared, they generally remained positive.

While it comes as no surprise that conservative and moderate elements within the Republic remained opposed to the military participation of women in the civil war, it is quite extraordinary that all the left-wing political groups in the Republican zone were able to form a consensus on the issue. Although the communists, anarchists and POUM had originally supported women's military participation in the civil war, by December their attitudes had changed drastically. As will be shown, the worst of the criticism of the female combatants came not from the public, but from political organizations. However, each of the left-wing political groups dealt with the issue in a distinct way. This can be seen most clearly through a systematic examination of the press controlled by each political group.

THE COMMUNISTS

To examine the changing attitudes of the communists toward the *milicianas*, two newspapers were studied: *Mundo Obrero*, the central organ of the PCE, and *Mujeres*, the newspaper of the CNFGF. Every issue of *Mundo Obrero* was examined for the period from July 1936 to July 1937. *Mujeres* was examined from its first issue in February 1937 until July 1937.

From the outbreak of the Spanish Civil War, the communists had supported women's military role in the struggle. As has been discussed in previous chapters, women were welcomed and even specifically recruited into communist militias and units, and in some cases were later promoted into leadership positions. The initial positive attitude of the communists toward the *milicianas* is also demonstrated by the treatment of the militiawomen in the communist press. While the depiction of militiawomen in the communist press shows that the communist leaders never wholeheartedly embraced women's equality and their full military participation, they nonetheless initially supported the inclusion of *milicianas* in the Republican fighting force. The positive attitude of the communists toward female combatants was also demonstrated by their treatment of militiawomen such as Odena and Sánchez de la Mora, who became war legends and were widely celebrated in the communist press and propaganda.[8]

Due to their demonstrated opposition to the social revolution and their role in its failure and the reversal of progressive gains, it might have been expected that the PCE and PSUC would become the strongest opponents of women's military participation in late 1936. However, in practice the communists were among the least visible protagonists in this debate. Instead of openly criticizing the *milicianas*, the communists replaced all references to them with images of women fulfilling their traditional gender roles through aiding the anti-fascist auxiliary. While the communist press did present several arguments for the removal of militiawomen from the front lines (as will be discussed below), these arguments focused on external factors such as the belief that women's military participation was unnecessary now that the initial urgency had passed, rather than any condemnation of the *milicianas* themselves.

As the months went on, fewer and fewer photographs of armed militiawomen were printed in *Mundo Obrero*. From four to six photographs featuring militiawomen were published in each of the months of August, September and October 1936. The three months after that witnessed a decline, with only three printed in November, two in December and one in January.[9] The type of photographs printed in these months is also significant. While in the earlier months of the war the photographs pictured armed women in the front lines, the photographs printed in the months November to January featured unarmed *milicianas* cooking, posing and smiling, and standing or marching in formation.

In late 1936, a new type of propaganda emerged and took the spotlight, glorifying the role of women in the home front and depicting women running kitchens, hospitals or orphanages, working in factories or sewing clothes for soldiers. When references to *milicianas* were made, they generally remained positive, but these occurred less and less often. [10] An article by Carlos Rodríguez entitled "Mujeres Antifascistas" is representative of the articles on the role of women in the struggle that appeared in *Mundo Obrero* around this time. [11] The article discussed the efforts of the Anti-fascist Women's Provincial Committee and the incorporation of women into work on the home front, and featured photographs of Federica Montseny, Dolores Ibárruri and women factory workers.

One widely distributed PSUC propaganda poster (produced jointly with the communist-dominated UGT) featured an illustration of a woman knitting demurely in the foreground, while the background depicted an armed man on the front lines. The slogan read, "Dones! Treballeu per als germans del front," ("Women! Work for our brothers of the front"). This poster was produced in 1937, and was later used in a PSUC/UGT calendar for 1938. [12] This type of image was common at the time, and its purpose was to define clearly the distinct roles men and women were expected to play in the anti-fascist resistance.

On the occasions after December 1936 when the communists openly supported a military role for women, this was generally only in the context of the training of civilian populations in the rearguard. [13] The fact that there is little evidence of communists openly criticizing *milicianas* (and that the communists continued to idolize war heroines such as Lina Odena and Rosario Sánchez de la Mora) does not negate the fact that the PCE and PSUC were firmly against the armed participation of women in the civil war. Several of the reasons cited for the need to remove women from their combat positions were put forward and publicized by the communists, who clearly felt that the "proper place" for women was in the home front.

An examination of *Mujeres* reveals interesting information about the communist change in attitudes toward the *milicianas* that occurred in late 1936, and about the developing belief that women were better suited to work on the home front. During the six months from February to July, *Mujeres* published eighteen photographs featuring *milicianas* (fourteen armed and only four unarmed, an average of one photograph per issue) along with fourteen articles and two poems on the same topic. Of the fourteen articles printed, only three argued against the military participation of women. [14] It is significant that the communist women's newspaper published a much higher ratio of photographs of militiawomen who were armed, as opposed to unarmed, than did *Mundo Obrero*.

The three articles that called for women to take up their "proper" place in the struggle in the rearguard, and the slogans, "Women, to the rearguard, and men, to the front lines of the fight,"[15] and "Men to the vanguard! Women to the rearguard!"[16] were published in the same issues as positive representations of female combatants. The first article, which argued for obligatory service for women in the auxiliary, claimed that this was more useful for women than military service, as a result of women's "sensibilities."[17] The second presented the argument that while there had been a place for women in the front lines in the first few crucial months, in February it was more important to ensure that all the able-bodied men should enlist, and that women should take up their rightful place on the home front.[18] The third article argued that it was simply not necessary for women to fight now that the initial urgency had passed— with the exception of extraordinary women who possessed special military ability.[19] While these articles were sexist, and clearly defined a limited role for women in the anti-fascist struggle, they stopped short of denigrating the individual militiawomen who had taken up arms.

Though it might appear to be a conflict that these articles were printed on the same pages as celebrations of *milicianas*, images of and references to women playing a military role and those playing an auxiliary role had existed side by side in the communist press since the outbreak of the war. At first the images of and articles about the *milicianas* were given a prominent place and were celebrated more openly, but later they appeared less frequently, and the focus shifted to the central role played by women on the home front.

Though fewer in number than in previous months, positive representations of *milicianas* were featured in *Mujeres* as late as May and June 1937, several months after the official decision to remove women from combat had been made. This is significant since the newspapers of other political groups ceased to publish positive references to militiawomen earlier in 1937. In May, an article entitled "La Mujer Española en el Fuego de la Guerra Civil" ("The Spanish Woman in the Fire of the Civil War"[20]), described the bravery and discipline of six militiawomen: Conchita from Toledo, her comrade Dolores, Juanita who fought with the Fifth Regiment of the Popular Militias, Odena, the communist military commander Aurora Arnáiz and the Catalan Marina Ginestá. Five of these women were said to be still participating in combat (Odena had been killed October 1936).

In June an article entitled "Nuestras Heroínas" ("Our Heroines"[21]), featured a photograph and information about the socialist María Elisa García, who at twenty-two years of age had been killed in battle on 10 May 1937 while fighting with her unit, the Third Company of the Asturias Battalion. García is described in overwhelmingly positive terms. The author, Olga Zubizaola, explained that the night before her death García had refused to leave her post: "she had to accomplish her task; and her task as a militiawoman was not to fail . . . but to resist. And she resisted. She resisted since life had been shaped by the anti-fascist spirit of struggle." García is described as "characterizing resistance and magnificent self-sacrifice."

Thus, while the changing attitude of the PCE and PSUC toward the *milicianas* manifested itself in a withdrawal of support for militiawomen, female combatants did not receive any harsh criticism from the communist press. Rather, it appears simply that a shift in emphasis took place, and that by late 1936 and early 1937 women were receiving strong messages from the communist leadership that their work on the home front was their most important and only acceptable contribution to the struggle. It is also significant that the changing attitude was represented in different ways in the organ of the PCE and the newspaper of a communist women's committee. This perhaps indicates that the essentially male leadership of the PCE maintained a harder line against women's military participation than did the women in its rank and file, and even those few women in its leadership.

THE UNITED COMMUNIST AND SOCIALIST YOUTH

The changing attitudes toward *milicianas* demonstrated in *Ahora*, the organ of the JSU, are intimately linked to those presented in communist newspapers like *Mundo Obrero* and *Mujeres*. However, since the JSU also represents a socialist and a youth viewpoint, it has been discussed separately.[22] This daily paper was examined in its entirety for the period from July 1936 to July 1937.

The change in attitudes toward the militiawomen that occurred in late 1936 is manifested in the organ of the JSU in a way that is notably different to the communist press. While *Mundo Obrero* began to replace photographs of *milicianas* in the front lines with images of women on the home front working in the auxiliary, the newspaper of the JSU actually demonstrated the change in the roles for militiawomen that occurred in the front lines. As the views of political parties became more critical of female combatants toward the end of 1936 and in early 1937, some women who had been serving in combat on the front lines began to carry out a solely supportive role, and this change is reflected in *Ahora*.

The first photograph of a woman in militia uniform undertaking a domestic task appeared in *Ahora* on 26 August, and featured a *miliciana* ironing.[23] It was published between two other photographs of uniformed and armed militiawomen standing in front of a barricade on the front lines. The next of its kind was not published until 16 September, and depicted four women in militia uniform and caps, crouching around a bucket. The caption indicates that these *milicianas* are cleaning the "kitchen" (which appears to be some equipment on the back of a cart), before preparing a meal.[24] Once again, this photograph is printed on the same page as two others depicting *milicianas*, the first of which shows two armed Andalusian women from the front being given weapons instruction, and another that features a uniformed woman who is described as just having "taken part in the reconquest of towns in the region occupied by fascists."[25]

On 26 September, two photographs were printed with the title "Militiawomen Fighters and Their Services in the Front" showing uniformed *milicianas* cooking.[26] A small photograph underneath featured a militiawoman crouched behind some bushes, aiming her rifle at an unseen enemy. On 30 September, five photos with the title "The Valiant and Self-Sacrificing Labor of Women in the Front"[27] were printed, featuring only one where a militiawoman is armed. She is stationed on a balcony and aiming her rifle. The other four photographs are of *milicianas* carrying a stretcher, checking papers, and washing clothes. All women pictured are referred to as *milicianas*, though the women washing clothes are not in uniform or armed. One photograph is particularly revealing of gender roles. It shows two women on their hands and knees scrubbing clothes, and a militiaman standing, towering above them with his hands on his hips and his rifle slung over his shoulder, watching them work.

Only one photograph depicting a militiawoman undertaking a non-combat task was published in October, showing two smiling militiawomen in uniform, holding large stacks of plates to be washed.[28] Though this is the only photograph of its type, as opposed to seven in September, it is significant that this photograph is not featured among others showing armed *milicianas* in combat. In November, the number of photographs of *milicianas* playing a strictly auxiliary role increased, as did the number of images of women working or undertaking military training in the rearguard as opposed to the front.[29]

In a manner similar to *Mundo Obrero* and *Mujeres*, images of *milicianas* in *Ahora* dissipated in a matter of months. December 1936 saw a steep decline in the number of photographs and articles about *milicianas*; only one photograph was printed during that month,[30] as compared to six in November and fifteen in October. However, significant coverage was maintained until March 1937. On four occasions in January, the paper featured militiawomen, twice with photographs alone,[31] and twice with an article and photographs.[32] In February an article appeared that included a discussion of women's participation in combat at the front, and that was illustrated with photographs of *milicianas*.[33] The final image of a *miliciana* was printed on 14 March 1937, but significantly, this image was a full-page photograph featured on the cover of the newspaper.[34] The caption is highly significant as it was overwhelmingly supportive of women's participation in combat. It read:

> Women of the Asturias. A brave *miliciana* who fought from the first
> days of the insurrection, rifle over her shoulder, alongside her com-
> rades in arms. Now she is in *San Esteban de las Cruces*. Before, she
> fought on other fronts. All the Asturian women are like her, self-deny-
> ing to the point of sacrifice, valiant to the point of heroism.[35]

The changing attitude of the JSU as presented in its newspaper shares
some characteristics with the communist press. The militiawomen were
not directly disparaged, and though references to them appeared less and
less often, when they were printed they remained positive, even in March
1937 at the peak of the denigration of *milicianas*. However, there is a
significant difference. Before images of and references to militiawomen
simply disappeared, *Ahora* provided evidence of the changing roles of
militiawomen in the front lines.

THE ANARCHISTS

The initial anarchist support for women's military participation, similar
to that of the communists, can be seen from the ready acceptance of
women into militias to fight. As explained in previous chapters, the majority of *milicianas* were anarchists, or members of anarchist militias. Despite this, it is also clear that the presence of large numbers of anarchist
militiawomen did not mean that the essentially male leadership of anarchist organizations such as the FAI and CNT completely accepted or
deliberately advocated women's equal military participation.

As has been discussed at length by Martha A. Ackelsberg in her work
on anarchism and women's emancipation, the anarchist movement in
Spain did not have a genuine commitment to feminism or a strategy to
achieve women's liberation. As she explains, "the subordination of wom-
en was at best a peripheral concern to the anarchist movement as a
whole. Most anarchists refused to recognize the specificity of women's
subordination, and few men were willing to give up the power over
women they had enjoyed for so long."[36] There was a minority within the
anarchist movement that had a different view on women's liberation,
seeing the particular nature of women's oppression and the need for a
separate movement to overcome it. These women established *Mujeres
Libres* in May 1936.[37] *Mujeres Libres* had a view on women's rights that
was quite distinct from that of the FAI and CNT. It was largely from
within *Mujeres Libres* that the militiawomen gained their anarchist support, rather than from the leadership of the anarchist movement.

The initial attitude of the FAI toward *milicianas* and women's military
contribution was thus quite ambiguous. Certainly, the right of women to
engage in combat was not seen as necessary for their liberation. These

equivocal attitudes eventually developed to become highly negative toward militiawomen and their continued presence in the front lines.

Three newspapers from the anarchist press were studied in order to provide a picture of the change in anarchist attitudes toward the militiawomen. The weekly Barcelonan newspaper *Tierra y Libertad* was examined in its entirety for the period from July 1936 to July 1937. There was limited availability of the newspaper *CNT*, which was examined only for the period from July to December 1936. Similarly, only a few issues of *Mujeres Libres* from the period of January to July 1937 were held on microfilm.

Unlike in the communist press, the militiawomen did not feature prominently in anarchist newspapers. This is surprising, since all sources indicate there were more anarchist than communist women fighting with the militias.[38] During the first year of the Spanish Civil War, *Tierra y Libertad* published only six photographs and five articles containing any information about the militiawomen. The last reference to a *miliciana* in *Tierra y Libertad* came in the form of an article about a foreign volunteer named Carmen and an illustration of a militiawoman, and was printed on 13 February 1937.[39] In the period from July to December 1936, only two images of militiawomen, and no articles, could be found in the newspaper *CNT*.

The *milicianas* received harsh criticism in *Tierra y Libertad*. One poignant example is an article printed on 21 November 1936, entitled "Mujeres Asturianas," in which Cruz Salido accused militiawomen in Asturias of being prostitutes:

> They [the women] knew perfectly well the noises of war and they distinguished our detonations from the enemy detonations. They situated themselves safely [away from] the action by the echo of the shots. Where have they come from? Nobody knows. The news that I picked up about them was very confusing and vague. The militiamen winked an eye at me expressively, and in it made clear their ideas about these women. The women were young. Some had a truly childish, infantile air about them. They constituted a feminine entourage that followed the columns. They moved themselves discretely with the militiamen and hid themselves from them in these damp and green meadows. Love here [at the front] has an unexpected manner. These women don't seem to be professionals, surrounded by the parapets and crouching in the trenches, in the hope of soliciting militiamen.
>
> They get up and clear out, not so far away so that one can't hear them sighing. He does not approach the women to ask them, "you want to?" He threatens them with a dry, "let's go." There aren't invitations, only orders. Everything was quick, dry and urgent. There was no foreplay, nor even the pleasure of a smile. Love in the war is like another gun shot. And at the *reveilles*, white with lust, they took them [the women] as if they were a parapet, and their resulting love was like

> a brief and quiet explosion, with which they shook the one whom they
> had between their arms. [40]

Nothing in this article clearly identifies these women as *milicianas*, since
they are not described as wearing uniforms or carrying weapons, and
there is no information given about any participation in combat. In fact,
the first two sentences of the quotation above indicate that the women
described were purposely avoiding danger or contact with the enemy.
The implication of the article, however, especially since it is written about
Asturias, a sector in which a number of militiawomen were fighting, is
that prostitution was rife in the front lines and that the removal of wom-
en was necessary to combat it.

However, the treatment of the *milicianas* in the newspaper *Mujeres
Libres*, the organ of the anarchist women's organization of the same
name, differs from that of both *Tierra y Libertad* and *CNT* in that until
March 1937 it demonstrated solid support for women's military contribution. Since it was not possible to examine the monthly *Mujeres Libres*
newspaper as a series, no comprehensive study of the treatment the militiawomen received in the newspaper can be made. However, from the
issues that were available on microfilm and the information about the
newspaper and propaganda available elsewhere, it is clear that the organization *Mujeres Libres* consistently presented the militiawomen in a
positive light. [41]

Given this initial solid support for female combatants, the change in
attitudes demonstrated in the newspaper *Mujeres Libres* is quite remark-
able. After *milicianas* were featured on the cover in March 1937, no further
images of or references to militiawomen were published until July, when
an article was printed denigrating those women who had taken up arms
in the struggle at the outbreak of the war. [42] By this time, *Mujeres Libres*
was staunchly advocating that women's contribution to the anti-fascist
cause must be limited to the social services. [43] The article began by prais-
ing the working-class women who had armed themselves at the outbreak
of the war, explaining that "seamstresses resisted the tyranny of the needle to realize their dreams of adventure." However, this suggests the
attitude that these women were devoid of political motivations for their
participation in the struggle. The article then goes on to explain how
these "dreams" were dispelled, and how militiawomen returned to fulfill
roles on the home front:

> And they offered up their young lives, teeming with youthful enthu-
> siasm, on the first days of the heroic struggle, when every man was a
> hero, and every woman was as good as a man. But in this long, con-
> stant fight between two classes filled with deadly hatred of one an-
> other, courage is not everything. Women understood this: they re-
> flected and realized that street skirmishes are quite different from me-
> thodical, regular, exasperating trench warfare. They realized this fact,

and knowing their own value as women, they chose to trade the gun for the industrial machine and the fighting spirit for the sweetness of their womanly souls. She has known how to imprint the delicate sweetness of her female psychology on the vulgar ambience of the war. She has a mother's care for those who, tired of long days' fighting return to their homes and she tries to keep optimism alive when morale is low. [44]

Strobl relates her belief that to the *milicianas,* this article must have seemed "pure cynicism and betrayal."[45] The article not only demonstrates beliefs about gender differences that are clearly sexist, but also reports inaccurately that the decision to return to the home front was made by the women themselves, in the absence of any political or public pressures, or indeed official decisions regarding their removal.

Among the anarchists, the change in attitudes toward the *milicianas* manifested itself somewhat differently from among the communists. The same strategy was used of decreasing the coverage of militiawomen in the press until the only reference to women's participation in the struggle highlighted their contribution to the rearguard or home front, but it is less noticeable since the militiawomen were never featured as prominently in the anarchist press as they were in the communist media. Arguments were presented for the removal of militiawomen from the front lines, but these included attacks on the *milicianas* themselves, in particular the accusation that they were prostitutes.

The fact that the anarchist press seemed to be more vehement than its communist counterpart in arguing that women should not occupy combat positions is peculiar, and the evidence available does not give any clear indication of why this was the case. One possible explanation is that since the anarchists had a greater number of militiawomen within their ranks than did the communists or other political groups, they needed to go to greater lengths to remove them. Another possible explanation is that the communists purposely avoided any disparaging of the militiawomen. Many historians believe that the communists were the source of the conservative push that saw many of the achievements of the social revolution reversed,[46] and the focus placed squarely on winning the war rather than pursuing the revolution. Given this fact, there was perhaps a deliberate attempt by the communist press to distance itself from arguments for the reversal of social gains, such as the cessation of women's military involvement. This and other differences between the anarchists and communists on the question of removing militiawomen from the front will be discussed further in part 2 of this chapter.

THE POUM

Early in 1937, amid the general outcry against women's armed participation in the war, even the POUM women's organization began to publish statements endorsing the idea that men and women had different roles to fulfill in the anti-fascist struggle. The Female Secretariat of the POUM, which had been the organization that most staunchly defended women's right to military training,[47] now claimed that a woman's "proper place" was at the home front, not in combat.[48]

The POUM still supported a limited military role for women, since it maintained its own women's battalion of over 100 women who participated in military and combat training in the rearguard and played a role in the military defense of Barcelona. The English-language POUM newspaper *The Spanish Revolution*, edited by Mary Low, included in its December issue an article entitled "The First Women's Battalion."[49] The article gave information about the POUM Female Secretariat and its formation of a rearguard women's battalion. Two photographs of the battalion undergoing military training accompanied the article, showing the battalion, composed of more than 100 women marching in formation.

The article demonstrates the POUM's continued support for the military participation of women in the war, albeit limited to the rearguard. The article gives the reason for the formation of the battalion, explaining that:

> From the very first moment . . . many women with great generosity and courage, enlisted in the people's army, offering voluntarily to fight for the total triumph of the working class. From the days of make-shift street fighting up to these present times of modern equipment and all the magnified dangers of modern warfare, women have done every-thing for the cause which could have been asked of them, and much more besides. . . . Up till the present, individual women had gone to the front in various columns of the militias, serving bravely with the men and doing their share as well as they could, but no effort had been made to provide them with adequate military training. The P.O.U.M. was the first to put forward the idea that so much eager willingness should be properly trained and organized, and in this way our plan for military instruction began.[50]

The change in attitude of the POUM was less overt than that of the communists or anarchists, since not only did the POUM continue to publish in its press positive statements and references to women's military participation, but it maintained its women's battalion in Barcelona.

THE SOCIALISTS

As previously discussed, the PSOE had never approved of women's military participation in the civil war. For the socialists, who could be considered the most conservative of the left-wing political parties on gender issues, the contribution of women to the struggle was limited to the home front. The attitude of the PSOE toward the militiawomen in late 1936 could not therefore be described as a change.

Nonetheless, in order to investigate this attitude, *Claridad*, the daily newspaper of the left-wing of the PSOE, was examined in its entirety for the first year of the Spanish Civil War.[51] During this time, the paper published only nine photographs of militiawomen and four articles containing information on women's military actions. While *Claridad* reported on news stories that were also widely covered in the communist press, such as the deaths of Francisca Solano and Odena, it did not demonstrate solid support for female combatants. *Claridad* ceased to include any photographs or positive references to *milicianas* at the end of October, much earlier than the communist, anarchist or POUM press.

The very last reference made to *milicianas* in the socialist press came in the form of an article published on 4 March 1937,[52] when it was insinuated that a majority of women who joined the militias at the beginning of the war had in fact been prostitutes working with the Nationalists to infiltrate the Republican troops:

> At first prostitutes joined the Popular Militia, apparently with great decisiveness and much enthusiasm; but when the heads of military divisions realized the ravages that certain well-dressed *milicianas* cause, they immediately put an end to their activity, which undoubtedly obeyed a preconceived plan of the fascists to initiate the counterrevolutionary movement.[53]

The socialist attitude toward female combatants was markedly different from that of the other left-wing political groups, since they maintained their opposition to women's military participation throughout the civil war.

CHANGING ATTITUDES OF THE PUBLIC

The shift of public opinion against the *milicianas* was clearly influenced by the change in attitude of political groups toward them. The attitude toward female combatants shown by the public, militiamen and foreign observers was overwhelmingly positive when women first took up arms during the insurrection in July. This positive attitude remained, and indeed intensified, when these women joined the militias and traveled to the front lines to fight. These sentiments were demonstrated through the number of militiawomen who were raised to the status of war legends, and through the prominence of art, poetry and photography featuring *milicianas*.

The treatment of militiawomen in the Republican independent press is a noteworthy demonstration of the positive feelings that the *milicianas* inspired in the general population. Female combatants were celebrated as symbols of bravery, and of the strength and commitment of the Republican cause. They were often used as examples to encourage and motivate others. It is significant that while public opinion certainly did swing away from supporting women's military involvement in the war, there is little evidence of such a change in attitudes in the independent press, or in the testimonies of militiamen and foreign observers. This is further evidence that the public's view of the *milicianas* was influenced more by political opinion and by the press and propaganda of political groups than by any other source.

The initial positive attitude of the public toward the *milicianas* can be seen in many ways. Communist *milicianas* such as Odena and Sánchez de la Mora became war legends for their contribution to the anti-fascist cause. These women were treated with adulation not just by the communists, but also by the public in general. Both women figured prominently in widely distributed communist and Republican propaganda publications and posters. Sánchez de la Mora, after an accident during training in which she lost her hand, became known as *La Dinamitera*, and became famous when the renowned poet Miguel Hernández wrote a poem dedicated to her.[54] A military school,[55] a street in Barcelona[56] and a women's battalion[57] were all named posthumously after Odena, who also featured in several works by poets such as Carlos de Rokha.[58]

These women maintained their status as war legends, and continued to be celebrated for their armed participation in the struggle, even as other women were being compulsorily removed from combat positions. Such was the fame of the most acclaimed *milicianas* that they became symbols of the anti-fascist resistance itself, and no longer directly represented real women who had fought at the front. As discussed previously, Spain had a history of idealizing individual women combatants, such as Aida Lafuente and Agustina de Aragón, but this had not meant that militancy or armed resistance was considered acceptable behavior for women in general.

Clearly, the social revolution saw a blurring of traditional gender roles, and for a short time, female military participation was considered acceptable. During these six months war heroines such as Odena and Sánchez de la Mora may have been viewed as real women and celebrated for their achievements, much in the same way as were male combatants who rose through the Republican ranks as a result of their bravery or military prowess. However, this soon changed when public attitudes shifted, and these women were refashioned into personifications of the Republican cause.

Lesser known or even anonymous women from all backgrounds, political and non-political, also played a part in war stories and legends. Women such as Francisca Solano, who became known as the Heroine of El Espinar, the Catalan communist Caridad Mercader and Angelina Martinez, a member of the JSU who took part in an attack on *El Cuartel de la*

Montaña, all featured in war legends that told of bravery and determination, and that encouraged others in the Republic to continue to fight.[59]

A further demonstration that the public viewed the militiawomen in positive terms was the prominence of *milicianas* in art during the Spanish Civil War. The artwork of Sim (*nom de plume* for Vila-Rey), which was also used for propaganda posters and calendars, included paintings that featured *milicianas* storming barracks, charging with rifles and fists in the air, patrolling the streets and eating in restaurants and coffee shops.[60] One of Sim's most recognizable paintings is a portrait of a *miliciana,* wearing a cap and shouldering a rifle.[61]

The photographs of Robert Capa were used in the press to report news of the civil war, but were also works of art in their own right. Capa's photographs of *milicianas* include one particularly paradoxical image of a woman in militia uniform sitting outside a café, her rifle resting upright against her chair, reading what is clearly identifiable as a women's beauty magazine, featuring a model on the cover who clearly represents the traditional gender role that the *miliciana* herself is so obviously defying. As previously mentioned, *milicianas* were often the subject of poetry, and even featured in cartoons.[62]

The *milicianas* themselves felt that public opinion toward their military contribution was very positive. Concha Pérez Collado remembers that as a militiawoman traveling through towns and villages as she moved from different fronts during the war, she was greeted with congeniality. When asked how the public reacted toward women who had volunteered for the front, Pérez Collado replied, "very well, there was great friendliness toward us everywhere."[63]

However, these positive attitudes began to dissipate in late 1936. Where once the militiawomen had been celebrated as heroines of the Republic, they were now largely seen as figures of ill-repute. Images of armed and uniformed *milicianas* were no longer widely featured in any press organ or propaganda medium, and these figures began to fade from the public eye. As noted earlier, one of the central elements in the shift of opinion against the *milicianas* was the belief that the majority of the militiawomen were in fact prostitutes. George Orwell described the process through which the *milicianas,* within a matter of months, went from being extolled to being openly disparaged and scorned. He noted that men had to be kept away from the POUM women's battalion while it was training, because otherwise they would laugh and ridicule the women.[64]

The leadership of the left-wing political groups in the Republican zone appears to have been largely responsible for the changing attitude of the public, since as previously noted, the harshest criticisms of the *milicianas* and the most powerful arguments for their removal from the front lines came from political groups rather than the general population. This can be demonstrated by an examination of the treatment of the militiawomen in the independent press, in comparison with the political press. Four newspapers from the independent Republican press have been examined in their entirety for the first year of the war: the popular and widely circulated daily newspaper *ABC*, the weekly newspapers *Crónica* and *Estampa* and the daily *La Voz*.

The representation of the *milicianas* in the independent press seems largely to have been unconnected with the politics surrounding women's military role in the war. *ABC*, *Crónica*, *Estampa* and *La Voz* did not publish any harsh criticisms of the *milicianas* or make any negative references to them, and put forward very few arguments for the removal of women from the front.[65] Instead, fewer and fewer photographs of the militiawomen were published as they disappeared from the front lines. Positive representations of the *milicianas* continued to appear in several of the independent newspapers for several months after they had stopped in the newspapers published by political parties.

Coverage of militiawomen in *ABC* began to decrease slightly in November 1936; nevertheless, photographs of *milicianas* still appeared every second or third day. Significantly, these representations remained positive. *ABC* featured militiawomen on its cover ten times in the first year of the war, and four of these occasions were in December, the month during which criticisms and negative opinions about the *milicianas* began to circulate among political groups.[66] It was not until January 1937 that a sharp decrease occurred. The last article written about women fighting at the front appeared on 16 January 1937.[67] Photographs disappeared almost completely after February 1937, the *ABC* printing only one in April,[68] three in May[69] and then no more. It is significant, however, that the last ever photograph of an armed female combatant featured in *ABC* was of a woman referred to as "La Chata," a sergeant in the 3rd Mixed Brigade of the 10th Division of the Popular Army.[70] Thus, while the figure of the *miliciana* in blue overalls and militia cap had disappeared by 1937, *ABC* demonstrated that a small number of militiawomen had been incorporated into the regular army.

The last significant reference in *Crónica* to the military participation of women was printed on 20 December 1936, and consisted of a two-page article discussing the military training of women's battalions in the rearguard.[71] *Estampa* did not publish its last article about a female combatant until May 1937. Significantly, this was two pages long and detailed the military activity of a communist volunteer from Holland named Fanny, who had been fighting in the militias since the first day of the war.[72] *La Voz* published its last photograph of a female combatant on 17 November 1936.[73] As with *ABC*'s last image of a female combatant, this pictured a woman who had also been incorporated into the regular army.

As used in the independent press, the slogan "Men to the Front, Women to the Home Front" clearly contended that men and women had different roles to play in the war, but did not seem to indicate that those militiawomen already fighting at the front should return home. Rather, it seemed to be aimed at encouraging the participation of those who had not yet taken up roles in the anti-fascist resistance. This is clear because the slogan co-existed in the independent press with the continued positive representations of *milicianas* in the front lines. The cover of *ABC* on 20 December 1936 demonstrates that even at the end of 1936 the independent press was not as prescriptive as the political press in spelling out the roles women should play in the anti-fascist struggle. The cover depicted photographs of women both fighting on the front line and working in the home front.[74]

No great change in attitudes toward the *milicianas* was evidenced in the independent Republican press. Similarly, there is little evidence that militiamen or foreign observers ever changed their positive view or support for the military involvement of the *milicianas*. When militiamen spoke of their female comrades, they did so in positive terms. The journalist Hans Kaminski interviewed a militiaman in Barcelona early in the war who expressed a common viewpoint among the left on women's right to contribute militarily to the revolution and anti-fascist resistance: "everyone has the right to do what they wish with their lives. We would be bad revolutionaries if we wanted to prevent a woman from giving her life in the fight against fascism."[75]

As late as July 1937, militiamen were still demonstrating positive attitudes toward the *milicianas*. An article printed in *Hombres Libres* about the actions of an anarchist militiawoman, Tata, in an attack on the Aravaca front ends with a description of the reaction of a *miliciano* named Roman: "he lifts her up . . . and fraternally takes her right hand and deposits a kiss of respect on it. . . . Roman does not know what to do and his lips mumble these tender words full of emotion. 'Comrade, you are a brave and valiant woman.'"[76]

Some foreign observers, while expressing a positive opinion of militiawomen and their military participation, also articulated a level of surprise upon witnessing women's actions in battle. Kaminski recorded his own opinion of the *milicianas* whom he saw fighting:

> Another thing that shocks me and that one does not normally see so close to the enemy is that there are women. They wear pants just like the men. It is useless to mention that here vanity serves no purpose and that women do not use lipstick or powder. The majority wear short hair like the men, to the point that often it is difficult to distinguish them. I do not think that any human beings are made for war, especially women. But the truth is that women carry out their duties with the same devotion as their masculine comrades. Many have distinguished themselves for their bravery.[77]

Accounts from many other foreign observers highlight the bravery of militiawomen and express support for their military involvement without indicating any surprise at the actions. Franz Borkenau wrote of the *milicianas* in positive terms throughout his account, describing them as acting with "self assurance"[78] and emphasizing their bravery in action. He spoke of one group of militiawomen as "more courageous even than the men."[79] As previously mentioned, Tom Clarke, a Scottish volunteer, spoke of the bravery of three *milicianas* in the Battle of Jarama in January 1937.[80] Mary Low and Juan Breà, in their roles as foreign observers and members of a POUM militia, continually wrote of the militiawomen in positive terms throughout their memoirs, even dedicating an entire chapter to the subject. John Tisa in his memoirs also portrayed militiawomen very positively, even after the change in attitudes of political parties and the public toward *milicianas* had taken place. He related a meeting in June 1937 with a group of anarchist militiawomen who had remained fighting on the Madrid front.[81] There is no evidence of these foreign observers changing their views on the militiawomen.

It is important to note that during my interview with Pérez Collado she put forward the argument there never was a change in attitudes toward women in combat. When asked what month she felt that public opinion began to change toward the *milicianas*, Pérez Collado answered that she did not believe there was a change at all. She related that when she returned from the front to work in a factory, she "never encountered any difference" in attitude compared to the positive, welcoming and friendly attitude that she had experienced at the beginning of the war.[82] She was aware of the change in attitude of political groups, and of the fact that *milicianas* had been asked to leave the front by the anarchist political leadership. She also recalled the negative opinions about *milicianas* that had circulated at the time, as was shown by the fact that she began, without prompting, to discuss the allegation that the existence of prostitution in the front lines had caused problems for the anti-fascist resistance. She spent a substantial amount of time refuting this allegation, which she attributed solely to the leadership of political groups and not to members of the public.

ARGUMENTS FOR THE REMOVAL OF WOMEN FROM COMBAT

During the period from late November until March 1937, arguments against the presence of women in combat roles were developed, propounded and discussed. A dynamic relationship existed between these arguments and the changing attitudes, since the arguments for removal were both produced by and contributed to the transformation of public opinion.

This section will examine the broad range of arguments put forward to justify the view that militiawomen should be removed from their combat positions. Some of these arguments have been accepted by contemporary historians as the true reasons why women were forcibly removed from the front. Others were not widely believed even at the time, and can clearly be seen as nothing more than thinly veiled pretexts. While many of the arguments presented for removing women from combat positions do indeed seem to have contributed to the decision that was made, none of them took into account the most fundamental reason why this occurred—the general reversal of progressive gains and policies that came about as a result of the failure of the social revolution.

The first of the reasons put forward came from the communists. The claim was that the presence of fighting women at the front was no longer necessary now that the urgency of the first days and months of the war had passed. The first mention of this idea came in early November, when the PCE printed an article in its organ *Mundo Obrero* explaining that while women's participation had been necessary during the first days after the insurrection, women now were more urgently needed in the home front.[83] The article was signed by M. Andiano, "in the name of the Party." The tone of this article was not derogatory toward the *milicianas*. While firmly asserting that women should leave the front lines of combat to serve the Republican cause on the home front, Andiano stated that the militiawomen had fought with "as much or more courage than the men."[84]

The communist *Comité Nacional Femenino contra la Guerra y el Fascismo* (National Women's Committee against the War and Fascism, CNFGF), presented this same argument in February 1937, when they published in their newspaper *Mujeres* an article entitled "Las Mujeres, en la Retaguardia, y los Hombres, en los Frentes de la Lucha" ("Women in the Rearguard, and Men, in the Front Lines of the Fight").[85] The article argued that the incorporation of women into the militias was "no longer necessary," and that women "have a lot to do in the second rank."[86]

This argument partly incorporated the idea that women had volunteered only due to a sense of urgency, rather than as a result of a genuine political decision to serve the anti-fascist cause in a particular way. One piece of evidence against this notion is the fact that in late 1936, after the "initial urgency" had passed, there were still women wishing to volunteer for front line combat. On 20 December, *Crónica* published an article written by Etheria Artay, who reported the existence of "a great number of women in Barcelona who wish to put themselves in a position to be able to intervene directly in the struggle for freedom, fighting at the side of men and renouncing the comfortable role of being weak and protected."[87] This article and others demonstrate that there were a significant number of women in Barcelona and in other areas of Spain who, as late as December, still wished to join their comrades in the armed resistance against fascism. They were in fact preparing to do so by forming battalions and completing military training.

Another common complaint leveled against the *milicianas* was their supposed lack of military training, which, it was argued, meant that they were less effective as combatants than were the men. This line of reasoning had existed since the beginning of the war, and had been referred to often by the small number of proponents of the view that women should never have entered combat positions in the first place. This alleged lack of military training was a grievance against the *milicianas* that Mary Nash explains was shared by both women's organizations and by political groups.[88]

In September, the communist newspaper *Treball* published an article that contended the view that a lack of training was grounds for removing women from the front lines of combat:

> We must acknowledge the merit of those brave girls who in the flower of youth offered their lives in defense of freedom, but we must not forget that one must have a certain degree of knowledge and preparation in order to assist an operator who is trying to save a life that is in serious danger. Unfortunately, not all women have such knowledge. This is the reason why, despite the enthusiasm of these beautiful *milicianas*, on many occasions they are of little use.[89]

There are several flaws in the argument that women's alleged lack of military training rendered them ineffective combatants. Firstly, it is not true that militiawomen had no training or experience in weapons handling. Evidence has already been presented that demonstrates that most women received training when they were issued their weapons, and that others already had experience even prior to the outbreak of the war. Women also learned the necessary skills very quickly at the front. The author of this article himself writes that "not *all* women" (italics added) possessed the military knowledge necessary, thus admitting that some in fact did. When this is the case, why is the argument put forth that *all* women should be removed from combat positions, rather than only those who did not possess suitable military skills?

Meanwhile, no one ever argued that the militiamen who had not had any military training, or who proved themselves to be militarily ineffectual, should return from the front. A great many militiamen had had little or no experience with weapons or any military training prior to the war. While many women may not have had any previous experience in the use of weapons at the time of enlistment, the same was true for many of the young male recruits to the Republican and revolutionary militias.

Orwell noted this fact on several occasions in his memoir, *Homage to Catalonia*.[90] During the brief instruction his militia received in the use of arms, he observed that "many of the militiamen had never had a gun in their hands before, and very few, I imagine, knew what the sights were for."[91] Dan Kurzman, in his study of the Battle for Madrid in November 1936, reported that of the 50,000 Republican fighters, "most were civilians, with little or no military training."[92] Nevertheless, no criticisms were made of these men by any political party or group at the time. Instead, they were praised for their heroic and successful defense of Madrid. If the presence in the Republican ranks of untrained men was discussed at all, it was in the context of the need for training to be provided.

The existence in the rearguard of women's battalions consisting of hundreds of armed and trained women also surely disproves the argument that women needed to be removed from the fronts because a lack of training made them militarily ineffectual. By December, these women would have received a great deal more training, and would have been far more militarily proficient than a great many of the young men who had initially gone off to fight in the front lines. The readiness of these women to be stationed if necessary in the front lines shows that the alleged need to remove women because of a lack of training was not a genuine concern, since there was never any talk of replacing "untrained" women with those from these battle-ready battalions.

Another reason advanced for women's supposed unsuitability for combat was the contention that women by their very nature were far better suited to fulfilling roles on the home front. Though not always clearly articulated, this idea was closely connected with most of the other arguments calling for the removal of women from combat positions. It was believed that the biological nature of women, along with their social conditioning, meant that they were far more effective in the home front performing auxiliary tasks. These tasks included working in hospitals, running orphanages and kitchens, organizing supplies for the male soldiers, and working in factories.

Though his views do not appear to have been widely accepted, the anarchist sexologist Ibáñez presented several reasons why he felt the removal of women from the front line of combat was imperative. Early in 1937, Ibáñez published a pamphlet entitled *Tres Mensajes a la Mujer* (*Three Messages to Women*), which put forward the peculiar and highly sexist theory (by today's standards) that militiawomen should be removed from the front in order that the militiamen could conserve their sexual energy for combat.[93] In December 1936, Ibáñez had been one of the leaders in the movement for the legalization of abortion in Catalonia, which would seem to indicate that he held progressive ideas on women's rights. However, by 1937, Ibáñez's views had clearly changed, and he was adamant that the problem of Republican military failures could be solved by simply forcing the *milicianas* to take up non-military roles in the rearguard, thus imposing chastity on the militiamen:

> And you, mercenaries of half virtuous women . . . who in the midst of a Revolution tried to convert the sacred land of the war front, covered with proletarian blood, in a garden of pleasure, go back! If the militiaman seeks you out, let it be in his free time, and under his own moral

responsibility, helped by existing hygienic resources. But do not make
him stray from his path nor put the softness of erotic fatigue in the steel
of his muscles. . . . You cannot give up your previous lifestyle by sow-
ing the battle front with venereal diseases. . . . Venereal diseases must
be extirpated from the front, and in order to do so, women must first be
removed. [94]

It is interesting to note that Ibáñez called specifically for militiawomen to
be removed from the front in order to solve what he saw as the "problem" of male and female combatants having sex in the front lines. While a
great many female nurses were stationed in the front lines, Ibáñez makes
no mention of these women nor the possibility that they could also be
having sex with militiamen. It is also telling that Ibáñez did not simply
call for all members of militias to stop having sex. It seems he felt that it
was the very presence of women that made that impossible, taking away
all responsibility from the militiamen themselves.

Also circulating at this time, and also clearly sexist, is the "chivalry"
argument for removing the *milicianas* from their combat positions.
Though it is not clear from which political group or sector of society this
idea originated, some people felt that the ingrained chivalry of Spanish
men meant that they would take unnecessary risks to save the lives of
endangered militiawomen, thus compromising the success of military
operations.

Low reported in her memoirs having come across this argument early
on in the war, on the first day that the POUM women's battalion went to
the barracks to begin their military training. While standing at the gate, a
young French volunteer who had recently returned from the front ran up
to the women to protest at their presence. When he discovered that the
women were members of a battalion who had come to begin their training, he proclaimed, "I wouldn't have women at the front at all, if I had
the choice. I've been there and I know." When questioned about this, the
young man explained that the reason for his comment was not that he felt
women were not brave enough or capable of performing well in battle.
Instead, he revealed his belief that:

> It makes everything altogether too heroic. Especially for the Spaniards.
> They're conscious of being males every moment of the day and night,
> you know. They haven't got rid of their old-fashioned sense of chivalry
> yet, however silly they may think it is. If one of you girls get caught by
> the enemy, fifteen men immediately risk their lives to avenge her. All
> that kind of thing. It costs lives and it's too much effort. [95]

Once again, this argument relies on the idea that men cannot be held
responsible for their actions. Low felt that the principles of the social
revolution dictated that these men should be trained to overcome their
sexist attitudes and learn to treat women as equals. This was pointed out
to the young French man by one of the militiawomen from Low's batta-

lion. "They must get over it," she declared. "And they never will unless we go on as we're doing."[96] However, it is clear that among many Spanish men chivalry was deeply ingrained, and not something they felt could be helped. A *miliciano* explained to Kaminski, "when I see a woman in the line of fire, I would like to run and protect her. I think it's a natural masculine sentiment and it is impossible for me to avoid it."[97]

A Mexican communist and foreign observer, Blanca Lydia Trejo, gave chivalry as the reason why she felt that "the collaboration of women as milicianas has been a total failure." She explained that the militiamen would come to the aid of wounded or dying *milicianas* without thinking, which would cause more deaths.[98] Sections of the British press reported the chivalry of Spanish men as the deciding factor in the removal of women from positions of combat. The magazine *Woman To-day* reported in December 1936 that rather than cowardice on the part of the militia-women, as some had reported, it was in fact the "curious reactions" of the militiamen that had made this action necessary.[99] The article explained that "these men, seeing their women fellow-soldiers fall dead, or lie writhing, lost their heads. Horror, or furious rage, took possession of them; forgetting discipline, they would rush upon the enemy, calling them Butchers and Fascists, and get needlessly killed themselves. And since there was no time to train away this instinctive chivalry, it was thought best to withdraw the women from the fighting ranks."[100]

The argument for removing women from combat positions that was most often cited and which received the most attention was the accusation that among the *milicianas* there were a great many prostitutes, who were causing severe problems among the Republican ranks by spreading venereal disease. It is believed that this accusation was initially leveled against the *milicianas* by the anarchists,[101] and was widely accepted by other political groups and the public. The argument that the presence of prostitution in the front lines was causing great difficulty for the Republican forces and became so widely believed that even contemporary historians, such as Ángel Moraga, have cited it as the real reason that militia-women were stripped of their combat positions in the anti-Nationalist resistance.[102]

Extreme action appears to have been taken by anarchists against women accused of being prostitutes at the front. Teresa Pàmies and Hans Kaminski both report in their memoirs that Buenaventura Durruti gave orders for a group of alleged prostitutes to be executed after they refused to return to the rearguard, and instead had sought to keep fighting on the Aragon front.[103] Ibáñez, mentioned above, was one of the notable anarchists to blame women very publicly for the spread of venereal disease at the front.[104]

The PSOE later joined in the slander campaign against the *milicianas* that focused on prostitution, even going so far as to insinuate that groups of prostitutes in the Republican ranks were Nationalist infiltrators working with the "Fifth Column." In March 1937, the PSOE put this position in its newspaper *Claridad*, claiming in an article written by Leoncio Perez, "at first prostitutes joined the Popular Militia, apparently with great decision and much enthusiasm; but when the heads of military divisions realized the ravages that certain well-dressed *milicianas* cause, they immediately put an end to their activity, which undoubtedly obeyed a preconceived plan of the fascists to infiltrate the counterrevolutionary movement."[105]

In her memoirs, Low reported a conversation with a POUM militiaman about prostitution in Barcelona. In the conversation, she suggested that one solution might be to retrain the women to perform other jobs or to go to the front to fight. The *miliciano* replied, "they did go to the front at first. But being hardened by prostitution doesn't necessarily make one cool under fire. A lot of them were in the way, and then the men were always being sent home with venereal disease because there was no control."[106] This conversation demonstrates that the view that prostitution among the *milicianas* was damaging the Republican forces was present even among dissident Marxists.

The spread of venereal disease did cause severe problems for the Republicans. The well-known adage that more Republican casualties were caused by venereal disease than by enemy bullets did have some truth to it.[107] However, many believe that these problems were not the result of sexual contact in the front lines, but arose as prostitution on the home front developed to meet the needs of militiamen and soldiers on leave.[108] It is interesting to note that the blame for these problems was placed squarely on the prostitutes, rather than on the men who sought out their services. Without the readiness of men to pay for sex, the prostitution industry would not have existed.

As for sexual relations between men and women in the front lines, it is of course natural to assume that it occurred. As has previously been established, many women joined the militia along with their husbands, partners or lovers. In addition, there is evidence of militiamen and women forming genuine bonds with each other during the war. The Basque anarchist Casilda Méndez spoke of the natural bonds that developed between men and women while fighting at the front:

> There was an end to [the type of] woman who could only hope to please her husband through housework and the bed. What they say about women going to the front in order to go to bed with the militians . . . all that is a lie. Now, it is unavoidable for empathy and affinities to develop between women and men; some call it chemical or cellular attraction; and relationships develop, particularly in areas isolated from urban areas, like the Aragon Front. Physical, moral and spiritual contacts can exist between a man and a woman who are at the war fronts. The contrary would be an aberration.[109]

Many of these couples even went on to marry.[110] Newspapers often reported these marriages, and many even took place at the front.[111] Conversely, several *milicianas* have commented that due to the harsh conditions caused by the weather, hunger, lack of sleep, lice and the constant threat of enemy attack, life at the front was so difficult and tiring that there was never time to concern oneself with sexual interactions.[112]

It is reasonable to expect that some women who were or had been prostitutes did go to the war fronts to fight during the war. While it is impossible to determine the number, it is clear that these women constituted only a very small minority and may not have stayed in the front lines for an extended period.[113] However, there is no evidence of women disguising themselves as *milicianas* in order to create business for themselves as prostitutes at the front.

The alleged presence of prostitution at the front has caused a great deal of anger and distress among the *milicianas* themselves, who have since spent a great deal of time in their memoirs and oral testimonies refuting the claim. Many *milicianas* felt that these accusations of prostitution represented a malicious attack against them. Even today, Pérez Collado becomes visibly angry and indignant when she speaks on the subject. During my interview with her in Barcelona in February 2005, prostitution was one of the very first subjects that she wanted to talk about, as if she was still determined to clear the names of the militiawomen who fought at the front. Pérez Collado related her understanding that the alleged presence of prostitutes at the front was the reason that the militiawomen were recalled from their combat positions, but affirmed that she had never met a single prostitute at the front, and nor had anyone she knew.[114]

Sánchez de la Mora is another *miliciana* who has expended a great deal of effort since the war trying to correct the historical record on this point. At the conference held in Salamanca in October 1987 to discuss the role of women in the Spanish Civil War, Sánchez de la Mora and several other *milicianas* denounced the smear campaign centered on prostitution that was orchestrated against the militiawomen by both the Nationalists and the Republicans during the war.[115] Sánchez de la Mora criticized the treatment that the *milicianas* had received from the Spanish public, as well as most male historians:

> Spaniards are very critical: They called the *milicianas* prostitutes and the militiamen thieves. And when the brigades arrived, they called them every name in the book. I don't understand it. Precisely the reason I came here today was to explain this to you. I never saw anything. First of all, one would have to be very stupid to go to the front lines to be a prostitute, where you can get your head blown off.[116]

During an interview with Sánchez de la Mora conducted by Ingrid Strobl later that same year, the issue was raised once again. When asked a personal question, presumably about her sexual relations while at the front, Sánchez de la Mora became so angry that she almost threw Strobl out of her house.[117] However Strobl points out that in her anger Sánchez de la Mora made comments that were more revealing than if she had simply answered the question. Sánchez de la Mora angrily replied:

> Those are filthy remarks! In the front we were all fighters, people with leftist ideology and with incredible ideals for which we were ready to die. I was sixteen years old when I went to the front. I arrived a virgin, and a virgin I returned. All this is only fascist propaganda to offend and to defile women![118]

The communist *miliciana* Teófila Madroñal also eschewed arguments that the militiawomen were nothing more than prostitutes that spread disease.

> After [the war] the militiawoman was morally maltreated, she went down in history as a sexual object, as one says these days. But it wasn't that way. It happened that some professionals took advantage of the circumstances and went to the front, but it isn't true that they spread venereal diseases and provoked scandal, this served their propaganda well. But it wasn't that way, the *milicianas* were brave, and during the time that they were at the front they acted as the men did, sometimes even more fearless than they. Women jumped out of the trenches like demons. . . . If the women had not gone into the streets [to fight fascism], I repeat, many men would have shit their pants.[119]

Fidela Fernández de Velasco Pérez also commented in an interview with Strobl that the rumors about the *milicianas* being prostitutes persist today, even among communists. She notes bitterly that while the *mono azul* was a symbol of honor when worn by men, when worn by women the uniform only served to represent prostitution. "Yes, there were prostitutes [in Spain at the time]," Fernández de Velasco Pérez explains:

> But they were in the rearguard most of all. There they carried out their business. But this had nothing to do with us, with those who fought. And our comrades knew it very well. None of them dared to approach us too much. They did not see us as women. Nor did they want to. We were in the dirty and lice infested trenches just like them, fighting and living just as they were. For them we were not women but simply one more [fighter].[120]

Lastly, the process of the militarization of the popular militias that began to take place in late 1936 and that was finalized in March 1937 brought with it one final argument for the removal of women from combat positions. The militias had been formed spontaneously as a response to the Nationalist insurrection, and had mostly been organized by trade unions, anarchist organizations and the POUM. The majority of these militias were organized by and consisted of revolutionaries, and they took on revolutionary forms. The traditional military hierarchy did not exist.

There were no official uniforms or saluting, officers were elected, and important decisions were made democratically. This model was open and inclusive, and allowed for the participation of women in combat. When the communists began to take control of the Republican government in late 1936, as has been discussed above, they began a process of establishing a conventional army, embracing formality and military discipline. At this time, it seems to have been simply concluded that the professional military was no place for women at all. Without a great deal of discussion or debate, the idea that the *milicianas* were not suited to, and did not belong in, the regular army prevailed.[121] It is not clear why it was necessary for this to be the case. While women had never fulfilled combat positions in a regular army in Spain before this time, neither had they ever done so within militias. Why was it not possible for these trained militiawomen simply to be incorporated into the regular army, the way that their male comrades were, unless there was some other reason why it was no longer considered acceptable for them to participate in combat?

As a result of these changing attitudes and arguments against women's military participation, the numbers of *milicianas* began to diminish. Orwell remarked that while the militias still contained female combatants in December, there were not as many as before.[122] Some female combatants became convinced by arguments that they would serve the Republican cause better in a non-military capacity, and thus voluntarily left the front lines.[123] Low also observed that by January "there were less women mingled among the men going to the front."[124] Due to the change in attitudes and practices of left-wing political parties, it had become increasingly difficult for new female volunteers to enlist. Having returned to Spain in late 1936 after a brief trip to Switzerland, Clara Thalmann joined the German anarcho-syndicalist unit on the Aragon front. At first, Thalmann was advised by Augustin Souchy that she might not be allowed to fight with the militia. On this occasion, the militia took a vote and decided to allow Thalmann to join their group as a militiawoman, because of her previous experience.[125] Other female volunteers, however, were not given the same opportunity.[126]

THE EXAMPLE OF WAR NURSES

It is useful to examine the issue of nurses at the war fronts (the vast majority of whom were female) in order to provide a contrast between the treatment of women who were playing a role that was traditionally considered acceptable for them, and of the *milicianas* who had decidedly stepped out of their conventional gender boundaries. While arguments were being developed to remove the *milicianas* from the fronts, the presence of female nurses in the front lines was never questioned. This was despite the comparable danger presented to them by their proximity to the front lines, the fact that in many cases they had also received little or no medical training prior to the war, and the equal possibility that they might enter into sexual relations with militiamen.

What is significant about the example of the war nurses is that almost every argument that was applied to the *milicianas* in an effort to prove the necessity of their forced removal could *also* have been applied to the nurses stationed in the front lines. However, these arguments were never directed at the war nurses, and this is highly telling. It is possible from this example to make further deductions about the true reasons why women were removed from combat positions during the Spanish Civil War. The argument that the militiawomen had not undergone the necessary training in order to be militarily effective could equally have been leveled at the many war nurses who fulfilled the role without any prior medical training. Many young women simply volunteered to become nurses at the outbreak of the war, and went off to the fronts in much the same manner as did the *milicianas*. Just as it was claimed that the lack of training of the militiawomen could cost lives in combat, so too could the lack of medical training of the nurses have cost thousands of Republican lives.

The Republican side experienced a shortage of nurses, not only due to the immediate demand caused by the war, but also because the core of the medical profession in Spain had been organized by religious institutions and staffed by nuns. These medical personnel had mostly joined the Nationalist side of the struggle.[127] In order to combat this shortage, the normal requirements of age, previous academic studies and training that had been necessary to work as a nurse were waived, and many women underwent short and intensive training courses[128] —much like those that the *milicianas* received in the use of weapons once they had reached the front lines. Some nurses were as young as fourteen.[129] Later in 1937, the Republican government and other anti-fascist bodies began to show concern that the removal of many requirements for performing nursing work was causing problems in the medical services. The response, however, was to facilitate further training—not to remove these women from their positions, as was the case with the *milicianas*.[130]

The argument that the front was no place for militiawomen, due to the dangerous proximity to the enemy in the front lines, could equally have been applied to the nurses who were stationed at or close to the fronts. Many nurses were assigned to field hospitals at the fronts, and others were stationed in hospitals not far behind the lines. The idea that the *milicianas* needed to return to the home front because of the chivalry of the Spanish militiamen, who supposedly would risk their lives unnecessarily to save the women if they were in danger, could equally be applied to nurses. Being stationed in such dangerous zones, their lives were also constantly in danger. Nash reports that many nurses were killed in field and military hospitals as a result of shelling or other forms of enemy attack.[131] Thus, this argument clearly was not a real reason for recalling militiawomen to the rearguard, since if it had been the case, nurses would have been recalled also. Nor does it explain the fact that the *milicianas* were allowed to remain with their units in the front lines so long as they gave up their weapons, and instead performed solely the auxiliary tasks of cooking, cleaning, sewing and laundry for their male comrades.

Concern over the wasted sexual energy of the male Republican fighters, or more significantly over the spread of venereal disease, appeared to be one of the main concerns of those advocating the removal of the *milicianas* from their combat positions in the front lines. However, no efforts were made to remove war nurses or to restrict their sexual relations with the militiamen or male soldiers. Once again, if this had been the main factor motivating the removal of women, it does not make sense that the *milicianas* were allowed to remain at the fronts if they confined themselves to fulfilling auxiliary tasks. Borkenau in his account implied that nurses had sexual relations with militiamen.[132]

Clearly, the reason that war nurses were not removed from the front is quite different. It has nothing to do with the fact that in many cases they had insufficient training, were positioned in dangerous proximity to the fronts and were having sex with militiamen. The real reason is that these women were playing a supportive and nurturing role that had long been considered acceptable for Spanish women. It was the fact that the *milicianas* had stepped outside their traditional gender boundaries that attracted negative attention. In the context of a general reversal of progressive gains as a result of the failure of the social revolution and the conservative push from the communists, it was the *milicianas'* transgression of these boundaries that gave rise to the sentiment that they should be stripped of their combat positions, and forced back into their traditional gender role in the home front.

The changing attitudes of both the public in the Republican zone and of left-wing political parties toward the *milicianas* is a complex issue. It is not simply the case that attitudes toward women's military participation were positive in July, and then became negative toward the end of 1936. The reality was that the full military participation of women, and indeed complete sexual equality, was never fully accepted or wholeheartedly embraced by any political group, except *Mujeres Libres*. It is also clear, however, that inroads were being made. Gender relations were transformed for a time, advances in women's rights were made, and consequently women's armed participation in the civil war was accepted and even encouraged to a certain extent. Certainly, during the civil war women experienced new opportunities and were able to fulfill roles that had been previously denied to them, albeit only for a brief period.

PART TWO: FORCED REMOVAL FROM COMBAT

When approximately 1,000 women in the Republican zone took up arms to fight on the front lines during the civil war, they stepped outside their traditionally defined gender role in a way that had never occurred in Spain on such a scale. Several thousand more armed women in the rearguard began military training and preparation, claiming for women a new definition of citizenship, which included the right to bear arms. For eight months these Spanish women, and the female international volunteers who joined them, fought alongside their male comrades and contributed to the anti-fascist cause. However, a change in attitudes toward the *milicianas* took place at the end of 1936, and by early 1937, it was no longer seen as acceptable for women to participate in combat. Consequently, in March women's military contribution ended when an official decision (or series of decisions) was made to compel the *milicianas* to lay down their arms. Militiawomen were sent back home to knit sweaters for the soldiers, run orphanages and work in factories.

The official decision to remove women from combat is one of the questions over which there is much debate among the historical community. Historians are not yet certain who gave this order, precisely when it was made and for what reasons *milicianas* were sent home from the fronts. While this question may never be completely resolved due to a lack of conclusive primary evidence, it is most likely that a series of decisions were made primarily by both Prime Minister Francisco Largo Caballero and the anarchist leader Major Antonio Ortíz,[133] and came into effect in March 1937. While the political leadership within the Republic presented numerous arguments to justify removing women from combat positions, it is clear that the reason why it was initially acceptable for women to fight, and then seen as deplorable eight months later, is connected to the course of social revolution in Spain.

The primary aim here is to discuss the impact on the *milicianas* themselves of the decision to exclude them from combat, and to indicate their reaction to the subsequent development of events. Part 2 of this chapter will examine the way in which the militiawomen were informed of the decision, and the steps that were taken to remove the majority of them from the front. While a consensus on these moves existed among the essentially male leadership of political groups within the Republican zone, it is clear that female combatants viewed this turn of events differently. The majority of the militiawomen had deep reservations about their recall from the front, and saw it as a retreat from the gains women had made during the war and revolution. It was for this reason that many *milicianas* needed to be forcibly removed from their front-line positions. A further demonstration that many militiawomen disagreed with the decision is the fact that a number of them stayed on to fight, regardless of orders to the contrary.

THE OFFICIAL DECISION

Since concrete documentation of the order to remove women from combat has not yet been found, and indeed may never have existed, it is impossible for historians to know precisely what occurred. However, circumstantial evidence exists to suggest that both the socialist Largo Caballero and the anarchist Ortíz gave the same order, the former possibly as a decree of parliament or a series of military ordinances, and the latter as an internal order given to the members of anarchist organizations. In addition, it appears likely that the order came as a series of decisions that were relayed to different sections of the fighting force at different times, which would account for the varied response. While there is evidence to suggest that talk of such an order, or perhaps preliminary advice to militias on the removal of *milicianas* began to be circulated in late December 1936, it was not until March 1937 that concrete orders were given, because it was not until March that most militias acted on the order and removed the majority of the militiawomen from their ranks.

Scanlon, who in 1976 was the first historian to discuss the issue, refers to this order as if it were a parliamentary decree passed by Largo Caballero, though unfortunately she does not provide a reference for this information.[134] Mary Nash notes that she has not found any record of such a decree in the *Gaceta Oficial del Estado* (Official Gazette of the State).[135] Nash nonetheless still agrees with Scanlon that it was Largo Caballero who gave the order officially, though possibly as an internal military order.[136] This would explain why documentation has not yet been found, and may never be. Other historians such as Josefina Serván Corchero, Mónica Carabias Álvaro and Pilar Folguera Crespo also agree with Scanlon that the decision to remove women from combat came in the form of a parliamentary decree sanctioned by Largo Caballero.[137] Corchero also notes that the communist deputies of the *Cortes* were particularly pleased with the decree.[138]

An order of whatever form made by the Republican government would not necessarily have affected the anarchist militias. It is believed that a separate order was given to anarchist organizations. The *miliciana* Concha Pérez Collado names Ortíz as the man responsible for the order to remove anarchist women from combat.[139] In my interview with Pérez Collado in 2005, she related that even though many have since said the order came from Durruti, it came in fact from Ortíz. This was the information that Pérez Collado received during the war, and she corroborated it by referring to conversations she had with Ortíz after the war. Pérez Collado explained:

> At first it was always said that it was Durruti, but the first [to give the order] was Antonio Ortíz and later we spoke of it many, many times, because he was a friend of mine. We met up, and we spoke of it.[140]

Pérez Collado is supported by the historian Dolors Marín, who also lays responsibility for the order with Ortíz.[141]

Separate from the question of who gave the order is the issue of *when* the order was given. Opinions on this question vary widely, with one notable proponent arguing that the order was given as early as September 1936, and others asserting that it did not occur until much later, in March 1937. The timing of the order is significant, as it is linked with the reasons *why* women were removed from combat. If the order was given and followed in September 1936, it would be unlikely to have been linked either with the failure of the social revolution or with the militarization of the popular militias, both of which did not occur definitively until months later. However, if this removal did in fact occur in March 1937, then both of these events can be connected with the decision.

Circumstantial evidence suggests that the forced removal of the *milicianas* from the front lines did not occur until March 1937, though some militiawomen appear to have been encouraged to leave earlier. Ronald Fraser relates that the call for *milicianas* to leave the front was made after the Battle of Guadalajara in March 1937.[142] He does not reference this information, but shortly afterward he does recount the oral testimony of a nurse and member of the JSU, Justina Palma, who claims that Dolores Ibárruri herself traveled to the front in March 1937 and told the militiawomen to leave, explaining that their proper place was on the home front.[143] The implication is that Fraser has relied on information received from his interview subjects to provide the date the *milicianas* were recalled. Historians such as Catherine Coleman[144] and Caroline Brothers[145] agree with Fraser that the directive was not made until March 1937.

Some historians relate that the order was given around the same time as the popular militias were incorporated into the Regular Army, but do not specifically mention the month in which they believe this occurred. These historians include Ingrid Strobl,[146] Crespo[147] and Gina Herrmann.[148] It is the opinion of these historians that the order was given as a direct result of the militarization of the Popular Army, though none offers an explanation as to why. Only Herrmann attempts to explain, stating that "part of the Republican rationale for this decree regarding militiawomen held that the survival of the Republic depended on the formation of a solid military organization that could compete with the enemy in an escalating 'total' war."[149] Perhaps these historians feel it is unnecessary to spell out that the connection between the militarization of the militias and the removal of the *milicianas* was the traditional belief that a conventional army does not include female combatants.

Of course, this comment does not explain why the exclusion of female combatants from the army was necessary in order for it to become "a sol d military organization," and relies on the sexist assumption that wo nen do not make good soldiers. This is an ahistorical viewpoint, wh ch disregards the success and military capability demonstrated by wo nen as members of the popular militias. In fact, the removal of the *milicianas* from their combat positions was only connected to the professionalization of the militias in so far as both these events occurred in the context of the failure of the social revolution and the rise to power of the communists within the Republican government. There is no basis upon which to assume that militiawomen were withdrawn from the front lines simply as a result of the belief that they could not be included in the professional military.

Nash appears to be the only historian who believes that the order was given as early as September 1936. She claims that "by September, a policy was being implemented to coerce them to leave the fronts."[150] Nash is able to argue that this occurred so early, when all others sources point to a later date, because she believes that it was originally military ordinances that ordered *milicianas* to leave the fronts, and that Largo Caballero then sanctioned these orders later, after the order had already been put into practice.[151] Nash also says that not all women left the fronts immediately, but that most had done so by the beginning of 1937.[152] It is interesting that Nash references Fraser for her assertion that the number of *milicianas* had been drastically reduced by 1937, since Fraser himself argues that this was because the order to remove them was not given until March 1937.[153]

It is arguable that the decision made in March was a formalization of what had already begun to take place in practice. A more likely possibility is that as a result of the changing attitudes, a series of military operational decisions and perhaps decisions within various political groups led to the events of March 1937. The Republic did not function in such a way that all obeyed decisions made at higher levels, even decisions of the Republican government. This was a result of the strength of the various left-wing political groups that operated within the Republic, and that generally made their own decisions, and as a result of the grassroots decision-making practices of the popular militias and anarchist groups. However, during the course of the war central control and decision-making did become more important.

The reaction of the *milicianas* to what took place was complex and varied. One peculiar reaction is the belief of a notable communist militiawoman, Rosario Sánchez de la Mora, that in fact no order was ever given to compel women to cease their military participation in the war. In her 1987 interview with Strobl, Sánchez de la Mora was adamant that no such order ever existed, and that women were never forced to leave the front. She explained that she never heard of such an order, and neither did she want to believe it.[154] Sánchez de la Mora maintained this position in an interview with Álvaro in 2001, again asserting that the *milicianas* were never expelled from the front.[155] Certainly, it is possible that Sánchez de la Mora never heard of the order, and it is true that she remained travelling and working in the front lines until the end of the war, although she did not participate in combat after the accident in which she lost her hand. Sánchez de la Mora's assertions would not lead a historian to disregard the plethora of other primary sources that indicate that an order was in fact made, and that women were removed from combat, but her belief nonetheless remains significant. It allows insight into the attitudes of the *milicianas*, and demonstrates that the order was not widely publicized and may not have reached every *miliciana* fighting in the civil war.

HOW MILICIANAS WERE INFORMED OF THE DECISION, AND THEIR REACTION

The press in the Republican zone had been publishing the various arguments for preventing *milicianas* from participating in combat since late 1936. The vast bulk of the evidence pertaining to the change in attitudes toward the *milicianas* in the Republican zone comes from the press and propaganda. However, the order that women had to cease their military activities and either leave the front or remain in a purely supportive capacity was never published in any newspaper. The fact that the decision had been made was never reported or discussed. Nor was the fact that *milicianas* had begun to leave the front in significant numbers, until only a small minority remained. Rather, the press coverage of the *milicianas* simply dissipated. Fewer and fewer references to the militiawomen were made, until by July 1937 they had all but disappeared.

No posters were ever displayed in the streets informing the public of the decision, nor were any plastered at the fronts where they would be visible to members of the militias. Rather, it seems that the order was relayed entirely by word of mouth. This being the case, it is not surprising that *milicianas* such as Sánchez de la Mora claim to have never heard of the decision, and that others such as Pérez Collado were able to stay on fighting at the front without ever being forced to leave. The studiously quiet removal of women from combat may have been designed to forestall any form of protest against the decision. The fact that the order appears to have been relayed verbally means that fewer primary sources are available on the subject. It is most likely for this reason that the majority of historians do not discuss the issue in any depth. The lack of evidence has also limited the depth of the discussion possible here.

One way or another, most of the *milicianas* clearly did receive the message that they were no longer allowed to fight against the Nationalists, since they began leaving the front in large numbers. Oral testimonies tell the story of a government or party official arriving at the front, relating the order, and removing the *milicianas* from their positions. Palma related that Ibárruri traveled to the front to explain to the *milicianas* that they would be more useful in the rearguard.[156] Andreas Bohl reported that many *milicianas* were in tears as they were forced to climb onto buses that would take them back to the home front.[157] Margarita Nelken gave an account in July 1938 that referred to militiawomen crying as they left in trucks.[158]

There is one known case where it was not an official who traveled to the front to relay the news, but a woman who had been a *miliciana* herself. The communist Trinidad Revolto Cervello, a member of the JSU, was a *miliciana* who had already returned to the home front when the order was given for the militiawomen to leave the front lines. (Revolto Cervello returned to Barcelona after participating in the attack on Majorca in September.[159]) In an interview with Antonina Rodrigo, Revolto Cervello explained the particular role she played in the removal of women from combat, which included traveling to the front to convince a group of *milicianas* that they should return home:

> Then the Party [JSU] decided to incorporate me into the Committee of Barcelona, to be responsible for the work of women [on the home front.] Above all [I was responsible for] the incorporation of women into posts of employment left by men who had marched to the front. . . . At the beginning of the war, many women had joined units of combatants, which had certainly caused disorder because not all of them had enlisted for exclusively political reasons. To explain the situation, they sent me to the Huesca front, in the Tardienta sector, where the Carlos Marx Column was stationed, and was commanded by our comrade José del Barrio. Despite a rigorous inquiry, the commission that I directed, which was composed of the female combatants, arrived at the conclusion that with the exception of a group of women who had acted admirably in the Communications and Health section, it was preferable that the rest [of the women] return to the rearguard.[160]

In some cases, the news of the order was not accompanied by a forced removal. While some *milicianas* simply left the front lines upon hearing the order, not all *milicianas* reacted in the same way. The anarchist Pérez Collado's story is quite different from that of women who were obliged to leave immediately upon receiving the order. She relates that when the women in her militia heard the news, "we laughed and we stayed at the front and nothing happened to us."[161] This type of reaction was not limited to the anarchist combatants.

Although no concerted or organized campaign was launched from any sector to defend the right of women to take up arms against fascism, it is clear that many *milicianas*, from all political backgrounds, did not welcome the decision. On an individual basis, women voiced their discontent with the decision and their continued belief that they could make an effective and useful military contribution to the war. On 27 March 1937, *Mujeres*, the organ of the communist CNFGF, printed an article that supported women's military contribution to the war, and argued specifically that women in the rearguard should still be receiving military training, because it remained possible that they would be needed at the front.[162] The author, Perdi, stated that "women are not only useful . . . as the kitchen-maid of a house, or as the adornment of a man."[163] She contended that women must be prepared militarily, asking, "can someone guarantee that tomorrow [a woman] will not have to go to the front?"[164]

The Catalan Carme Manrubia organized a small protest upon being refused entry into the School for War Commissaries.[165] The most significant ways in which women expressed their reservations about the order to remove them from combat were in their often anguished response to the instruction to depart, in the fact that a small number simply refused to leave the front and in the highly critical comments voiced by various *milicianas* in later interviews.

While Nash has expressed puzzlement that no large-scale protest was made against the decision to withdraw women from combat, [166] this fact is not surprising when examined in the context of the political setting in which it took place. The removal of the *milicianas* from the fronts came at a time when society in the Republican zone was taking a step back from revolutionary ideals. Depending on the point of view of Spanish men and women at the time, the revolution either had ended, or was being "put on hold" until after the war was won. It is for this reason that a campaign against the reversal of only one of the gains made by the revolution was not likely to occur.

Evidence indicates that most *milicianas* began leaving the front lines, or began to play a strictly auxiliary role in their militias, after March 1937, though it was a complicated process and did not occur all at once. The Spanish Civil War was being fought on many fronts, and different units would have heard the order at different times—perhaps a month or more apart. For this reason, and because many women did not welcome the decision, a simple mass exodus of *milicianas* from the front lines did not occur.

Historians cite various dates for the time when the majority of *milicianas* had been removed from combat. Herrmann states that by July 1937, no women were joining the armed resistance, and most who had played a military role had returned to the rearguard.[167] Coleman, Antony Beevor and Shirley Mangini cite a later date, claiming that it was not until 1938 that women had returned entirely to a supportive role.[168] Clearly, it took some time for news of the order to reach all the women fighting at the front. In addition, many *milicianas* did not simply lay down their weapons the moment they heard the news. Some women continued to fight with their militias even after they heard the order. Eventually, some of those women became convinced they would be more useful in the rearguard and left voluntarily, others were removed under protest and a small number of women actually continued to fight until their death or the end of the war, as documented below.

MILICIANAS WHO CONTINUED FIGHTING

There is evidence of a small number of *milicianas* defying their orders and remaining on the front lines to fight the Nationalists. This is perhaps the clearest demonstration that the militiawomen did not agree with the decision to remove them from their combat positions. Several of these women later claimed that they did so because they were never aware of the order, but the majority were well aware that they had been asked to leave, and simply refused to do so. Many *milicianas* considered that this order to abandon the fronts meant a return to the discrimination they had suffered before the outbreak of the war, and a regression to being forced to undertake work traditionally reserved for women.[169] Sofia Blasco refers to *milicianas* still fighting on the front lines as late as 1938, though she notes that they had been "decimated" by exhaustion and the harsh conditions.[170] Strobl indicates that some *milicianas* continued fighting with their units until they were wounded or killed, or until the end of the war when the majority were executed or put in prison.[171]

It is clear that the order to withdraw women from combat was never fully enforced in any area of the Republican fighting force, since the women who remained came from all left-wing political backgrounds. It does appear, however, that in general those women who stayed behind either held leadership positions or had demonstrated a high level of military proficiency.

There is evidence of communist women remaining in the front lines as combatants well after the order had been given for their removal. Julia Manzanal continued fighting with her battalion for several months after she had first been told of the decision. Such was her determination to keep fighting that when she had discovered earlier in the war that she was pregnant, Manzanal had an abortion the next day and was back in the front lines the same afternoon. When finally the PCE did enforce the decision by specifically ordering Manzanal to return from the front to undertake political work, Manzanal recalled being very disappointed to have to obey.[172] Another communist woman who did not relinquish her combat position was Lena Imbert.[173]

The communist Fidela Fernández de Velasco Pérez also remained fighting at the front, despite the order that *milicianas* return to the rearguard. Fernández de Velasco Pérez related in an interview with Strobl in 1987 that even after the militias had been incorporated into the Regular Army, and many women had been forced to abandon their combat positions, she remained in the front lines "shooting at everything that moved."[174] She also related her belief that whether or not female combatants could stay on in their combat positions depended on the individual actions of each woman.[175] Fernández de Velasco Pérez explained that she would be the last person to tolerate being forcibly removed from the front and ordered to return to the rearguard: "I was always like that, I always wanted to fight. I have never been interested in women's gossip."[176]

After a year and a half fighting on the front lines, Fernández de Velasco Pérez was wounded and was ordered by the PCE to take a three-month period of convalescence. After this time she was assigned to the party's secret service, and once her training was completed she was sent behind enemy lines to fight as a covert agent.[177] Fernández de Velasco Pérez could not see why she, or any other women, should be affected by the professionalization of the militias and their incorporation into the Regular Army. She explained, "what I learned in the front is that women are braver than men, more resilient, they can withstand more, even the physical pain."[178] When asked by Strobl about the widely accepted belief that women by their very nature are not suitable for combat, and that they are better suited to domestic work, Fernández de Velasco Pérez answered very clearly and quickly, "it is nonsense. I have nothing more to say."[179]

Lola Iturbe believed that it was *only* communist militiawomen who were allowed to stay on. The anarchist Iturbe explained in her interview with Marín that it was only *milicianas* from anarchist battalions who were recalled to the home front.[180] Iturbe claims that in contrast to the orders given to anarchist *milicianas* to return to the rearguard, communist battalions not only allowed the fighting women to stay on, but also integrated them into the new army and allowed those who held leadership positions to keep them.[181] This is clearly incorrect, since there is evidence both of communist women being removed under duress and anarchist women being allowed to stay. But what Iturbe's belief does demonstrate is that the order was applied inconsistently, and also that *milicianas* from anarchist militias were not always aware of what happened to the militiawomen of communist militias, and vice versa.

Iturbe notes the exceptions of Mika Etchebéhère (though she was not an anarchist) and Pepita Urda who were incorporated into the Regular Army and allowed to keep their positions as captains. While her recollections and experiences do not prove that communist women were spared being recalled from positions of combat, since there is a great deal of evidence that shows that they were, what Iturbe's example does show is that enough communist women stayed on in the front and continued to fight to allow some people to form the opinion that there had never been an order to send them home.

Similarly, there is also evidence of anarchist militiawomen remaining in the front lines. Based on her interviews with *milicianas* from all political backgrounds, Strobl asserts that the prohibition against women fighting was never imposed comprehensively in those units dominated by anarchists.[182] Pérez Collado is one anarchist woman who remained fighting at the front after the order had been given. Other anarchist *milicianas* who remained in the front lines include Urda and Casilda Méndez.[183] Coleman relates that Urda stayed on as a combatant and sergeant of her unit after the order had been given for *milicianas* to return to the rearguard,[184] though Coleman does not reveal for how long she was able to stay or if she did indeed continue fighting until the end of the war. John Tisa published in his memoirs a letter he wrote to his brother from Spain, relating that he had met several anarchist militiawomen who were still fighting in the front lines in June 1937.[185] He wrote that "they had healthy tans from being on the Madrid front for several weeks. Their exuberance was contagious, but it gave way to seriousness when they spoke of their experiences in the combat zones."[186]

The POUM never completely enforced the order either, and nor did the Regular Army, since Etchebéhère remained a fighter and a commander until the end of the war, and was incorporated into the army in 1937 as a member of the General Staff. Etchebéhère had been the captain of the Second Company of the POUM's Lenin Battalion, and had fought on the Aragon front until December 1936. By this time her unit had suffered such terrible loses that only sixty members of the unit remained. The First Company was also decimated in January 1937 in a battle at Pinar de Humera. The remnants of both companies merged, and when the militarization of the popular militias took place, this unit became the Fourth Company Cipriano Mera's 38th Mixed Brigade. At this time, Etchebéhère was given a post on the Brigade General Staff, and served as second in command.[187]

The fact that women such as Etchebéhère and Fernández de Velasco Pérez stayed on as combatants and were incorporated into the Regular Army, where they proved to be effective and capable soldiers, tends to discredit the idea that the *milicianas* were ordered to return to the home front simply because of the notion that "the army is no place for women." On 28 January 1937, *Ahora* (the organ of the JSU) published an article highlighting the success of another *miliciana* named Cristina, who had just been incorporated into the Regular Army as a combatant.[188]

There were noticeable differences among the left-wing political parties in the way they expressed their changing attitudes toward the *milicianas* and their developing belief that women were not suited to combat. Conversely, there are no discernible differences between political groups in the way they enforced the decision to remove militiawomen from combat. It may be due to the shortage of evidence that no clear patterns are evident, but it is also likely that this is due to the inconsistent and haphazard manner in which the removal of *milicianas* was carried out.

After experiencing eight months of relative liberation, the vast majority of Spanish *milicianas* thus returned to the positions they had occupied in society prior to the outbreak of the war. However, the return to pre-war gender roles was nothing compared to the harsh repression women would face later under the Franco regime.

NOTES

1. R. M. G., "Los Hombres, al Frente; las Mujeres, al Trabajo," *Crónica*, 8 November 1936, 2. This is the earliest the slogan appeared in any of the newspapers that I examined. For a list of the newspapers and the dates of the issues examined, see the Bibliography.

2. Félix Martí Ibáñez, *Tres Mensajes a la Mujer*, Barcelona, 1937.

3. Shirley Mangini, *Memories of Resistance: Women's voices from the Spanish Civil War*, Yale University Press, New Haven, 1995, 81.

4. Leoncio Pérez, "La Prostitución, el Arma Principal de la Quinta Columna," *Claridad*, 4 March 1937, 4.

5. Mary Nash, *Defying Male Civilization: Women in the Spanish Civil War*, Arden Press, Denver, 1995, 116.

6. It is not claimed that the reasons for removing *milicianas* from the front were considered sexist at the time, nor that the analysis presented here in relation to sexist ideas were commonly held views in Spain during the civil war. This is an assessment of these issues from today's perspective.

7. For a detailed study of the social revolution and the causes of its failure, see Burnett Bolloten, *The Grand Camouflage: The Spanish Civil War and Revolution, 1936–1939*, Pall Mall Publishers, London, 1968; Bolloten, *The Spanish Civil War: Revolution and counterrevolution*, University of North Carolina Press, Chapel Hill, 1991; Pierre Broué and Emile Témime, *The Revolution and the Civil War in Spain*, Faber and Faber, Paris, 1972; Helen Graham, *The Spanish Republic at War, 1936–1939*, Cambridge University Press, Cambridge, 2002; Felix Morrow, *Revolution and Counter-Revolution in Spain, including the Civil War in Spain*, Pathfinder Press, New York, 1974; and Hugh Thomas, *The Spanish Civil War*, 4th edition, Penguin, London, 2003.

8. The PCE produced several biographical pamphlets about Odena during the war. See Ángel Estivill, *Lina Odena: La gran heroína de las juventudes revolucionarias de España*, Editorial Maucci, Barcelona, 1936; and Dolores Ibárruri, Aurora Arnáiz et al, *Lina Odena: Heroína del pueblo*, Ediciones Europa América, Madrid, 1936.

9. *Mundo Obrero*, 3 November 1936, 2, 5 November 1936, 2, 12 November 1936, 3, 13 December 1936, 2, and 30 January 1937, 2.

10. See for example "¡También las Mujeres Irán a las Trincheras!" *Mundo Obrero*, 11 February 1937, 2.

11. Carlos Rodriguez, "Mujeres Antifascistas," *Mundo Obrero*, 8 March 1937, 4.

12. "1938 Calendar, PSU/ UGT, Printed 1937," Herbert Southworth Collection, item 2108, no. 2.

13. See for example *Mundo Obrero*, 11 February 1937, 4, caption reads, "¡Trabajadores de Madrid: Aprended de estas muchachas de Alerta! Instruiros en el manejo de las armas!" and *Mundo Obrero*, 27 February 1937, 3, caption reads: "Las Mujeres de Valencia Aprenden la Instrucción Militar, a Requerimiento de Nuestro Partido."

14. *Mujeres*, 20 February 1937, 6; 27 February 1937, 2; and 17 April 1937, 2.

15. *Mujeres*, 27 February 1937, 2.

16. *Mujeres*, 17 April 1937, 2.

17. *Mujeres*, 20 February, 6.

18. *Mujeres*, 27 February 1937, 2.

19. *Mujeres*, 17 April 1937, 2.

20. "La Mujer Española en el Fuego de la Guerra Civil," *Mujeres*, 15 May 1937, 8.

21. Olga Zubizaola, "Nuestras Heroínas," *Mujeres*, 5 June 1937, 9.

22. Early in the war the JSU and its organ were controlled by Francisco Largo Caballero, and thus represented a socialist viewpoint. However, as the war progressed Largo Caballero lost control of both the JSU and its newspaper to the communists. See Bolloten, *Spanish Civil War*, 130 and 478–479.

23. *Ahora*, 26 August 1936, 6.

24. *Ahora*, 16 September,1936, 7.

25. *Ahora*, 16 September 1936, 7.

26. *Ahora*, 26 September 1936, back cover.

27. *Ahora*, 30 September 1936, 2.

28. *Ahora*, 22 October 1936, 11.

29. *Ahora*, 4 November 1936, 7; 11 November 1936, 6; and 14 November 1936, 7.

30. *Ahora*, 11 December 1937, 4.

31. *Ahora*, 10 January 1937, 8; and 23 January 1937, 5.

32. "Mujeres: La mujer en la retaguardia y en la guerra," *Ahora*, 1 January 1937, 19, and "Cristina, en el Frente," *Ahora*, 28 January 1937, 4.

33. "¿Qué Opinan de Ellos los que Luchan?" *Ahora*, 12 February 1937, 6.

34. *Ahora*, 14 March 1937, cover.

35. *Ahora*, 14 March 1937, cover.

36. Martha A. Ackelsberg, "Separate and Equal? Mujeres Libres and Anarchist Strategy for Women's Emancipation," *Feminist Studies*, vol. 11, no. 1, Spring 1985, 66.

37. Ackelsberg, "Separate and Equal?" 67–68.

38. See chapter 3.

39. Kyralina, "Mujeres Heroicas: Apuntes de la revolución," *Tierra y Libertad*, 13 February 1937, back cover.

40. Cruz Salido, "Mujeres Asturianas," *Tierra y Libertad*, 21 November 1936, 3.

41. Josefina Serván Corchero and Antonio Trinidad Muñoz, "Las Mujeres en la Cartelística de la Guerra Civil," in *Las Mujeres y la Guerra Civil Española/ III Jornadas de Estudios Monográficos: Salamanca, octubre 1989*, Instituto de la Mujer, Madrid, 1991.

42. "Las Mujeres en los Primeros Días de Lucha," *Mujeres Libres*, no. 10, July 1937, 5.

43. Ingrid Strobl, *Partisanas: La mujer en la resistencia armada contra el fascismo y la ocupación alemana (1936–45)*, Virus, Barcelona, 1996, 46.

44. "Las Mujeres en los Primeros Días," *Mujeres Libres*, 5.

45. Strobl, *Partisanas*, 46.

46. It must be noted that a consensus on this point does not exist and indeed some historians question the extent to which the communist organizations took over the Republic. See for example, Graham, "Against the State: A Genealogy of the Barcelona May Days (1937)," *European History Quarterly*, vol. 29, no. 4, 485–542 and Graham, *Spanish Republic*.

47. Nash, *Defying*, 111.

48. *La Mujer Ante la Revolución*, Publicaciones del Secretariado Femenino del POUM, Barcelona, 1937, 7.

49. "The First Women's Battalion," *The Spanish Revolution*, 2 December 1936, vol. 1, no. 7, 4.

50. "First Women's Battalion," 4.

51. *Informaciones*, the newspaper of the right-wing of the PSOE, was not examined since Nash has indicated it contained no references to militiawomen.

52. Pérez, "Prostitución."

53. Pérez, "Prostitución," 4.

54. Miguel Hernández, *Obra Poética Completa*, 3rd edition, Zero, Madrid, 1977, 269.

55. Geraldine Scanlon, *La Polémica Feminista en la España Contemporánea (1864–1975)*, Siglo Veintiuno Editores, Madrid, 1976, 294.

56. Febos, "La Calle de Lina Odena," *ABC*, 17 November 1936, 12.

57. *ABC*, 31 October 1936, 4 and Scanlon, *Polémica*, 294.

58. Carlos de Rokha, *Lina Odena*, Herbert Southworth Collection, item 2016.

59. "Francisca Solano, Heroína de las Milicias," *Estampa*, 8 August 1936, 10–12; Amadeu Bernado, "La Dona i la Revolucion: Caritat Mercader, nervi de la frustrada

Olimpiada Popular de Barcelona," *Treball*, 1 September 1936; and "Angelina Martínez, la Miliciana que Tomo Parte en el Asalto al Cuartel de la Montaña," *Estampa*, 1 August 1936, 18–19. For further details of the actions of these women in combat, see chapters 2 and 3.

60. Frances Lannon, "Women and Images of Women in the Spanish Civil War," *Transactions of the Royal Historical Society*, Sixth Series, vol. 1, 1991, 217.

61. Sim, *Estampas de la Revolucion Española, 19 Julio de 1936*, Barcelona, 1937, Herbert Southworth Collection, item 2115.

62. A. S. de Leeuw, *Het Spaanse Volk Strijdt Voor Democratie Tegen Fascisme*, Amsterdam, 1936, Herbert Southworth Collection, item 557, and Harry Gannes, *How the Soviet Union Helps Spain*, Workers" Library, New York, 1936, Herbert Southworth Collection, item 836.

63. Lines, "Interview with Concha Pérez."

64. George Orwell, *Homage to Catalonia*, 3rd edition, Secker & Warburg, London, 1954, 5–6.

65. One of the few exceptions was an article written by Ramon Martorell and published in *Crónica* as early as 30 August 1936. Though it was printed in the independent press, the article appears to have been written from a right-wing socialist viewpoint, since the author presents and agrees with the arguments of the right-wing socialist leader Indalecio Prieto y Tuero. The article argued that the proper place for women was in the rearguard, and called for them to be sent there. He cited Prieto as arguing that, "in all wars, women have always occupied their posts in the rearguard," and Martorell agreed with him that women should be forced to return to the home front, especially since he believed there were thousands of men ready to take their places. Specifically, Martorell argued that women's correct place was in "the hospitals, the kitchens, [and] in the factories." The article concludes with the question, "But who will make these milicianas return?" This article serves more as an example of the socialists" continuing opposition to women's military participation, than of any change in attitudes of the general public as expressed in the independent press. Ramon Martorell, "Milicianas Aprendiendo el Manejo de Fusil," *Crónica*, 30 August 1936, 2–4.

66. *ABC*, 17 December 1936, 20 December 1936, 22 December 1936, and 27 December 1936.

67. "Una Mujer en el Frente," *ABC*, 16 January 1937, 8.

68. *ABC*, 29 April 1937, 5.

69. *ABC*, 4 May 1937, 5, 12 May 1937, 4, and 25 May 1937, 2.

70. *ABC*, 4 May 1937, 5.

71. "Las Mujeres de Barcelona se Preparan, por si Llegara el Momento en que Ellas, También, Tuvieran que Combatir," *Crónica*, 20 December 1936, 7–8.

72. "De las Jornadas Trágicas de Barcelona: Fanny, la heroína del Casal Carlos Marx," *Estampa*, 22 May 1937, 16–17.

73. *La Voz*, 17 November 1936, 4.

74. *ABC*, 20 December 1936, cover.

75. Hans Erich Kaminski, *Los de Barcelona*, Parsifal Ediciones, Barcelona, 1976, 210.

76. Aurelio Jerez Santa-Maria, "En los Frentes de la Libertad. Tata, mujer anarquista, interviene en un golpe de mano contra los facciosos de Aravaca," *Hombres Libres*, 9 July 1937, cited in Nash, *Defying*, 105.

77. Kaminski, *Los de Barcelona*, 210.

78. Franz Borkenau, *The Spanish Cockpit: An eyewitness account of the political and social conflicts of the Spanish Civil War*, Pluto Press, London, 1937, 72.

79. Borkenau, *Spanish Cockpit*, 164.

80. Ian MacDougall (ed.), *Voices from the Spanish Civil War: Personal recollections of Scottish volunteers in Republican Spain 1936–1939*, Polygon, Edinburgh, 1986, 62.

81. John Tisa, *Recalling the Good Fight*, Bergin and Garvey, Massachusetts, 1985, 113–114.

82. Lines, "Interview with Concha Pérez."

83. "Las Mujeres a la Retaguardia," *Mundo Obrero*, 8 November 1936, cited in Carmen Alcalde, *La Mujer en la Guerra Civil Española*, Editorial Cambio 16, Madrid, 1976, 125.

84. "Las Mujeres a la Retaguardia," *Mundo Obrero*.

85. El Comité, "Las Mujeres, en la Retaguardia, y los Hombres, en los Frentes de la Lucha," *Mujeres*, 27 February 1937, 2.

86. El Comité, "Mujeres, en la Retaguardia."

87. Etheria Artay, "Las Mujeres de Barcelona se Preparan," *Crónica*, 20 December 1936, 7.

88. Nash, *Defying*, 111.

89. Comité Local, "A les Dones de Catalunya. Organitzem els Grups de Reraguarda!" *Treball*, 12 September 1936.

90. Orwell, *Homage*, 7, 9–10, 17.

91. Orwell, *Homage*, 17.

92. Dan Kurzman, *Miracle of November: Madrid's epic stand 1936*, G. P. Putnam's Sons, New York, 1980, 18.

93. Ibáñez, *Tres Mensajes*.

94. Ibáñez, *Tres Mensajes*.

95. Mary Low and Juan Breà, *Red Spanish Notebook: The first six months of the revolution and the civil war*, Purnell and Sons, London, 1937, 187–188.

96. Low and Breà, *Notebook*, 188.

97. Kaminski, *Los de Barcelona*, 210.

98. Blanca Trejo, *Lo Que Vi en España, Episodios de la Guerra*, Mexico City, 1940, 42, cited in Mangini, *Memories of Resistance*, 80–81.

99. "A Girl of the Spanish People: A story from the special correspondent of *Woman To-day*," *Woman To-day*, December 1936, 6.

100. "Girl of the Spanish People," *Woman To-day*.

101. Nash, *Defying*, 113.

102. Ángel Luis Rubio Moraga, "El Papel de la Mujer en la Guerra a través de los Carteles Republicanos," *Cuadernos Republicanos*, no 36, October 1998, 106.

103. Teresa Pàmies, *Cuando Éramos Capitanes: (Memorias de aquella guerra)*, Dopesa, Barcelona, 1975, 45 and Kaminski, *Los de Barcelona*, 210.

104. Ibáñez, *Tres Mensajes*.

105. Pérez, "Prostitución," 4.

106. Low and Breà, *Notebook*, 197.

107. Ronald Fraser, *Blood of Spain: The experience of the Civil War, 1936–1939*, Allen Lane, London, 1979, 286.

108. Nash, *Defying*, 114 and Strobl, *Partisanas*, 54.

109. Luís Maria Jiménez de Aberasturi, *Casilda, Miliciana: Historia de un sentimiento*, Editorial Txertoa, San Sebastián, 1985, 49–50.

110. It is significant to note that anarchists had specific views on marriage as it existed under capitalism, which held that these were most often forced unions based on property relations and the subordination of women. Instead they promoted "free love," which anarchists understood to be a union based on respect and mutual agreement, rather than on the bourgeois principles of state or religious marriage. See Richard Cleminson, "Beyond Tradition and 'Modernity': The cultural and sexual politics of Spanish anarchism," in Helen Graham and Jo Labanyi (eds.), *Spanish Cultural Studies: An introduction*, Oxford University Press, Oxford, 1995, 121.

111. See "Boda de Milicianos," *ABC*, 6 October 1936, 4, and *Crónica*, 27 September 1936, 10.

112. See de Aberasturi, *Casilda*, 44.

113. Nash, *Defying*, 113, Lines, "Interview with Concha Pérez," and Mangini, *Memories of Resistance*, 84.

114. Lines, "Interview with Concha Pérez."

115. Mangini, *Memories of Resistance*, 84.

116. Mangini, *Memories of Resistance*, 84.

117. Strobl, *Partisanas*, 74.

118. Strobl, *Partisanas*, 74.

119. Antonina Rodrigo, *Mujer y Exilio 1939*, Compañía Literaria, Madrid, 1999, 64.

120. Strobl, *Partisanas*, 54.

121. Nash, *Defying*, 116.

122. Orwell, *Homage*, 5.

123. One example is Pérez Collado, who left the front in early 1937 because she was convinced she would be more useful working in a factory in the rearguard. Marín, "Libertarias," 356.

124. Low and Breà, *Notebook*, 214.

125. Clara Thalmann, *Combats pour la Liberté*, translated by Caroline Darbon, Spartacus, Paris, 1983, 170–171.

126. Nash, *Defying*, 108.

127. Nash, *Deyfing*, 151.

128. Nash, *Defying*, 152.

129. Nash, *Defying*, 152.

130. Nash, *Defying*, 153.

131. Nash, *Defying*, 151.

132. Borkenau, *Spanish Cockpit*, 106.

133. José Manuel Márquez Rodríguez and Juan José Gallardo Romero, *Ortiz: General sin dios ni amo*, Santa Coloma de Gramenet, Hacer, 1999.

134. Geraldine Scanlon, *La Polémica Feminista en la España Contemporánea (1864–1975)*, Siglo Veintiuno Editores, Madrid, 1976, 294.

135. Mary Nash, *Defying Male Civilization: Women in the Spanish Civil War*, Arden Press, Denver, 1995, 110.

136. Nash, *Defying*, 110.

137. Josefina Serván Corchero and Antonio Trinidad Muñoz, "Las Mujeres en la Cartelística de la Guerra Civil," in *Las Mujeres y la Guerra Civil Española/ III Jornadas de Estudios Monográficos: Salamanca, octubre 1989*, Instituo de la Mujer, Madrid, 1991, 365; Mónica Carabias Álvaro, *Rosario Sánchez Mora (1919)*, Ediciones del Orto, Madrid, 2001, 18; and Pilar Folguera Crespo, "Las Mujeres durante la Guerra Civil," in Elisa Garrido González (ed.), *Historia de las Mujeres en España*, Síntesis, Madrid, 1997, 521.

138. Corchero, "Las Mujeres en la Cartelística," 365.

139. Lisa Lines, "Interview with Concha Pérez Collado," 13 February 2005, Barcelona.

140. Lines, "Interview with Concha Perez."

141. Dolors Marín, "Las Libertarias," in Ingrid Strobl, *Partisanas: La mujer en la resistencia armada contra el fascismo y la ocupación alemana (1936–45)*, Virus, Barcelona, 1996, 355.

142. Ronald Fraser, *Blood of Spain: The experience of the Civil War, 1936–1939*, Allen Lane, London, 1979, 287.

143. Fraser, *Blood of Spain*, 287.

144. Catherine Coleman, "Women in the Spanish Civil War," in Juan P. Fusi Aizpurau, Richard Whelan et al., *Heart of Spain: Robert Cap's photographs of the Spanish Civil War*, Aperture, New York, 1999, 50.

145. Caroline Brothers, *War and Photography: A cultural history*, Routledge, London, 1997, 77.

146. Strobl, *Partisanas*, 46.

147. Crespo, "Las Mujeres durante la Guerra," 521.

148. Gina Herrmann, "Voices of the Vanquished: Leftist women and the Spanish Civil War," *Journal of Spanish Cultural Studies*, vol. 4, no. 1, 2003, 14.

149. Herrmann, "Voices of the Vanquished," 14.

150. Nash, *Defying*, 110.

151. Nash, *Defying*, 110.

152. Nash, *Defying*, 110.

153. Nash, *Defying*, 214n.

154. Strobl, *Partisanas*, 46–47.
155. Mónica Carabias Álvaro, *Rosario Sánchez Mora (1919)*, Ediciones del Orto, Madrid, 2001, 32.
156. Fraser, *Blood of Spain*, 287.
157. Andreas Bohl, *Revolution in Spanien*, Munich, 1984, 150, cited in Strobl, *Partisanas*, 46.
158. Margarita Nelken, "Mujeres de España," *Frente Rojo*, 19 July 1938, 10.
159. Antonina Rodrigo, *Mujer y Exilio 1939*, Compañía Literaria, Madrid, 1999, 80.
160. Rodrigo, *Mujer y Exilio*, 80.
161. Lines, "Interview with Concha Pérez."
162. Perdi, "Reflexiones: La mujer en el frente," *Mujeres*, 27 March 1937, 9.
163. Perdi, "Reflexiones," 9.
164. Perdi, "Reflexiones," 9.
165. Nash, *Defying*, 108.
166. Nash, *Defying*, 111.
167. Herrmann, "Voices of the Vanquished," 14.
168. See Coleman, "Women in the Spanish Civil War," 50; Antony Beevor, *The Spanish Civil War*, Orbis Publishing, London, 1982, 89; and Shirley Mangini, *Memories of Resistance: Women's voices from the Spanish Civil War*, Yale University Press, New Haven, 1995, 80.
169. Corchero, "Las Mujeres en la Cartelística," 365.
170. Sofia Blasco, *Peuple d'Espagne. Journal de guerre de la madrecita*, translated by Henrietta Sauret, Nouvelle Revue Critique, Paris, 1938, 47.
171. Strobl, *Partisanas*, 46.
172. Strobl, *Partisanas*, 66.
173. Nash, *Defying*, 110.
174. Strobl, *Partisanas*, 51.
175. Strobl, *Partisanas*, 54.
176. Strobl, *Partisanas*, 51.
177. Strobl, *Partisanas*, 55.
178. Strobl, *Partisanas*, 54.
179. Strobl, *Partisanas*, 55.
180. Marín, "Libertarias," 348.
181. Marín, "Libertarias," 348.
182. Strobl, *Partisanas*, 46.
183. Nash, *Defying*, 110.
184. Coleman, "Women in the Spanish Civil War," 48.
185. John Tisa, *Recalling the Good Fight*, Bergin and Garvey, Massachusetts, 1985, 113.
186. Tisa, *Recalling*, 114.
187. Andy Durgan, "International Volunteers in the POUM Militias," Fundación Andreu Nin. Expanded version of a paper originally presented to the Conference on the International Brigades organized by the University of Lausanne, 19–20 December 1997. http://www.fundanin.org/durgan1.htm Accessed on Monday 19 April 2004.
188. "Cristina, en el Frente," *Ahora*, 28 January 1937, 4.

SIX

Representations of *Milicianas*

From the first days of the Spanish Civil War, the independent and left-wing political press in the Republican zone instantly took notice of the presence of women in combat, first during the street fighting that took place in response to the Nationalist insurrection, and then in the trenches as the battle lines were drawn and the militias were formed. Photographs and illustrations of *milicianas* wearing the *mono azul* (blue overalls) and shouldering rifles were strewn across the pages of many newspapers. The *miliciana* became the central Republican icon for the people's fight against fascism. The representation of the militiawomen that appeared in the media in the Republican zone from the beginning of the civil war amounted to a radical departure from the images of women that had hitherto been found in the Spanish press. These images depicted the *milicianas* in a manner that was revolutionary, militant and forceful. Women were seen demonstrating strength, bravery and purposefulness in a way that had never been shown before in Spain.

An examination of the cultural representation of the *miliciana*, involving a detailed investigation of gendered imagery, is integral to studying the experience of the militiawomen during the war. It is in this way the changing gender roles for women in the Republican zone can best be demonstrated. Through such an examination, it is possible to plot the course and the timing of the onset but also the failure of the revolution. The representations of *milicianas* in the press served a dual function, as reflections of reality and as ideal images designed to influence the actions of people in the Republican zone and bring about change. Tracing the development and subsequent reversal of these ideals can offer insights into the changing and competing views in Republican Spain on the issue of women's participation in the war, in both a military and non-military capacity.

In order to analyze the representation of the militiawomen in the left-wing political press and the independent Republican press, key newspapers from each group were selected and examined in their entirety for the first year of the Spanish Civil War, where available. Such a systematic examination of sources allows contrasts to be discovered and comparisons to be made between the representation of the militiawomen in the newspapers of each political group, and in the independent press. Examining the newspapers as a series, and inspecting every issue with a view to collecting information regarding the *milicianas* has allowed not only the study of each group's treatment of the militiawomen, but has also made it possible to trace the changes in this treatment over time. As previously discussed, a change in attitudes toward the *milicianas* in late 1936 saw them forced from combat positions around March 1937. This change in circumstances for the militiawomen is visibly reflected in the press.

It is of course necessary to use caution in the evaluation of images as evidence. Images can be read in various ways and on various levels, and it is often difficult to determine precise meanings. Further, the broader context of the production and reception of images must be taken into account.

The social revolution that took place in the Republican zone caused the rapid advance of women's rights, and the civil war gave rise to a situation in which women were called upon to fill new roles in the workplace. The war created a new discourse relating to women, and the role that women would play in the war was a subject often discussed on the radio, in newspapers and magazines, in meetings of political and women's groups and at conferences.[1] A new image of women appeared in the media in the Republican zone, an image most commonly identified with the figure of the *miliciana*. The *miliciana* not only looked and dressed differently, but she participated in activities previously unthinkable for women.

The photographs of *milicianas* that appeared in both the political and independent press were quite similar. The militiawomen most often wore the *mono azul*, but were also photographed wearing khaki uniforms or simply dresses with aprons. In the majority of photographs the militiawomen were shown carrying a rifle, but images depicting women engaging in combat, aiming or firing their weapon, were rare. The *milicianas* were photographed alone or in groups, and the vast majority of the photographs were posed, showing the militiawomen standing and smiling into the camera.

The *mono azul* worn by the *milicianas* held a double significance for women. It symbolized not only support for the Republican cause and social revolution, but also served as a challenge to the conventional gender role that dictated forms of dress and appearance for women. When thousands of women in the Republican zone donned these overalls during the civil war, it was the first time in Spain's history that women had worn male attire. For many women, wearing the *mono azul* was a physical demonstration of their adoption of the new gender role that was emerging.

A certain tension between the femininity of the *milicianas* and the supposed masculinity of combat existed in many representations of the *milicianas*. This was largely due to the social norms and conventions that had existed in Spain prior to 1936, which unequivocally viewed warfare as a masculine domain and held very strict ideas of what was acceptable behavior for women. This created a blurring of gender roles as women crossed into previously unacceptable spheres of activity. Those who wished to reassert traditional values, such as the independent press, emphasized this tension between the feminine qualities of the *milicianas* and their militancy, while progressive representations, such as those in *Ahora*, the organ of the JSU, sought to reconcile these seemingly conflicting ideas. Some representations of *milicianas* during the civil war, particularly those of the communist and anarchist press, signified a new gender role for women, albeit still taking shape and not devoid of the effects of previous ideas of what was considered feminine.

COMMUNIST PRESS AND PROPAGANDA

The newspapers *Mundo Obrero* and *Mujeres* were examined in order to analyze the communist representation of the militiawomen.[2] Every issue of the daily *Mundo Obrero* was examined for the first year of the Spanish Civil War. The fortnightly paper *Mujeres* was examined in its entirety from its first issue in February 1937 until July 1937.

During the first twelve months of the war, the daily newspaper *Mundo Obrero* featured twenty-eight photographs of *milicianas*, one poster, and four feature-length articles. The first photograph of a militiawoman appeared on 1 August 1936, and the last on 15 May 1937. In sixteen of these photographs the militiawomen were armed, and in twelve no rifles or weapons of any kind were visible. *Milicianas* were pictured traveling to the front, washing clothes, carrying blankets, marching in formation, posing and smiling for the camera, standing guard, participating in combat, firing their weapons, eating, standing in rank, cooking and undertaking military training. The four articles discussed the death of Lina Odena, the Republican war effort in which there were no spectators and everyone was needed to fight (including women at the front), a successful battle in which two *milicianas* fought and women's contribution to the Republican cause, including information on Odena and women's battalions.[3]

An analysis of the gendered representation of the *milicianas* in the communist press demonstrates many of the underlying beliefs about women, their contribution to the war effort and the behavior that was considered suitable for them. One poignant example is the photographs in which women in the rearguard are undertaking military training. In five of the seven photographs, which first appear on 30 October 1936, the women are pictured wearing shirts, skirts and high heels.[4] The other two photographs are of women in militia uniform. Since it is obviously impractical to participate in combat wearing this attire, the emphasis of these photographs is clearly not on the battle-readiness of these women. Rather, the traditional appearance of the women is emphasized, and these photographs represent women adhering to their traditional gender role. Also, in five of the seven photographs (though not the same five) the women are unarmed, despite the captions clearly indicating that they are undertaking military training.[5] This representation of women is in stark contrast to the manner in which men are featured on the same pages. Not one photograph appears featuring men undertaking military training.

In a discussion of the representation of women, it is important to recognize the meanings attached to women in images, and also how these meanings are constructed. In order to do this, rather than to compare different types of images of women, it is necessary to analyze the meanings signified by representations of women with reference to representations of men. A useful method for interpreting the gendered meanings of images is the use of female/male reversals.[6]

Imagine a photograph featuring rows of men in suits and ties (comparable male attire that can be considered unsuitable for combat, though no doubt less so than high heels), without any weapons, with a caption that reads, "young men of Madrid undergo military instruction." Such an image would clearly convey a meaning very different from the photographs featuring women described above. Such an image might appear ridiculous, and raise such questions as: "how can it be considered military training if they are not receiving instruction on how to use a weapon?"; "why are they wearing clothing that is not suitable for battle?" and most significantly, "is it really intended that these men will participate in some form of combat?" If the viewer of the photograph was a Republican during the civil war, perhaps he or she would think it odd in any case that men in the rearguard were receiving military training, when they could simply be sent to the front to fight, where they were needed. When the above photographs of women undertaking military training without rifles, wearing skirts and high heels, are viewed in this way, a double standard becomes obvious.

An interesting comparison can also be made between the photographs featuring women standing together in groups and posing for the camera, and those of men in a similar format. Two such comparable photographs are featured in *Mundo Obrero* on 4 August and 12 September 1936. The first photograph features nine militiamen from the Peñalver Column, three of whom are crouching in front, with the rest standing in a line behind them.[7] All the men are carrying rifles, most in front of them, one over his shoulder. The men are each wearing different pants and shirts, and different hats. In this photograph, one man has his head turned and appears to be talking to another. Only three of the men are half smiling with closed mouths, the others appear quite serious. (One face is not clearly visible on the microfilm.) Though all but one of the men are facing the camera, their gazes are not all focused in the same direction, so it seems they were not looking directly at the camera. In this photograph the men appear as individuals, all looking in a slightly different direction and standing or sitting in a different way. One man is in the middle of a conversation, and not paying attention to the camera at all. Thus, these men appear as active rather than passive subjects, even though the photograph is a group shot and they have clearly been asked to pose.

The second photograph features seven militiawomen, six of whom are crouching or sitting in a line, with one woman standing behind.[8] Each woman is wearing the militia uniform and holding a rifle upright in the same way. All seven women are directly facing the camera and smiling widely, most showing their teeth. This photograph is only subtly different from the first, but the result is that the women appear as passive rather than active subjects. Their big smiles, similar poses and uniforms emphasize their appearance in a way that is quite different from the photo of the men.

These two photographs are examples of a general trend in which images of women are posed for the benefit of the viewer, and tend to feature women who are standing and smiling, whereas photographs of men emphasize their activity, and tend to picture them in action or combat rather than standing still. Photographs of Republican militiamen in *Mundo Obrero* over this period typically picture them in combat, firing their weapons, and do not appear to have been staged. There are no photographs of militiamen cooking, cleaning, doing laundry or completing any of the auxiliary tasks such as those the militiawomen are pictured undertaking. Militiamen did not appear in photographs without their weapons, unlike the *milicianas*, who are pictured unarmed almost half the time.

Despite that the fact that communist representations of the *milicianas* contained a clearly gendered content, they did not display an overt emphasis on the beauty and youth of the *milicianas*, such as that contained in the independent newspapers in the Republican zone. *Mundo Obrero* never used any adjectives to describe the militiawomen that focused on their beauty or appearance. Instead, the organ of the PCE only ever used the adjective "valiant"[9] to describe female combatants and no other. Similarly, in 1937, *Mujeres* referred to the *milicianas* as "pretty" only once, and this was in a line of a poem, not a caption or article.[10] Instead, the communist women's newspaper described the militiawomen as "heroines."[11]

In general, the communist press presented the *milicianas* in a positive manner, but the main focus was always on the "glory" and "righteousness" of the Republican cause, in which female combatants played a symbolic role, rather than on any advance in women's rights that was represented by the military role played by the *milicianas*. In many ways, images of *milicianas* that featured in the communist press during the war served as symbols for the Republican cause, and embodied a set of ideas and values, rather than representing any particular woman or group of women.

A related example is the Phrygian woman in the illustrations by the artist Pyrol that were featured in communist newspapers and propaganda throughout the civil war. The woman appeared wearing the Phrygian cap that was a symbol for the Republican revolutions in France and Spain during the eighteenth and nineteenth centuries. In the best-known case, only her head appears in the background of a picture of a Republican militiaman.[12] This Phrygian woman can be compared to "Lady Liberty" in terms of her embodiment of specific and widely understood ideas and values.[13] When "Lady Liberty" appears in artwork baring her breast or raising a flag or a torch, the viewer is immediately aware that this image is symbolic of the ideals of the French Revolution of 1789 and does not represent a real woman. This was also the case not only for the image of the Phrygian woman, but also in the case of the many images of *milicianas*, especially illustrations, during the Spanish Civil War.

Perhaps the strongest demonstration that the images of *milicianas* in the communist press were often symbolic rather than representative of real women is the fact that these images were used to link the Republican cause with past heroic struggles of the Spanish people. Creating an association with the *milicianas* fighting for the Republic in 1936 and heroines of past struggles such as Mariana Pineda, Agustina de Aragón and Aida Lafuente was a highly successful method by which the communist media emphasized the righteousness and virtue of the Republican cause. One example was published on the cover of *Mundo Obrero* on 5 October 1936 with the title "In the War There Are No Neutral Zones nor Groups of Spectators. We Are All Fighters!"[14] The article was illustrated with two large photographs, the first of Odena and the second of Lafuente. Odena's caption compares her to Lafuente.[15]

Another example comes from a propaganda poster produced jointly by the CNT and UGT. Though this was created and distributed jointly by the anarchist and communist-dominated trade unions, it nonetheless best demonstrates a trend present in communist propaganda. The poster shows a female hand holding an olive branch, with four names printed down the center of the poster in a large cursive font. The names are Agustina de Aragón, Mariana Pineda, Aida Lafuente and Lina Odena. Underneath, a smaller caption reads "Heroínas de la Independencia y la Libertad de España" ("Heroines of the Independence and Liberty of Spain").[16] This was a clear and concise way of linking the civil war with past struggles. The fact that this poster provided no context for or information about the four names it features indicates an expectation that the audience was familiar with these women, and that their names held a precise and widely understood meaning.

In the five months between February and July 1937, *Mujeres* published eighteen photographs (fourteen of armed women and only four of unarmed women, an average of one photograph per issue), fourteen articles and two poems featuring *milicianas*. It is interesting to note that the ratio of photographs featuring armed women to those featuring unarmed women is much higher here than for photographs that were printed in *Mundo Obrero*, but the ratio of women who were pictured aiming or firing their weapons was similarly low. The photographs of militiawomen are all posed and picture them marching, or standing and smiling, with their rifles and arms at their sides, or their rifles or fists raised in the air.

Only one of the photographs features two women aiming their weapons, but it is clear that this is not a photograph of actual combat.[17] While two *milicianas* are crouching behind a parapet and aiming their rifles, a third woman stands immediately next to them, watching, with her rifle upright at her side, fully exposed to any enemy at whom the other women are supposedly shooting. Once again the photographs of *milicianas* are in stark contrast to those of militiamen, who are most often pictured in combat and never appear unarmed. The image of militiawomen was featured on the cover of *Mujeres* just once, in May 1937, in the form of an illustration by the artist Sim.[18]

The last image and reference to a *miliciana* in the communist women's newspaper was not printed until 5 June 1937. It was a photograph and article about the death of María Elisa García in May and her actions in battle.[19] It is significant not only that this was printed almost a month after the last reference to a militiawoman in *Mundo Obrero*, but also that it is a positive representation, clearly supportive of women's military contribution to the Republican cause.

Intricately linked to the communist treatment of the *milicianas* is the study of *Ahora*, the organ of the JSU. Though the JSU came to be dominated by the communists, *Ahora* specifically represents a youth viewpoint, and also a socialist viewpoint, though to a lesser extent. In the first year of the civil war, the newspaper published eighty-seven photographs of militiawomen, fifty-eight of which depicted armed *milicianas*, and in twenty-nine of which there were no weapons visible. Although the majority of female combatants pictured were armed, only eight photos out of the eighty-seven depicted women aiming or firing their weapons, which is only about 9 percent.[20] This is in complete contrast to the photographs of men, who were almost invariably photographed in battle. In July alone *Ahora* printed more photographs of men aiming and firing their weapons than were printed of women over a one-year period. During this same period, only four articles containing information about militiawomen were published,[21] though the newspaper did also print seven photo essays that contained lengthy captions.

In *Ahora*, the *milicianas* received a positive and triumphant representation. They were very often pictured with their fists or rifles raised, or after a successful battle. However, *Ahora* appears to have over represented *milicianas* on its pages early in the war, and then sharply decreased its coverage of the female combatants, possibly as their novelty wore off. This trend of over representation will be discussed further in relation to the independent press. As mentioned earlier, the percentage of women in combat was less than 2 percent of the total fighting force,[22] and yet in the issues of some newspapers they accounted for almost 50 percent of the photographs relating to the war. *Ahora* featured photographs of armed *milicianas* wearing *monos* in almost every issue in July and August 1936. During these two months alone *Ahora* published five photo essays on women in combat,[23] and featured *milicianas* on the cover in full-page photographs twice.[24] The first of these covers was a full-page photograph of a *miliciana* alongside two militiamen. All three were wearing the militia uniform and carrying equipment and rifles. The part of the caption relating to women referred to "brave girls who, like this one who appears in the photo, do not limit their enthusiastic action to aiding the fighters, but have also decisively taken up arms against the enemy."[25] The second cover featuring a woman in combat was a photograph of a *miliciana* and two militiamen crouching behind a rock, aiming their rifles at the unseen enemy.[26]

The symbolism connected to the representations of *milicianas* in the communist newspaper *Mundo Obrero* can also be seen on the pages of *Ahora*. While the photographs published in *Ahora* clearly depicted real women fighting in the front lines, they also took on a larger symbolic meaning, and at times could be seen to represent the Republican cause in general. The language used in captions and articles to describe the militiawomen, which often referred to their beauty, youth, enthusiasm and courage rather than any specific military actions, plays an important role in creating meanings and connotations that served to link the images of *milicianas* to *La República Bonita*, the (feminine) Beautiful Republic. In July and August 1936, nineteen out of thirty captions referred to militiawomen as "beautiful," "young," "brave" or "enthusiastic."[27]

It is also true that at times the presence of female combatants was used to indicate the level of morale. An article printed in *Ahora* on 5 August 1936[28] proclaimed that "the extraordinary enthusiasm with which the people of Catalonia throw themselves into the fight against the Nationalists, in the arduous defense of the liberties of the Republic, is most notably demonstrated through the cooperation of women, who accompany the combatants and share with them the danger at the front."[29] *Ahora* also used the militiawomen to link the anti-fascist resistance with struggles of the past, as has been discussed previously. On March 14, 1937, the cover of *Ahora* featured a full-page photograph of a *miliciana* from Asturias. The caption stated that this woman, like all other *milicianas*, "is of the strong race of Mariana Pineda, of Aida Lafuente (*La Libertaria*), of Lina Odena, of *Pasionaria.*"[30]

Overall, the representation of the *milicianas* in the communist press was positive, but it was presented in a highly gendered fashion with clear double standards. There are stark differences between the content of the photographs of militiawomen and those of the militiamen. While the militiawomen are pictured armed most of the time, they very rarely appear in combat or even aiming their weapons. Often the image of the *miliciana* was used by the communist press in a symbolic manner, rather than to represent real women fighting in the front lines. Thus, it is clear that the representation of the militiawomen in the communist press does not constitute a wholehearted acceptance of a new gender role for women.

ANARCHIST PRESS AND PROPAGANDA

Three newspapers from the anarchist press were studied in order to provide a comprehensive picture of the anarchist representation of the militiawomen. The weekly newspaper *Tierra y Libertad*, from Barcelona, was examined in its entirety for the first year of the civil war. Due to limited availability of *CNT*, this newspaper was examined only for the first six months of the war. Similarly, only a few issues of *Mujeres Libres* from the period of January to July 1937 were available.

The anarchist press did not feature the *milicianas* prominently, as was the case in the communist press. During the twelve months between July 1936 and July 1937, *Tierra y Libertad* published only six photographs of militiawomen (three showing armed women and three unarmed) and five articles relating to the *milicianas*. *Tierra y Libertad* printed as many illustrations as photographs of armed women. In five out of six cases, the images of armed women, whether they were illustrations or photographs, were printed next to articles that contained no references to militiawomen. The last image of a *miliciana* was printed in *Tierra y Libertad* on 13 February 1937, four months earlier than the last communist representation, and was an illustration accompanying a short article about a foreign volunteer named Carmen.

The six photographs of militiawomen pictured them raising their rifles or fists triumphantly, standing guard, standing and talking with their rifles in front of them and marching. In none of these photographs are women shown aiming or firing their weapons, or participating in combat. Only one illustration of armed women depicts them participating in combat and shows three armed and muscle-bound women charging into battle, a flag of the FAI in the background.[31] Another illustration features a woman raising her rifle above her head[32] and the last is of a woman standing guard.[33]

In the first six months of the war, from July to December 1936, only two images of a female combatant, and no articles, could be found in the newspaper *CNT*. The first image is an illustration of a woman wearing a dress and holding a baby; the woman is identified as a militiawoman only because she has a pistol strapped to her hip; this classification may not even be correct.[34]

The illustration conveys a clear message about the anarchist perception of the accepted roles of women in the war. Even if some anarchist women had taken on new roles in combat or in other areas in the public sphere as a result of the civil war, there was never any indication in the anarchist press (or in any other) of plans to revolutionize what had always been considered the primary and natural role of women—motherhood. A female/male role reversal in this instance clearly shows the gendered nature of this image. A photograph or an illustration of a man holding a baby with a gun strapped to his hip would seem highly irregular.[35] The second image found in *CNT* during the months from July to December 1936 is a photograph of two armed and uniformed *milicianas* standing on top of a tank.[36] Both of these images were printed early in the war, in August, and nothing more appears for the remainder of the year.

Anarchist propaganda posters, such as the joint CNT-UGT poster discussed above, did depict women in combat. A further example is a CNT poster featuring the slogan "¡No Pasarán!" ("They Shall Not Pass!")[37] The poster depicts an anarchist militia in battle, including a militiawoman who is firing her rifle at the unseen enemy. The militiawoman is situated in a position higher than the militiamen who surround her, as she is standing with one knee up on the wall. The two men next to her are crouching and the rest of the militia are in the background, charging forward. A dead militiaman lies over the wall in the foreground. This poster clearly represents *milicianas* in a positive light, as this particular woman can be seen to be leading her militia. However, some historians such as Kelly Phipps have argued unconvincingly that this female figure is not intended to represent real women fighters and instead fulfills a purely symbolic role.[38]

Some representations of *milicianas* in the anarchist press highlight the dichotomy between femininity and militancy, as the tension between the militiawomen's feminine qualities and the violence of the front is emphasized. One example, mentioned above, is that of the illustration of the woman holding her baby protectively against her chest, with a pistol (that appears to be almost the size of the baby) strapped to her hip.[39] A second example can be found in the article "Mujeres Heroicas" ("Heroic Women"), printed in *Tierra y Libertad* on 13 February 1937. The author describes the militiawoman in the following way: "her beauty and agility impress me, and I question her. Yes, I was not mistaken. She is a woman. And she paces back and forth, with a rifle on her shoulder, and she carries herself upright and severely, with strict attention, eyes watching to prevent a possible enemy attack."[40] The author demonstrates a sense of shock upon discovering that the armed, pacing guard is in fact a woman. The article contrasts the beautiful appearance of the *miliciana* with the militaristic images of her rigid posture, her pacing and her rifle, which all imply the masculine sphere of combat.

The representation of the *milicianas* by the anarchist women's organization *Mujeres Libres*, in their war posters and also in their newspaper of the same name, differs from that of both *Tierra y Libertad* and *CNT*. No comprehensive study of the amount and type of images of militiawomen printed in *Mujeres Libres* can be made, as it was not possible to examine the source in its entirety. Despite this, it is clear from those issues that were available, and also from information about *Mujeres Libres* that was available elsewhere, that the anarchist women's organization consistently presented radical and progressive images of women.[41] *Mujeres Libres* clearly demonstrated the new gender role that was being created for women in the Republican zone.

Josefina Serván Corchero and Antonio Trinidad Muñoz explain that these images depict women not only fighting against fascism, but also fighting for their own freedom against oppression.[42] *Mujeres Libres* was also more likely to refer to the *milicianas* as "heroic" or "brave" rather than "pretty" or "beautiful." The newspaper *Mujeres Libres* featured *milicianas* on its cover on 8 March 1937. The full-page illustration shows a group of women in battle, each woman holding or firing a rifle, with the Republican flag visible in the background. In the foreground, a woman lies dead. The caption clearly demonstrates support for the participation of women in combat. It reads, "with work and with arms, women will defend the liberty of the people."[43] However, even *Mujeres Libres* eventually exhibited the change in attitudes toward the militiawomen that took place across the political spectrum in Republican Spain, printing an article in July 1937 that disparaged the *milicianas* and their military contribution.[44]

The mainstream anarchist representation of the *milicianas* differs from that found in the communist press, showing much less interest in the militiawomen. There are also similarities, with the anarchist press just as unlikely as the communist press to show the militiawomen participating in combat. In general, the same differences exist between the photographs depicting militiawomen and those of militiamen. *Mujeres Libres*, like the communist newspaper *Mujeres*, treated the militiawomen in a more progressive way than did the mainstream anarchist and communist press. However, even the anarchist women's organization ultimately withdrew its support of women's military participation, and this was evidenced in the organization's newspaper.

PRESS AND PROPAGANDA OF THE POUM

Only very limited sources were available for studying the representation of *milicianas* by the POUM. The weekly newspaper of the JCI, *Juventud Comunista*, was examined for the period from July to December 1936 (with the exception of some issues missing from the series), but only two photographs of militiawomen were found. The first, featured on the cover in September, showed a *miliciana* wearing the *mono azul* raising her rifle with a flag above her head.[45] This photograph was printed alongside an article celebrating the contribution of young communists in the armed fight against fascism. While the article did not specifically mention female combatants, the inclusion of the photograph implies the involvement of both men and women in the conflict. The second depicted a militiawoman marching with her rifle at her side.[46] This photograph was printed next to an article entitled "Mujeres Proletarias: Nuestra Misión," which focused on the revolution and women's liberation in terms of women's contribution in the home front.

Since no newspaper of the POUM was available to be examined in its entirety, it is not possible to draw any firm conclusions about the representation of the militiawomen in the party's press. It is possible only to say that the information on militiawomen that was found, including in the English-language POUM newspaper discussed earlier,[47] was positive and supportive of militiawomen in a way that was devoid of any symbolism, negativity or criticism.

SOCIALIST PRESS AND PROPAGANDA

Claridad, the daily newspaper of the left wing of the PSOE, was examined in its entirety for the first year of the Spanish Civil War.[48] During this time, the paper published only nine photographs of *milicianas*, the least of any newspaper for which twelve months of issues was studied. Only one of these photographs pictured an unarmed woman, and this was the widely publicized photograph of the head and shoulders of Odena.[49]

Though the socialist press did select photographs that show the weapons of the *milicianas*, making explicit their military involvement, none of the images picture the women actually participating in combat. In seven of the nine photographs, *milicianas* were pictured standing and posing for the camera with their rifles over their shoulders or held in front of them. Only one photograph, featured on the cover on 26 July,[50] shows four militiawomen aiming their weapons. However, the position of the photographer—above and in front of the *milicianas*, and directly in the line of fire had the enemy been positioned where the women were aiming their guns—coupled with the fact that the women are smiling, makes it clear that this photograph was also posed.

Though the articles published in *Claridad* during the first year of the war are few in number, three of the four discuss the military actions of the militiawomen. The first describes the actions of Francisca Solano in a battle at El Espinar, the second discusses the participation in combat of several other women from the *Circulo Socialista del Oeste* and the third reports the death of Odena and recounts her military actions.[51] Despite publishing accounts of women's military involvement, *Claridad* did not express clear support for the militiawomen. The socialist newspaper ceased its representation of the *milicianas* much earlier than did the communist, anarchist or POUM press, printing its last photograph of a *miliciana* on 31 October 1936.[52] Further, the last article pertaining to militiawomen was in fact a malicious attack, accusing the *milicianas* not only of being prostitutes, but of collaborating with the Nationalists.[53]

INDEPENDENT REPUBLICAN PRESS AND PROPAGANDA

In many ways, the representation of the *milicianas* in the independent media is quite different to that found in the press and propaganda of left-wing political parties. In the independent media, militiawomen were overrepresented during the first months of the war, and appeared not in the context of new reportage but as "cover girls." Images of *milicianas* in the independent press demonstrated the new gender roles being created for women in the Republican zone, since these were armed women playing a military role in the war, asserting their independence and strength. However, traditional gender stereotypes were reinforced, since it was the physical appearance and femininity of the militiawomen that was emphasized, rather than their military actions. The daily newspapers *ABC* and *La Voz* and the weekly *Crónica* and *Estampa* were examined as a series from July 1936 to July 1937. The daily newspaper *La Libertad* was examined for six months, from July to December 1936.

The first indication that the independent press saw the presence of female combatants at the front as a novelty, rather than as a phenomenon worthy of significant coverage, is the clear photographic overrepresentation of the *milicianas* coupled with a lack of any information about their military actions. *ABC*, a daily mainstream newspaper with a wide circulation in the Republican zone, is a striking example of this trend. In the first year of the war, *ABC* printed 109 photographs of *milicianas*, which is out of proportion with the number of women actually participating in combat, when compared to the number of male fighters. This is more than any other newspaper examined, and twenty-two more photographs than were published in *Ahora*, the paper that printed the second highest amount. Of these photographs, sixty-nine showed the militiawomen with their weapons visible. Similar to *Ahora*, in some issues photographs of *milicianas* accounted for almost 50 percent of those relating to the war.[54]

ABC featured from one to five full- or half-page photos of *milicianas* in the photo section in almost every issue of the paper from July to December 1936. However, despite the great amount of attention paid to *milicianas* in the photo section of *ABC*, the paper rarely ran any articles or published any information about these militiawomen or their actions in combat. The issue of 31 July 1936, for example, contained five half-page photographs of a total of twenty-four *milicianas*, and yet the issue included no information about these women. The photos were accompanied by captions of little informative value, such as "a *miliciana* equipped to leave for the lines of fire,"[55] and "girls who form part of the women's battalion organized in Madrid."[56]

This trend to over represent *milicianas* photographically while failing to provide adequate information about their military activities is also found in the smaller independent newspapers, though not to the same extent as in *ABC*. *Crónica* featured forty photographs and four illustrations of *milicianas*, many of them full-page sized, in the first year of the war (twenty-seven armed, thirteen unarmed), and featured militiawomen on the front or back cover five times.[57] During this same period only eight articles were printed containing information on the *milicianas*, half of which contained only one paragraph pertaining to female combatants. *Crónica* also over-represented the numbers of *milicianas* in the front lines not simply through publishing a large number of photographs, but also through consistently stating that there were "many" militiawomen fighting. For example, the caption accompanying the full-page photograph of a *miliciana* on 2 August 1936 is "one of the many milicianas who fight."[58]

From July 1936 to July 1937, *Estampa* also published forty photographs of *milicianas*, a quarter of which were full- or half-page sized (twenty-six armed and fourteen unarmed), and featured *milicianas* on the cover of the paper three times.[59] During the same period, *Estampa* carried only five articles containing information about women in combat.[60] Similarly, the independent paper *La Voz* featured *milicianas* on its cover three times in July and August,[61] and regularly printed photos of *milicianas* on its page 4 from July until late November (though only twenty in total, nine armed and eleven unarmed). But aside from a caption, it never published a single article or piece of information about women in combat. Almost all of the photographs of *milicianas* published in the newspapers of the independent press appeared on their own without a supporting article. Some photos of armed women were used to illustrate articles that did not mention the presence of women in the battles described. There were even several instances in which photographs of *milicianas* were used to illustrate articles about the work of women on the home front.[62]

It is also significant that *La Voz* published proportionately more photographs of militiawomen undertaking domestic tasks than any other newspaper, depicting *milicianas* sewing in two, washing clothes in two and cooking in three.[63] Interestingly, one of these photographs was accompanied by the caption "in the front of the Somosierra, heroic militia-women provide useful services, swapping military activities without dismay for the private work of women. These brave women who, having stopped shooting bullets, now wash clothes in a stream for their combatant comrades."[64] These images communicated a strong message about the role of women in the war and in society generally, and this is revealed through the use of the female/male reversal. While photographs of women performing domestic tasks in the front lines were read by their audience as images of women performing their natural and traditional role, albeit outside of the home, an image depicting a man sewing, washing or cooking would appear very peculiar to a Spanish readership in the 1930s.

One explanation for the overrepresentation of the *milicianas* in the independent Republican press, other than their simply being seen as a novelty, is that the role of their images was not to represent real women fighting in the front lines, but to be symbolic of the Republican cause. While it is easy to see how illustrations, cartoons and poems could be interpreted as symbols or allegories representing the valor of the Republican cause, it is more difficult to understand how photographs served the same function. The case is complicated, since the representations of *milicianas* blurred the line between the "real" and the "symbolic." The photos of *milicianas* represented a group of real women who were actually alive at the time, and were playing a military role in the war. However, the way in which these images were presented meant they could also be viewed as symbolic representations. The language used in the captions and articles surrounding these celebratory representations of female combatants, as well as the way in which militiawomen were referred to in popular culture (for example in propaganda, posters and speeches), translated the actions of these women into symbols. *Milicianas* came to represent youthful enthusiasm, dedication, bravery and strength in the fight against fascism.

The representation of the *milicianas* in the independent press is clearly gendered, since there is a vast difference between the types of images featuring militiamen as opposed to militiawomen. The majority of photographs of militiamen showed them in battle, aiming and firing their weapons, hiding from the enemy, wounded, or even being shot or dying. In contrast, photographs of *milicianas* in the independent press were almost invariably posed and do not show the female combatants in action. Instead, these images show the militiawomen alone or in groups standing in a line and smiling at the camera, with their rifles at their sides or over their shoulders. In group shots of both men and women, the women invariably stand front and center.[65]

Only rarely did photographs in *ABC* show a *miliciana* aiming or shooting her rifle. Despite the fact that militiawomen were shown by *ABC* with their rifles or other weapons in sixty-nine photographs during the first year of the war, a mere six photographs showed women aiming or firing their weapons.[66] At least one of these photos is of a *miliciana* in training to use her rifle, rather than participating in battle. The most common military task that the *milicianas* are pictured performing is standing guard, most likely because the difference between this action and posing for the camera is almost imperceptible.[67] Despite not showing *milicianas* in combat, and in contrast to political newspapers such as *Ahora*, *ABC* only very rarely pictured militiawomen undertaking domestic tasks in the front lines. In the 109 photographs in *ABC*, militiawomen are depicted cooking in three, sewing in two, and washing clothes in one.[68]

Again, the smaller independent newspapers follow the pattern seen in *ABC*. Of the forty images published in *Crónica* between July and December 1936, only four show women aiming or firing their rifles.[69] However, one of these images was an illustration, and another was clearly posed since the four *milicianas* are crouching and aiming their weapons directly at the camera.[70] *Estampa* only ever printed two photos of *milicianas* aiming their rifles, but once again, one of these photos is obviously posed as the woman is smiling into the camera.[71] *La Voz* only ever published one photograph of a *miliciana* aiming her weapon,[72] and the newspaper *La Libertad* never published a single photo of a woman aiming a gun.

The independent press can be seen to have used the revolutionary image of the *miliciana* to confirm the traditional gender role for women, while at the same time justifying their participation in combat. One method used to do this was to represent combat in such a way that it fitted in with a conservative view of what was proper conduct for women. *Milicianas* were represented as fighting to protect their families, homes and their children, which was a way of fulfilling their traditional gender role. The underlying message was that the Republican cause was so righteous that even women were moved to cross gender boundaries in order to fight for it. In this way, women's entrance into what was traditionally considered a male sphere of activity served to emphasize the virtue of the Republican cause. The constant referral to the youth, beauty and feminine qualities of the *milicianas* was one way in which the independent press made fighting feminine. *Milicianas* were photographed in poses that Shirley Mangini describes as sexually provocative.[73] This emphasis on the femininity of the *milicianas* supported the idea that these women fought and killed because they were super-feminine, driven by their maternal instincts to protect their homes and families against the Nationalists.[74]

During the month of August 1936 *ABC* used the words "young," "pretty" or "beautiful" to describe *milicianas* in one out of every three captions (out of a total of thirty-one),[75] and used the words "brave" and "valiant" only three times.[76] In some examples, the captions purposely emphasize the beauty of the *milicianas*. In July, an *ABC* caption referred to "eight or ten girls of extraordinary beauty"[77] who belonged to the Acero brigade. In October, *La Voz* printed a photo of "real milicianas, who fight gun in hand. And moreover, very beautiful, as can be seen."[78]

Milicianas who matched the press's idea of what was a young and beautiful woman were singled out for discrimination. *La Libertad* even ran a sexist cartoon deliberately making fun of those women who did not fit the stereotype. The picture showed a uniformed *miliciana* talking to a much larger woman wearing a dress. The woman wearing the dress says, "I am indignant. I am told that there are no overalls for me." The uniformed woman replies, "of course! Because what you need isn't overalls [read 'a monkey'], it's an orangutan."[79] (The Spanish word for overalls is *mono*, which is also the word for monkey.) The "joke" here is that the larger woman cannot fit into the blue overalls the other, slimmer and more conventionally attractive *milicianas* were famous for wearing. It is also significant that the uniformed militiawoman pictured in the illustration is wearing high heels.

An article in the newspaper *Crónica*, printed on 2 August 1936,[80] attempted to justify this emphasis on beauty by arguing that it was the *milicianas* who were most preoccupied by their appearance. The article was written about a number of women who had enlisted in the popular militias, and their subsequent weapons training. The author describes his interactions with one of these women, "a dark woman, very pretty."[81] The author relates that the woman asked him to take a photograph of her, and then took out a small mirror and a comb from her bag in order to check her appearance first. The final line of the article reads, "and as such she will go this afternoon to the Sierra, with her rifle, her cartridge belt, her mirror and her comb."[82]

It is interesting to note that Mary Low discounted this claim that it was the *milicianas* who were most concerned with their appearance. She wrote that:

> I had been in the [POUM] local a week before I noticed that I had given up looking at myself in a mirror. One of the things which had always annoyed me about revolutionary women up till then was the lack of care they took over their appearance. Now, I realise that one only bothers over feminine coquetry because of the shortage of larger interests allowed us in life under the capitalist regime. Nobody dressed up during the revolution in Spain. They forgot to think about it.[83]

Even though the physical attributes of these militiawomen were valued more highly by sections of the press than their military ability, it is nonetheless positive that these progressive representations of women were so appealing to the press and its readers. While it is sexist to refer constantly to the youth and beauty of the *milicianas* in lieu of any other characteristic, the writers of these captions clearly intended to present the *milicianas* in a positive light. The representation of *milicianas* in the independent press demonstrated a form of support for women in combat. The fact that the independent press remained positive about the presence of *milicianas* at the front provides some insight into the attitudes held by the public toward the militiawomen.

Incontestably, a great deal of tension existed in the independent press between the representation of new gender roles and efforts to reassert traditional stereotypes of femininity. An article printed in *Estampa* on 1 August 1936[84] is a notable example of such efforts, even in the context of women's military participation. The two-page article features an interview with Angelina Martínez, and discusses her role in the assault that took place in the *Cuartel de la Montaña*. It is Martínez's physical appearance that is first discussed, before any mention of her military actions.

The very first line of the article relates that "Angelina Martínez is a young blonde woman, a student, who lives in Madrid. She is pretty and, above all, graceful and self-confident. She has a fine figure for what she is: a proper and intelligent lady."[85] It is quite clear that the emphasis here is on the physical appearance of Martínez, and moreover that her beauty meant she was fulfilling her proper role as a woman. When her actions in battle are discussed, Martínez relates that "Compañeros were falling on all sides of me and I realized that, after every shot, my weapon was still working. . . . Boom! Boom! I shot to kill. I assure you. I could not hurt a fly. But what a pleasure to crush a fascist!"[86] Martínez describes continuing to fight even after the men in her militia had stopped. But the fact that she is generally a pacifist is also emphasized, since this is a trait considered in keeping with proper femininity.

The independent press in some ways promoted the new gender roles that were being created by and for women in the Republican zone. On 2 August 1936, *Crónica* published on its cover an illustration that was clearly intended to demonstrate the new gender roles for women.[87] It featured two women walking hand in hand, using their other hands to break through a heavy chain. One woman is wearing the militia uniform (shirt and pants) and cap, with a munitions belt around her waist and a rifle over her shoulder. The second woman is wearing a white nurse's uniform (blouse and skirt). Behind them is a banner that says "19 July," and the caption describes the women as "Las Heroínas." This image clearly represents women breaking out of the restrictive, traditionally accepted behavior for women, to fulfill new roles created by the war and revolution. Both roles, militiawoman and war nurse, represented a new freedom for women to assert their strength and independence. The facial expressions of these women imply determination and courage, and their sleeves are rolled up to reveal bulging biceps muscles.

A second image printed in *Crónica* that displays an aspect of the new gender role for women is a photograph of a couple who have just been married. However, in stark contrast to traditional wedding photographs, this image shows the woman and man in their militia uniforms, with their rifles strapped to their backs. They are kissing and holding hands. This image demonstrates an equality between the couple who are the same height, and wearing identical uniforms. Whereas traditional expectations of a married woman in Spain would suppose her role is purely domestic, and to be fulfilled in the home, this image shows the new wife making an equal contribution to the Republican cause on the war fronts. Not only is she the equal of her husband, but she is outside the home, and playing a role in the previously masculine sphere of combat.

As political and public attitudes began to change toward the *milicianas* in late 1936, and as moves began to be made to remove militiawomen from their combat positions, the representation of the *milicianas* in the independent Republican press began to decrease. While the nature of the representations of militiawomen in the independent press did not change, fewer and fewer of them appeared, until after several months they ceased to be published completely. In *ABC*, a noticeable decrease in the number of images of and references to *milicianas* occurred in January 1937. The last article was printed in late January,[88] and the last photographs appeared in May.[89] The last references to *milicianas* in the four other newspapers examined, *Crónica, Estampa, La Voz* and *La Libertad*, were printed in December, May, November and October,[90] respectively.

Examination of the representation of *milicianas* in the left-wing and independent press clearly demonstrates that while a new gender role for women was emerging in Republican Spain, it had not yet fully developed or been wholeheartedly accepted either by the general public or by those on the left. It is apparent that the social revolution had not been successful in revolutionizing gender relations. The differences between the left-wing groups in their treatment of the militiawomen also reveals a great deal about the attitudes of these groups toward women's roles in the war and gender issues more broadly. This issue is inextricably linked with the fate of the militiawomen who, after eight months of military participation in the civil war, were sent home to fulfill a strictly auxiliary role on the home front.

NOTES

1. Geraldine Scanlon, *La Polémica Feminista en la España Contemporánea (1864–1975)*, Siglo Veintiuno Editores, Madrid, 1976, 291.

2. *Mundo Obrero* was the central organ of the PCE. *Mujeres* was the newspaper of the CNFGF.

3. *Mundo Obrero*, 22 September 1936, 4, 5 October 1936, 1, 13 December 1936, 2, and 8 March 1937, 4.

4. *Mundo Obrero*, 30 October 1936, 2, 3 November 1936, 2, 5 November 1936, 2, 5 February 1937, 2, and 5 February 1937, 3.

5. *Mundo Obrero*, 30 October 1936, 2, 3 November 1936, 2, 5 November 1936, 2, 30 January 1937, 2, and 27 February 1937, 3.

6. Griselda Pollock, "What's Wrong with Images of Women?" in Manuel Alvarado (ed.), *Representation and Photography: A screen education reader*, Palgrave, New York, 2001, 78.

7. *Mundo Obrero*, 4 August 1936, 4.

8. *Mundo Obrero*, 12 September 1936, 2.

9. *Mundo Obrero*, 4 August 1936, 4, and 26 August 1936, 3.

10. *Mujeres*, 27 February 1937, 7.

11. *Mujeres*, 20 February 1937, 2, and 5 June 1937, 9.

12. *Mundo Obrero*, 22 July 1936.

13. "Lady Liberty", or Marianne, became the most famous symbol of the French Republic during the revolution of 1789. She represents liberty, reason and republicanism. For a detailed discussion of the origins, meaning and interpretations of "Lady Liberty", see Maurice Agulhon, *Marianne into Battle: Representation, imagery and symbolism in France, 1789–1880*, Cambridge University Press, Cambridge, 1981.

14. "En la Guerra Actual no hay Zonas Neutrales ni Grupos de Espectadores: ¡Todos somos beligerantes!" *Mundo Obrero*, 5 October 1936, cover.

15. *Mundo Obrero*, 5 October 1936, cover.

16. Jorge Semprún et al (eds.), *Mujeres en la Guerra Civil Española*, publisher unknown, Salamanca, 1989, 80.

17. *Mujeres*, 10 April 1937, 8.

18. *Mujeres*, 1 May 1937, cover.

19. Olga Zubizaola, "Nuestras Heroínas," *Mujeres*, 5 June 1937, 9.

20. *Ahora*, 30 July 1936, 16, 1 August 1936, 1, 3 August 1936, 23, 5 August 1936, 14, 6 August 1936, 12, 26 September 1936, back cover, 30 September 1936, 2, and 15 November 1936, 2.

21. *Ahora*, 26 August 1936, 6, 14 September 1936, 7, 28 January 1937, 4, and 12 February 1937, 6.

22. See chapter 3, "Quantitative Significance: Numbers of Women in Combat."

23. *Ahora*, 25 July 1936, 27, 30 July 1936, 16, 3 August 1936, 23, 5 August 1936, 10–11 and 6 August 1936, 12–13.

24. *Ahora*, 30 July 1936, cover, and 1 August 1936, cover.

25. *Ahora*, 30 July 1936, cover.

26. *Ahora*, 1 August 1936, cover.

27. *Ahora*, 25 July 1936, 27, 29 July 1936, 23, 30 July 1936, cover and 16, 1 August 1936, cover and 23, 3 August 1936, 23, 5 August 1936, 10 and 11, and 6 August 1936 12 and 13.

28. "La Organización de la Milicias Expedicionarias en Barcelona," *Ahora*, 5 August 1936, 10–11.

29. "Milicias Expedicionarias," 11.

30. *Ahora*, 14 March 1937, cover.

31. *Tierra y Libertad*, 16 January 1937, back cover.

32. *Tierra y Libertad*, 5 November 1936, 5.

33. *Tierra y Libertad*, 13 February 1937, back cover.

34. *CNT*, 15 August 1936, 2.

35. Though I did not examine the newspapers with the purpose of locating images of men with children, I cannot recall coming across any during my research of these Spanish newspapers for the first year of the war.

36. *CNT*, 22 August 1936, 4.

37. Semprún, *Mujeres en la Guerra*, 73.

38. Kelly Phipps, "Gender and the Language of Struggle: Republican representations of women in the Spanish Civil War," Honours Thesis, April 2003, Gender Studies, Brown University, Providence, R.I., USA, 41.

39. *CNT*, 15 August 1936, 2.

40. Kyralina, "Mujeres Heroicas," *Tierra y Libertad*, 13 February 1937, back cover.

41. Josefina Serván Corchero and Antonio Trinidad Muñoz, "Las Mujeres en la Cartelística de la Guerra Civil," in *Las Mujeres y la Guerra Civil Española/ III Jornadas de Estudios Monográficos: Salamanca, octubre 1989*, Instituto de la Mujer, Madrid, 1991.

42. Corchero and Muñoz, "Las Mujeres en la Cartelística," 366.

43. *Mujeres Libres*, 8 March 1937, cover.

44. "Las Mujeres en los Primeros Días de Lucha," *Mujeres Libres*, no. 10, July 1937, 5.

45. *Juventud Comunista*, September 1936, cover.

46. *Juventud Comunista*, 24 December 1936, 3.

47. "The First Women"s Battalion," *The Spanish Revolution*, 2 December 1936, vol. 1, no. 7, 4.

48. *Informaciones*, the newspaper of the right-wing of the PSOE, was not examined since Nash indicated it contained no references to militiawomen.

49. *Claridad*, 23 September 1936, 8.

50. *Claridad*, 26 July 1936, cover.

51. "La Heroína de El Espinar," *Claridad*, 27 July 1936, 3; "El Circulo Socialista del Oeste", 28 July 1936, 6; and "Lina Odena ha Muerto", 23 September 1936, 8.

52. *Claridad*, 31 October 1936, 5.

53. Leoncio Pérez, "La Prostitución, el Arma Principal de la Quinta Columna," *Claridad*, 4 March 1937, 4–5.

54. *ABC*, 2 August 1936.

55. *ABC*, 31 July 1936, 7.

56. *ABC*, 31 July 1936, 9.

57. *Crónica*, 2 August 1936, 6 September 1936, 4 October 1936 and 13 December 1936.

58. *Crónica*, 2 August 1936, 2.

59. *Estampa*, 25 July 1936, 1 August 1926, 8 August 1936.

60. *Estampa*, 1 August 1936, 18–19, 8 August 1936, 10–12, 29 August 1936, 25–26, 10 October 1936, 15 and 22 May 1937, 16–17.

61. *La Voz*, 31 July 1936, 7 August 1936 and 8 August 1936.

62. See for example *Estampa*, 13 February 1937, 3 and 5 June 1937, 11–12.

63. *La Voz*, 3 September 1936, 4, 15 October 1936, 4, 9 September 1936, 2, 10 November 1936, 1, 22 September 1936, 4, 24 September 1936, 4 and 17 October 1936, 4.

64. *La Voz*, 9 September 1936, 2.

65. See for example *ABC*, 28 July 1936, 4, 30 July 1936, 3 and 2 August 1936, 4.

66. *ABC*, 2 August 1936, 4, 2 October 1936, 3, 17 December 1936, 1, 25 December 1936, 2, 12 January 1937, 1 and 19 January 1937, 2.

67. See for example *ABC*, 10 September 1936, 8, 7 January 1937, 2 and 21 January 1937, 12.

68. *ABC*, 6 August 1936, 6, 18 October 1936, 14, 25 May 1937, 2, 18 October 1936, 14, 23 November 1936, 8 and 13 November 1936, 4.

69. *Crónica*, 6 September 1936, back cover, 27 September 1936, 10, 22 November 1936, 14 and 6 December 1936, 5.

70. *Crónica*, 22 November 1936, 14.

71. *Estampa*, 1 August 1936, 19, and date unknown, January 1937, 5.

72. *La Voz*, 20 October 1936, 4.

73. Shirley Mangini, *Memories of Resistance: Women"s voices from the Spanish Civil War*, Yale University Press, New Haven, 1995, 81.

74. Joanna Bourke, *An Intimate History of Killing: Face-to-face killing in twentieth century warfare*, Granta Books, London, 1999, 320. In her chapter "Women go to War," Bourke explains the notion of justifying women's participation in combat through "making fighting feminine," using British, Australian and U.S. examples.

75. *ABC*, 6 August 1936, 6, 9 August 1936, 5, 11 August 1936, 5, 12 August 1936, 2, 13 August 1936, 4, 14 August 1936, 1, 15 August 1936, 5, 16 August 1936, 4, 19 August 3 and 19 August 1936, 5. Ten captions out of a total of thirty-one.

76. *ABC*, 1 August 1936, 37, 4 August 1936, 7 and 8 August 1936, 15.

77. *ABC*, 30 July 1936, 23.

78. *La Voz*, 13 October 1936, 4.

79. *La Libertad*, 6 August 1936, 11.

80. "¡Mujeres! ¡A formar!" *Crónica*, 2 August 1936, 6.

81. "¡Mujeres! ¡A formar!" 6.

82. "¡Mujeres! ¡A formar!" 6.

83. Mary Low and Juan Breà, *Red Spanish Notebook: The first six months of the revolution and the civil war*, Purnell and Sons, London, 1937, 40–41.

84. "Angelina Martínez, la Miliciana que Tomó Parte en el Asalto al Cuartel de la Montaña," *Estampa*, 1 August 1936, 18–19.

85. "Angelina Martínez," 18.

86. "Angelina Martínez," 18.

87. The same image was also later published on the back cover, *Crónica*, 30 August 1936, back cover.

88. "Una mujer en el frente," *ABC*, 16 January 1937, 8.

89. *ABC*, 4 May 1937, 5, 12 May 1937, 4, and 25 May 1937, 2.

90. Etheria Artay, "Las Mujeres de Barcelona se Preparan, por si Llegara el Momento en que Ellas, También, Tuvieran que Combatir," *Crónica*, 20 December 1936, 7–8; "De las Jornadas Trágicas de Barcelona: Fanny, la heroína del Casal Carlos Marx," *Estampa*, 22 May 1937, 16–17; *La Voz*, 17 November 1936, 4. *La Libertad*, 27 October 1936, 6.

Conclusion

THE HISTORY OF THE MILICIANAS

The military participation of thousands of women in the Spanish Civil War was a significant historical event, and unique in Spain's history. Thus far, the bulk of the secondary literature concerning the civil war has omitted any reference to the existence of these female combatants, and even sources that do discuss their involvement have underestimated or downplayed its extent and significance. A detailed examination of the history of those women who took up arms in the anti-fascist struggle in Spain during the first year of the war reveals a great deal, and not only about their self-motivation, their numbers and the nature of their military role both in the front lines and in the rearguard. The information revealed by this book also has implications for other fields such as gender and politics in Spain, and women in war and revolution more generally.

An understanding of women's position in Spain prior to the outbreak of the civil war is necessary in order to appreciate the significance of the transformation in gender roles that occurred during the years 1936 to 1939. Accepted gender behaviors during these years existed in stark contrast to the traditional roles played by women during the nineteenth and early twentieth centuries, when they experienced severe oppression and occupied a strictly subordinate position in society. An examination of the policies and practices of left-wing political groups in relation to women's rights and gender issues exposes their record of lack of commitment to this question, though it is clear improvements were being made. During the first two years of the Second Republic, 1931–1933, the rights of Spanish women were advanced, and they became the legal equals of men for the first time. Women also became increasingly involved in political and social movements during these years. These developments helped to create the favorable conditions in which women were able to play a military role during the civil war.

The most significant preconditions for women's ability to play a combat role, however, were those created by the intersection of the war and the social revolution in July 1936. These two events transformed gender roles, albeit for a limited time. It is evident, however, and highly significant to the fate of the *milicianas*, that while gender lines were blurred, they were not definitively and permanently changed. Women in the Republican zone experienced extended rights and newly found freedoms, but they were not fully liberated. They had not achieved full and lasting equality with men.

Women played an important military role in the spontaneous uprising of the people against the Nationalist military coup in July. Chapter 3 also revealed the extent of the self-motivation of those women who went on to join the militias and fight in the front lines, and their political motivations for doing so. It is also clear from an examination of this early period of the war that some historians have underestimated the number of *milicianas*. In fact, there were around 1,000 militiawomen fighting at the front, and several thousand more forming sections of the armed rearguard.

As chapter 4 demonstrated, the *milicianas* stationed in the front lines and those who were members of women's battalions in the rearguard played an extensive and sophisticated military role. While it has been suggested that the *milicianas* incorporated into mixed-gender militias and battalions on the front lines mainly played an auxiliary role (to the detriment of their participation in combat), it is evident that the majority of militiawomen did in fact participate in combat equally with their male comrades. While most *milicianas* also carried out domestic tasks in the front lines, as a result of the persistence of traditional ideas about women's natural skills and abilities, these responsibilities were carried out as well as their normal combat duties.

Milicianas of rearguard battalions played an important military role in the defense of their cities and towns, and in some cases participated in battle, for example in Madrid in November 1936. Since these women did not leave their homes and communities, they were often more visible to society than were their front-line counterparts. As such, these *milicianas* served as models to the wider community, demonstrating the new roles and opportunities for women created by the war and social revolution. They presented a serious challenge to traditional gender roles, and constructed a revolutionary definition of female citizenship, which included the right to bear arms.

Even during the peak of women's military involvement, however, in the first six months of the war, the limits of the revolution in relation to women's liberation were clear. While most *milicianas* report being treated as equals by their male comrades, there is evidence that some women suffered discrimination and harassment while serving the anti-fascist cause. Toward the end of 1936, the positive attitude of the public and political parties that the *milicianas* had first enjoyed began to dissipate. Arguments began to circulate as to why women should be removed from their combat positions and return to the home front to fulfill roles that were considered better suited to their feminine nature.

As evidenced in chapter 5, sexist undertones can be detected in each of the arguments presented by the left-wing political groups as to why the *milicianas* should cease to fulfill a military role in the war. Proponents of the view that women should not fulfill combat roles argued that it was no longer necessary now that the initial urgency had passed; women had not received sufficient training to be militarily useful; the biological nature of women precluded them from such a role and rendered them better suited to roles on the home front; the *milicianas* were causing problems as a result of sexual relations with militiamen; and among them were a number of prostitutes spreading venereal disease among the Republican fighting force. It is clear that these arguments were merely pretexts for the removal of women from combat, which occurred not in isolation but came in the context of a larger reversal of progressive attitudes and policies that coincided with the failure of the social revolution.

In March 1937, most women's military contribution came to an end when an official decision (or series of decisions), was made to oblige the *milicianas* to lay down their arms and return home from the front. Chapter 5 showed that though there existed a consensus around this issue among the essentially male leadership of the Republican government and left-wing political groups, it is clear that female combatants viewed this turn of events differently. The majority of the militiawomen had deep reservations about their recall from the front and saw it as a retreat from the gains women had made during the war and revolution. While the political leadership within the Republic presented numerous arguments for why it was necessary to remove women from combat positions, it is clear that the reason it was initially considered acceptable for women to fight, and then seen as deplorable eight months later, was connected to the course of the social revolution and its failure.

While the end of the social revolution saw the reversal of many progressive gains for the working class in the Republican zone, and the removal of women from combat was in a way simply one of these, this was not the only contributing factor to the demise of the *milicianas*. An examination of this period reveals that women's participation in combat was never fully accepted or wholeheartedly embraced in the Republican zone by any political group, except *Mujeres Libres*. This is confirmed by the examination in chapter 6 of the representation of the militiawomen in the press and propaganda of left-wing political groups, which in many ways served to reinforce traditional gender roles, whether overtly or subtly. This reluctance to prioritize or accept the complete transformation of gender roles and the liberation of women meant that the essentially male leadership of the communists, anarchists, POUM and socialists were quickly able to achieve a rare consensus on the removal of militiawomen from their combat positions.

It is significant to note, however, that while there were many similarities between these groups on the issue of the militiawomen, there were also important differences. The history of the *milicianas* brings to light important information about the connection between women's rights and left-wing political groups. It might be assumed that the radical left, in particular the anarchists, would be most committed to women's liberation as an extension of their commitment to the social revolution. However, the evidence suggests that in fact the anarchists appear to have been less interested in the issue. An examination of the anarchist press for the first year of the war reveals that they were relatively reluctant to report on and represent women in military roles. Conversely, politically more moderate forces, in particular the communists, seem to have devoted more attention to the issue. Communist newspapers contained far more images of, references to and information on the militiawomen than did the anarchist press. It is also significant that the female combatants who were raised to the status of war legend, such as Rosario Sánchez de la Mora and Lina Odena, were communist women and made famous by communist propaganda.

However, it is also clear that while that leadership of anarchist groups (and their press) did not prioritize the question of women's rights and women's military role, this was not necessarily true of the rank and file membership. It is significant that there were far more anarchist militiawomen than communist, and that it was from the anarchist rank and file that the most militant feminist group in Spain, *Mujeres Libres*, emerged. It was this women's organization more than any other that supported women's liberation and encouraged women's equal participation in the anti-fascist resistance, including in a military capacity. While the communist public profile on gender issues and women's combat roles in the war was certainly more advanced than that of the anarchists, this did not necessarily equate with a greater commitment to women's equality in practice. In any case, the commitment of all left-wing groups to women's equality and indeed their right to bear arms was short-lived.

BROADER CONCLUSIONS

The history of the *milicianas* confirms wider theories relating to women in war and revolution. As discussed in the introduction, Alan Milward and Angus Calder theorize that wars do not cause any social or economic changes, but rather only highlight or accelerate processes that already exist within the society, and consequently that women's experience during war is only a deviation from traditional gender relations that will be returned once the war is over.[1]

Further, the experience of the *milicianas* confirms Marxist theory that explains that women cannot achieve full equality without the removal of the preconditions for their oppression, specifically the existence of private property and class society.[2] A social revolution that attempts to transform gender roles will not be successful in changing the position of women in society without the accompaniment of both a fundamental and lasting social, political and economic revolution. It is for this reason that women in the Republican zone initially experienced an extension of their rights and were able to fulfill new roles in the public and military spheres during the war and revolution, but were ultimately returned to their traditional positions of subjugation.

As the social revolution came to an unsuccessful end eight months after it had begun, many questions relating to what might have been the course of the women's liberation movement in Spain remain unanswered. Given the poor record of left-wing groups on gender issues, and the fact that their broad ideological radicalism did not always equate with a genuine commitment to gender equality, would the fate of the *milicianas* have been the same had the social revolution not come to an end? Or, since inroads were being made into the public's consciousness on the rights and roles of women, and given that improvements in the policies and practices of progressive groups in relation to gender issues were being made, is it possible that if the revolution had continued unfettered women would have continued to enjoy enhanced rights and opportunities? What might Spain have looked like if the social revolution had not only continued, but in the event of a Republican victory? Given the actual course of events, it is clearly only possible to speculate on these issues.

As it was, in 1937 women in the Republican zone lost the progressive gains they had won as a result of the social revolution. While women continued to enjoy enhanced rights and opportunities within the public sphere, in particular in the work force, due to the necessities created by the war, they were no longer able to fulfill more radical roles such as that of a militiawoman. As has been the case for many female revolutionaries globally,[3] at the end of the revolution women put down their gun, but were left holding the baby.

It is useful to revisit Valentine Moghadam's theory on gender and revolution (examined in the introduction), which proposes that there are two categories of revolution: the "woman in the family" model that adheres to traditional gender roles, and the "women's emancipation" model that seeks to transform these roles and liberate women.[4] It is clear that while the left-wing groups in the Republican zone exhibited multifarious attitudes toward gender issues, overall it was the "woman in the family" model that dominated. It must be noted, however, that initial support for women's military participation was a radical departure from such a conservative model, and there were also some notable exceptions such as *Mujeres Libres* who demonstrated an ideology that adhered to the "women's emancipation" model. While the failure of the social revolution was the primary cause for the removal of women from combat, it is evident that the relationship between left-wing groups and gender issues was a significant factor in the timing and nature of this removal.

THE DEFEAT OF THE LEFT AND FRANCO'S PUNISHMENT

In May 1937, the fate of the social revolution was sealed when the PCE crushed the workers' struggle in Barcelona and began a campaign of brutal persecution against anarchists and members of the POUM. The weakened anti-fascist resistance was dealt its final blow two years later when in March 1939, army commander Colonel Segismundo Casado staged a coup and rapidly organized the surrender of the Republicans.

The rights and freedoms for women that had been won during the Second Republic and enhanced during the civil war were immediately reversed at the end of the conflict with the triumph of the Nationalist forces. The victory of Franco's forces meant a new era of repression for women. Traditional gender roles supported by Catholicism were swiftly reinforced, and women were once again confined to the private sphere, and brought under the control of the patriarchal head of the family.

This repression of Spanish women in general was coupled with brutal reprisals against Republican women. In the aftermath of the civil war, Republican activists (or indeed anyone who had been denounced by a fascist)[5] were hunted down and arrested.[6] Even elderly women with no political history were imprisoned because of their children's or husband's activities.[7] Jails were literally overflowing.[8] It is estimated that thousands of women were executed in the early years of Franco's rule and some 30,000 imprisoned.[9]

Conditions in the overcrowded prisons were miserable. Prisoners were granted only the barest rations,[10] water was often contaminated and water-borne diseases such as typhoid were rife.[11] Countless imprisoned women died of hunger.[12] Prisoners' children often had to live with their mothers inside the jails, where there was insufficient food and a desperate lack of medical care. Many of these children died of hunger and preventable diseases.[13] Some children were removed from their mothers by the regime to "protect" them from Marxist ideology.[14] Prisoners were beaten and tortured to near death—or in some cases death—in an effort to extract information.[15] Many of the nuns in charge of female political prisoners were responsible for the torment and cruel treatment of the women.[16]

There was a great deal of stigmatization of those who had been on the losing side of the war.[17] In an effort to demean and humiliate women prisoners, some had their heads shaved or were brandished with tar on their foreheads.[18] Rape, which had been used by the Nationalists as a weapon in the civil war,[19] was employed by fascists after their victory, both on the streets against random victims and as a specific punishment for Republican women.[20] For those prisoners not arbitrarily executed, trials heard "evidence" from fascists acquainted with the accused, and prisoners were sentenced to death or long jail terms.[21]

LIFE UNDER FRANCO

After the war, the economic conditions were harsh and starvation was common. Many families were forced from their homes or lost their houses in the bombings.[22] Many Republican workers ended up in difficult jobs with poor conditions and security as a result of being sentenced to exile or having fled their hometowns to avoid the authorities.[23] Widescale purges were conducted in various fields of employment to eliminate Republicans and anti-fascist sympathizers.[24]

Women whose husbands had joined the armed resistance to Franco were excluded from employment, leaving them with no means to survive. Money and property were confiscated from many households where a family member had been accused of political crimes.[25]

In addition to the political persecution and desperate economic situation, the regime overturned the advances in the status of women that had been made during the Second Republic and the revolution. According to Catherine Davies in her 1998 book *Spanish Women's Writing 1849–1996*, "the fall of the Republic delayed women's emancipation by some 50 years."[26]

The highly conservative moral purification campaign by the Catholic Church under Franco insisted on women's alleged natural and eternal place as moral guardians in the home.[27] Women were relegated to the subordinate position they had occupied in previous centuries.

Those women who had defied this image of womanhood and participated in the anti-fascist resistance and political struggle (especially the *milicianas* who had participated in combat) were singled out for retribution.[28] Republican women were also blamed for failing their central purpose as mothers by raising the generation that produced so many revolutionaries.[29]

The regime made it compulsory for all Spanish women to become members of the women's section of the fascist Falange Party.[30] Women caught engaging in "impure" acts, such as selling items on the black market to feed their families, were also subject to acts of "purification." Some were forced to drink castor oil or had their heads shaved.[31] Humiliation and shame were used as tools to control and demean women.

Laws targeting women outlawed abortion, adultery and divorce. Sex education and contraception were also banned, along with co-education in schools.[32] Women were prohibited from many professions. However, the regime's hypocrisy, in addition to the trying economic times, meant that prostitution flourished under Franco's rule.[33]

CONTINUED RESISTANCE

Resistance existed throughout the life of the fascist dictatorship. The PCE continued to organize underground, guerrilla struggles took place in rural Spain and illegal trade unions operated. During the later decades of the dictatorship, workers and students collaborated to organize strikes.[34] Many women risked their lives by taking part in the resistance.

Inside the prisons, women engaged in daily battles to secure water and other basic necessities. They also organized to obtain packages from friends and family on the outside, often passing on food to prisoners in worse health or otherwise greater need.[35] Women prisoners organized hunger strikes to protest the treatment of particular prisoners.[36] Women also conspired in jail to prepare escape attempts and many prisoners were successful in securing their freedom.[37]

Educated prisoners taught illiterate women how to read and write.[38] Women also continued political discussions inside their jail cells. More experienced activists educated the younger prisoners.[39]

Many women on the outside also worked hard to support the political prisoners, bringing them food and letters. Some also did what they could to defend those imprisoned, holding round-the-clock vigils outside prisons to prevent the fascists from removing political prisoners for execution.[40] Women contributed to the resistance on many fronts, acting as messengers, helping to produce clandestine publications, and in some cases participating in the guerrilla struggle. The sacrifices made by women were many and varied, including long separations from children and other loved ones.[41]

Women successfully fought for reforms, and changes were gradually made to the anti-women Civil Code during the 1950s, 1960s and 1970s.[42] Economic development also brought greater opportunities for women, which began to be reflected in changing attitudes toward women.

Despite the extent of abuse and suffering endured by the Spanish people during the long years under Franco's rule until his death in late 1975, countless women refused to ever bow down or allow their hopes for the future to be crushed.[43] There are countless stories of courageous women who continued to fight for what they believed in and never gave up. One example is Antonia García. After eleven years in Franco's jails, García, a political prisoner who suffered severe injuries as a result of torture, was offered an early release in exchange for signing a statement that she repented. She flatly refused. She would not surrender her dignity, not even in exchange for freedom.[44]

Former guerrilla fighter Esperanza Martínez, who spent fifteen years in Franco's prisons, recalled one New Year's Eve in her cell:

> At midnight I got up to toast happiness for the New Year, for freedom, for so much we had fought for. In those moments I wasn't thinking

about being alone, not at all, because as soon as I lifted my hand with the glass, I thought about how thousands and millions of people were lifting their glasses to toast with the same desires and goals for which I had fought and for which so many people in the world had fought.[45]

This memory of resistance and solidarity is a fitting way to conclude. Despite her physical solitude and the suffering she endured while imprisoned, Martínez nonetheless felt connected to the greater struggle, and all those who fought alongside her, against fascism and for a better world.

NOTES

1. Alan Milward, *War, Economy and Society, 1939 – 45*, Allen Lane, London, 1977 and Angus Calder, *The People's War: Britain 1939 – 45*, Cape, London, 1969, cited in Margaret Higonnet and Patrice Higonnet, "The Double Helix," in Margaret Randolph Higonnet, Jane Jenson, Sonya Michel and Margaret Collins Weitz (eds.), *Behind the Lines: Gender and the two World Wars*, Yale University Press, New Haven, 1987, 31.

2. For the Marxist theory on the origins and cause of women"s oppression, see August Bebel, *Woman Under Socialism*, translated by D. de Leon, New York Labour Press, New York, 1904, Friedrich Engels, *On the Origins of the Family, Private Property and the State*, Foreign Languages Press, Peking, 1978 and Pat Brewer, *The Dispossession of Women*, Resistance Books, Chippendale, 2000.

3. For an in-depth study of this issue, in particular in relation to women who participated in the wars fought by liberation armies, and their consequent treatment by the new state once the revolutionary war is successful, see Cynthia Enloe, *Does Khaki Become You? The militarisation of women's lives*, South End Press, London, 1983, 160–172.

4. Valentine Moghadam, "Gender and Revolutions," in John Foran (ed.), *Theorizing Revolutions*, Routledge, London, 1997, 137–167.

5. Tomasa Cuevas, *Prison of Women: Testimonies of war and resistance in Spain, 1939–1975*, translated and edited by Mary E. Giles, State University of New York Press, Albany, 1998, 110.

6. Cuevas, *Prison of Women*, 21.

7. Cuevas, *Prison of Women*, 34.

8. Cuevas, *Prison of Women*, 23.

9. Michael Richards, *A Time of Silence: Civil war and the culture of repression in Franco"s Spain, 1936–1945*, Cambridge University Press, Cambridge, 1998, 53.

10. Cuevas, *Prison of Women*, 25.

11. Cuevas, *Prison of Women*, 27.

12. Cuevas, *Prison of Women*, 87.

13. Cuevas, *Prison of Women*, 184.

14. Julius Ruiz, *Franco's justice: Repression in Madrid after the Spanish Civil War*, Oxford University Press, Oxford, 2005, 118.

15. Cuevas, *Prison of Women*, 25.

16. Cuevas, *Prison of Women*, 80.

17. Richards, *A Time of Silence*, 52.

18. Cuevas, *Prison of Women*, 26.

19. Richards, *A Time of Silence*, 52.

20. Cuevas, *Prison of Women*, 21 and 26.

21. Cuevas, *Prison of Women*, 34 and 110.

22. Cuevas, *Prison of Women*, 14.

23. Cuevas, *Prison of Women*, 213.

24. Ruiz, *Franco's justice*, chapter 5.

25. Richards, *A Time of Silence*, 52.

26. Catherine Davies, *Spanish Women's Writing 1849 – 1996*, Athlone Press, London, 1998, 177.

27. Richards, *A Time of Silence*, 54.

28. Richards, *A Time of Silence*, 55.

29. Filipe Ribeiro De Meneses, *Franco and the Spanish Civil War* , Routledge, New York, 2001, 103.

30. Davies, *Spanish Women's Writing 1849 – 1996*, 173.

31. Richards, *A Time of Silence*, 55.

32. Davies, *Spanish Women's Writing 1849 – 1996*, 177.

33. Richards, *A Time of Silence*, 55 and De Meneses, *Franco and the Spanish Civil War* , 7.

34. Davies, *Spanish Women's Writing 1849 – 1996*, 177.

35. Cuevas, *Prison of Women*, 28–29.

36. Cuevas, *Prison of Women*, 87.

37. Cuevas, *Prison of Women*, 80.

38. Cuevas, *Prison of Women*, 122.

39. Cuevas, *Prison of Women*, 54.

40. Richards, *A Time of Silence*, 53.

41. Cuevas, *Prison of Women*, 227.

42. Davies, *Spanish Women's Writing 1849 – 1996*, 180.

43. Cuevas, *Prison of Women*.

44. Cuevas, *Prison of Women*, 123.

45. Cuevas, *Prison of Women*, 205.

Notes on the Sources

The vast bulk of the research underpinning this book is based on Spanish-language primary source material, mainly in the form of memoirs, oral testimonies, observer commentaries, newspapers and propaganda. Some of these sources, while not disregarded by historians, may never have been read with an eye to discovering information about the militiawomen. Some of the primary sources that will be introduced in this book have not previously been cited by historians of this field.

While a significant proportion of the research materials were collected in Australia, the most important sources were collected during a trip to Spain. A great deal of research was undertaken in Madrid, in *La Biblioteca Nacional* (the National Library), *El Instituto de la Mujer* (the Women's Institute) and *La Universidad Complutense* (the Complutense University), as well as in *El Archivo General de la Guerra Civil Española* (the General Archive of the Spanish Civil War) in Salamanca. The National Library and General Archive were particularly valuable, as they held comprehensive and, in most cases, complete microfilm collections of Spanish newspapers from the period. The National Library also held the largest collection of both primary and secondary sources pertaining to the civil war. The Women's Institute held only a small collection, but this contained several autobiographies and biographies of *milicianas* that were not available elsewhere. The Complutense University also held several secondary sources unavailable elsewhere. A trip to Barcelona allowed for an interview with the anarchist *miliciana* Pérez Collado.

ORAL HISTORIES

Oral history sources have been integral to the research for this book. The use of sources focused on the subjective experiences and perceptions of the *milicianas* has allowed a greater understanding of their point of view.

The use of oral history is integral to a grassroots history of the Spanish Civil War. Without the use of oral history, the evidence available on a subject is usually limited to that produced by a social, political or intellectual elite, and will not necessarily reflect the experiences of the majority of people and in particular of working-class women. In the case of the Spanish Civil War, the use of oral history becomes even more critical due the limitations placed by the Franco regime on the publication in Spain of sources from a Republican or left-wing viewpoint. Without the use of oral history, much of the history of the Spanish Civil War would have been lost.

Due to the fact that over seventy years have passed since the beginning of the Spanish Civil War, I was able to conduct only one interview of my own, with one of the last surviving *milicianas*. The vast majority of militiawomen have now died, and most of the few remaining women appear to be no longer willing or able to tell their stories.

In February of 2005, I conducted an interview with Pérez Collado in Barcelona. This absorbing interview with a lifelong activist enhanced my research and provided further insight into the motivations of the militiawomen. Conducting this interview with Pérez Collado allowed me to discover information about her actions in combat as part of the initial resistance in the streets of Barcelona, and later as a member of an anarchist militia that took part in many battles, most notably that at Belchite in 1937. Other interviews conducted with Pérez Collado by historians such as Nash and Marín do not appear to have focused on her actions in battle nor on her daily life in the front lines. It is for this reason that my interview with Pérez Collado is significant for my purposes.

Information gained during this interview on Pérez Collado's initial reaction to the civil war, and on her journey to the Huesca front to fight, has been included in chapter 3. This information helped me to analyze further the varying reasons that women had for volunteering for combat. Details pertaining to Pérez Collado's participation in battle, as well as her opinion that women took part in combat on equal terms with men, have been included in chapter 4.

Oral testimonies have also been collected from the work of historians of the field who have either published entire interviews with their subjects, or incorporated sections into their research. The most significant examples are Mangini, Strobl, Marín and Nash.[1] Each of these sources played a vital part in the research for this book, primarily because they are among the few historians to have undertaken substantial research in this field, interviewing militiawomen and publishing their accounts.

The interviews conducted by Mangini and Nash were particularly useful for examining the motives that drove the women to volunteer for combat. However, they did not provide as much insight into the combat actions of the women at the front. The work of Strobl and Marín helps to fill this gap, since their interviews contain more information on their subjects' actions in battle. These oral history sources contribute to the argument of this book by allowing the reader to gain a fuller understanding of the experience of the Spanish Civil War from the perspective of the women who played an active part in the conflict.

While the use of oral testimonies allows insight into the subjective experiences of the *milicianas*, it must be noted that there are several dangers with relying on evidence presented in this way.[2] The most obvious is that interviews with individual women provide a personal rather than a broader view of the war. The historian may be tempted to generalize, and argue without supporting evidence that the opinion or experience presented is representative of a larger number of women, which is not always the case. For example, if a historian with little experience in the field had interviewed Fernández de Velasco Pérez, who was one of the few women who continued fighting in the militias until the end of the war, he or she might mistakenly believe that women were never removed from combat. This is obviously an extreme example, but it nonetheless demonstrates the point.

Further, the historian must be aware of the bias present in oral testimonies. No interview can be totally objective, since each person's opinions and experiences have been shaped by their own circumstances and beliefs. Spain during the civil war was a highly politicized environment, and often the women who participated in combat held firm political beliefs. If one were to ask a communist *miliciana* a question regarding the anarchist militias, for example, one might not receive the most reliable evidence, and vice versa. However, the discerning historian would perhaps gain insight into the attitudes held by one political group toward another. This demonstrates that so long as the historian is aware of bias, valuable evidence can still be extracted.

Another pitfall in the use of oral history is that often subjects are interviewed many years after the events took place, as with the study of the militiawomen. A person's memory is fallible, and becomes less reliable over time. My interview with Pérez Collado took place almost seventy years after the event in question. In 2005, Pérez Collado was ninety years old, and at that point in life it is natural that one cannot always recall many details. However, it is also true that some events that have had a great impact on a person are never forgotten. While Pérez Co lado was unable to remember her date of birth for several minutes, she was able to speak in great detail about the death of her brother, a mil tiaman killed during the war.

The historian is able to deal with the problem of fallible memory through further research. I have been able to corroborate much of the information provided by Pérez Collado using other sources, such as interviews that were conducted with her at a younger age, and also secondary sources that confirm the dates of battles and other events that she mentioned. Where I was able to check information, I did not find any discrepancies. Therefore, there is no compelling reason to doubt the accuracy of the new information that Pérez Collado gave me.

If the historian is aware of these drawbacks, it is possible to overcome them. Taking into account the constraints, the use of oral testimony allows the historian to develop a more personal and emotional understanding of the war. Due to the historical erasure throughout the Franco era of leftist—and especially women's—wartime experiences, the use of oral history is one of the only ways for these women's stories to be told and for their experiences to be shared. Oral testimonies are a valuable resource, especially for the purpose of this book, which, as a grassroots history, is intended specifically to highlight the participation of these fighting women in the war as *they* experienced it.

MEMOIRS AND AUTOBIOGRAPHIES

The use of various memoirs has been important to the research for this book. Firsthand accounts written by women who participated in combat have been particularly useful, since these allow insight into the attitudes and beliefs of the *milicianas* themselves, as well as accurate accounts of their actions in battle. The two most useful memoirs in English and Spanish respectively are Mary Low and Juan Breà's *Red Spanish Notebook*,[3] and Etchebéhère's *Mi Guerra de España*.[4]

In *Red Spanish Notebook* the (Australian and Cuban respectively) Trotskyists Low and Breà recorded their day-to-day experiences during the first six months of the Spanish Civil War. Both were directly involved in the conflict, Breà as a member of the Lenin International Column of the POUM and Low as both a member of the POUM women's militia and editor of the English edition of the POUM newspaper, *The Spanish Revolution*. During their six months in Spain, Low and Breà worked at the POUM headquarters in Barcelona, traveled to the fronts in Aragon, Tierz and Madrid and encountered many *milicianas*. The chapters written by Low, including one specifically focused on women, are particularly insightful concerning the experiences of women in combat. Low's text is useful to the historian both in terms of relaying her own experiences as a fighter during the war, and also because as a *miliciana* herself she was able to relate more easily to the other militiawomen, who might not have been so willing to tell their stories to an outside observer, or who might have told their stories in different terms. Low recounted the experiences and stories of many *milicianas* in detail.

Low and Breà's text is useful due to its particular perspective. While there are many accounts written by journalists and other observers, it is rare to find a record by international revolutionaries involved in the civil war. Further, this primary document was written immediately after the experiences, and while the civil war was still raging, in contrast to the memoirs written by participants many years later. This certainly adds to the usefulness and reliability of the source.

Etchebéhère's *Mi Guerra* is the detailed memoir of an Argentinean woman who was not only a *miliciana* but also a commander who led her troops into many battles in the front lines. *Mi Guerra* allows insight into many of the trials and experiences faced by a woman in combat during the Spanish Civil War.

Etchebéhère and her husband Hipólito[5] volunteered immediately when the civil war broke out. Hipólito became the first commander of the POUM's Motorized Column and Etchebéhère worked as a medic and undertook some administrative duties. After only one month, Hipólito was killed in battle, and Etchebéhère joined his column as a combatant to take his place. Shortly afterward, having shown bravery and decisiveness during the siege at the Sigüenza Cathedral in September 1936, Etchebéhère was promoted to the position of first commander of the Second Company of the POUM's Lenin Battalion. She went on to fight in the trenches at Moncloa in Madrid and toward the end of the war led shock troops in dangerous missions. *Mi Guerra* serves as one of the most valuable records of an international *miliciana's* experiences.

In her *Entre el Sol y la Tormenta*,[6] Sara Berenguer plays a role similar to that of Low, as both a participant and an observer. Unlike Low who began to write about her experiences only weeks after they occurred, Berenguer recorded her experiences much later and did not publish her autobiography until 1988. Berenguer chronicled the experiences of many of the anarchist women from the group *Mujeres Libres*, of which she was a part.

Several other memoirs that have also been useful in the research for this book include Clara and Pavel Thalmann's *Combats pour la Liberté*,[7] and Jessica Mitford's *Hons and Rebels*.[8] It must be noted here that the use of memoirs and autobiographies must be approached with the same caution as oral histories, due to the similar drawbacks and dangers of using evidence of this kind.[9]

COMMENTARIES FROM OBSERVERS AND OTHER PARTICIPANTS

Accounts from people who were either in Spain as observers of the civil war, or who took part personally in the fighting, have also been used to enhance the stories of the *milicianas*. These people include Teresa Pàmies, George Orwell, Claude Cockburn, Donald Renton, Tom Clarke, Robert Capa, Hans Erich Kaminski, and Franz Borkenau, among others.[10] The observations of the *milicianas* by these people bear out the bravery and confidence of the fighting women.

THE PRESS IN THE REPUBLICAN ZONE

This book has also relied on evidence collected from articles and photographs that were published in newspapers in the Republican zone during the Spanish Civil War. The use of these newspapers provided information regarding the *milicianas* and their military actions that otherwise would have been unavailable. These daily, weekly or monthly newspapers and their teams of journalists relayed to the Republican people, and eventually to historians, a wealth of information. Significantly, these newspapers appear to be a resource untapped until now by historians in the field of the militiawomen.

While the abundance of newspaper information pertaining to the *militianas* has never before been utilized in a systematic way, general historians of the Spanish Civil War have seen the value of newspapers as a primary source. Bolloten in particular, discusses this value at length:

> Above all, this work reflects the extensive use I have made of Spanish Civil war newspapers and periodicals. Unlike those historians who do not appreciate the value of using newspapers as a primary source, I strongly believe that it is impossible to understand the passions, the emotions and the real issues that touched the lives of the Civil War participants without consulting the press. I have found that newspapers, more than any other source, reflect clearly the views and feelings of the numerous and diverse factions that were engaged in the terrible conflict.[11]

Historians studying the *milicianas* have quoted from newspapers in discussing the imagery surrounding these women, and in arguing that the enthusiastic media coverage of the *milicianas* rendered them symbols of the Republican cause. Until now, however, historians have not utilized these publications as a source of information about the attitudes of left-wing political groups toward the *milicianas*. It is for this reason that one of the research methods used for this book was a systematic analysis of these newspapers based on their political affiliations, across the period from July 1936 to July 1937 (where available). Newspapers from each of the left-wing political persuasions have been included in this research, and these publications have been studied not as individual issues or editions, but as a whole resource—every available issue of each newspaper has been examined with an eye to discovering the information regarding the militiawomen contained within.[12]

Also, it is significant that these newspapers reveal a great deal of information not only about the attitudes of progressive political groups toward the *milicianas*, but also the names and numbers of women who participated in combat, and information regarding the battles in which they fought. Thus, these publications have been used to construct a more comprehensive picture of what life in the front lines was like for these fighting women. The information gathered from these newspapers has been incorporated into the research for all six chapters. Chapter 6, however, as an examination of the representation of the militiawomen in the press and propaganda in the Republican zone, contains the bulk of the information collected from these sources.

The communist newspapers that were examined are *Mundo Obrero*, the official organ of the PCE, *Treball*, the paper of the PSUC and *Ahora*, the newspaper of the socialist and communist youth, the JSU. One newspaper produced by a communist women's anti-fascist group was examined. This was *Mujeres*,[13] the paper of the CNFGF.

Three anarchist newspapers were examined: the *CNT* from Madrid; *Tierra y Libertad*, from Barcelona; and *Mujeres Libres*, produced by the anarchist women's group of the same name.

Only one newspaper from the POUM was available to be examined at length, this was *Juventud Comunista*, which was actually the newspaper of the POUM youth, the JCI. The POUM were the revolutionary (or anti-Stalinist) communists of Spain, most often referred to as dissident Marxists or Trotskyists. It was possible also to examine a single issue of the English edition of the POUM newspaper, *The Spanish Revolution*,[14] which contained an article on the POUM's women's battalion.

Claridad was the newspaper of the PSOE. *Ahora* also serves to highlight the socialist perspective, since it was the newspaper of the JSU, the group that came into being through the unification of the socialist and communist youth groups.

The independent and mainstream Republican newspapers that were examined are the *ABC*,[15] *Crónica, Estampa, La Libertad* and *La Voz*. These newspapers provided a great deal of information and, overall, contained by far the most photographs and images of the *milicianas*.

Also included in the research are some editions of newspapers for which the whole series from July 1936–1937 was not available, either because the paper was only published for a short period or because the newspaper, for whatever reason, has not been preserved on microfilm at the National Library or General Archive. These publications include *El Diluvio, L'Instant, El Mono Azul* and *La Noche*.[16]

One particular instance in which the inclusion of hitherto unused primary evidence from newspapers has proven valuable is the case of an article published on the cover of *L'Instant* on 9 September 1936.[17] This article contains an interview with a woman who related that her organization, the MFAC, had by that time recruited, trained and sent to the front over 500 women to fill combat positions. This information is relevant to the debate concerning the number of *milicianas*.

It is significant to note that in the case of most newspapers (with some notable exceptions such as *ABC* and *Estampa*) the majority of editions contained no mention of the *milicianas*, or featured photographs of female combatants without any supporting article or information. In many cases, however, conclusions can also be drawn from the absence of such information.

It is of course necessary to acknowledge the ever-present bias in the media, since it is the role of newspapers to carry the message of their owners and editors to specific audiences, for specific purposes. In the case of the press during the Spanish Civil War, the issue of bias is even more pertinent. During this conflict, the press in the Republican zone was often used deliberately as a tool to motivate the Spanish people to defend the Republic against the Nationalists. Clearly, one must take this bias into consideration and recognize, for example, that accounts of the bravery of particular women in battle may have been exaggerated in order to motivate and mobilize others.

If the historian maintains an awareness of the political bias in the media, it is nevertheless possible to view the information published in the press as valuable primary evidence. Clearly, the press is an indispensable resource for the historian examining the attitudes held by different political groups toward the *milicianas*, as well as the attitudes that political groups wanted their audience to hold. In addition, the press often contained interviews with *milicianas* that reveal important information. It is unlikely that dates, details of battles and names and numbers of militiawomen would have been fabricated, because in most cases this would serve no significant purpose.

PROPAGANDA: PUBLICATIONS AND IMAGES

Several publications from the civil war period have been used to convey the attitudes of particular political parties toward the *milicianas*. One of these is a detailed pamphlet published by the JSU in 1936, after the death of Lina Odena. Written by Angel Estivill, the document *Lina Odena: La gran heroína de las Juventudes Revolucionarias de España* (Lina Odena: The great hero of the Revolutionary Youth of Spain) provides a great deal of information about Odena's life, political activity, and armed participation in the civil war. Once again, the fact that this pamphlet was written for propaganda purposes must be taken into account, but it is nonetheless a valuable resource.

The Herbert Southworth Collection, an extensive microfilm collection of primary source documents on the Spanish Civil War, contains numerous examples of propaganda and imagery featuring the militiawomen. Examples of relevant sources include political cartoons; a calendar produced by the UGT; the artwork of Sim (pseudonym for Vila-Rey) and poems about Odena, as well as many pamphlets and posters produced by political groups. This collection, which includes a large amount of material from outside Spain, demonstrates the world's fascination with these fighting women.

NOTES

1. Mangini, *Memories of Resistance* and "Memories of Resistance"; Strobl, *Partisanas.* Marín, "Libertarias"; Nash, *Defying* and "Women in War."

2. For a discussion on the methodology behind the use of oral histories, see Sherna Berger Gluck and Daphne Patai (eds.), *Women's Words: The feminist practice of oral history*, Routledge, New York, 1991.

3. Mary Low and Juan Breà, *Red Spanish Notebook: The first six months of the revolution and the civil war*, Purnell and Sons, London, 1937.

4. Etchebéhère, *Mi Guerra de España*, Alikornio, Barcelona, 2003.

5. Spelling of name taken from Etchebéhère, *Guerra*, 11. Also spelled Hipolyte.

6. Sara Berenguer, *Entre el Sol y la Tormenta*, Seuba Ediciones, Barcelona, 1988.

7. Clara and Pavel Thalmann, *Combats pour la Liberté*, translated by Caroline Darbon, Spartacus, Paris, 1983.

8. Jessica Mitford serves as an example of a woman who was unable to make the military contribution she had hoped to during the war. Mitford, *Hons and Rebels: An autobiography*, Victor Gollancz, London, 1989.

9. For a discussion on the critical use of memoirs and autobiographies, see Samuel Hynes, *The Soldiers' Tale: Bearing witness to modern war*, Penguin Books, New York, 1998, xi–xvi.

10. Teresa Pàmies, *Cuando Éramos Capitanes: (Memorias de aquella guerra)*, Dopesa, Barcelona, 1975; George Orwell, *Homage to Catalonia*, 3rd edition, Secker & Warburg, London, 1954; James Pettifer (ed.), *Cockburn in Spain: Dispatches from the Spanish Civil War*, Lawrence and Wishart, London, 1986; Ian MacDougall (ed.), *Voices from the Spanish Civil War: Personal recollections of Scottish volunteers in Republican Spain 1936–1939*, Polygon, Edinburgh, 1986, 21; MacDougall, *Voices from the Spanish Civil War*, 62. Fusi Aizpurau, Whelan et al, *Heart of Spain*. Hans Erich Kaminski, *Los de Barcelona*, Parsifal Ediciones, Barcelona, 1976; Franz Borkenau, *The Spanish Cockpit: An eyewitness account of the political and social conflicts of the Spanish Civil War*, Pluto Press, London, 1937.

11. Bolloten, *Spanish Civil War*, xvii.

12. Where possible each issue from the time period has been examined. In some cases the newspapers were not produced continuously for the entire period in question. There are also cases in which several issues were missing from the collections.

13. There were two newspapers with the name *Mujeres* within the Republican zone during the Spanish Civil War. The first was produced in Bilbao, and all references to the newspaper *Mujeres* are references to this paper. The other was produced by the *Comité Nacional de Mujeres Antifascistas* (National Committee of Anti-fascist Women), and this paper has not been referenced in this book.

14. "The First Women's Battalion," *The Spanish Revolution*, vol. 1, no. 7, 2 December 1936, Barcelona.

15. In Spain at the time there were two different newspapers with the name *ABC*. One was produced in Madrid and was a Republican newspaper, the other was produced in Seville and was Nationalist. This book will only refer to the Madrid newspaper. Therefore all references to *ABC* are to *ABC* Madrid.

16. *El Diluvio*, Barcelona. Issues examined were from the months of September, November and December 1936 and January 1937. (All others missing from the collection.) *L"Instant*, Barcelona. Only issues from 1936 held in the collection. *El Mono Azul*, written by Maria Teresa Leon et al. Only numbers 1 and 4–8 held in the collection. *La Noche*. Only issues from 1936 held in collection, with a majority of those missing.

17. To the best of my knowledge, this newspaper has never been used in the published research of a historian of this field. This is evident from the bibliographies of monographs, articles and chapters written about the *milicianas*.

Bibliography

ENGLISH-LANGUAGE SOURCES

Primary Sources

Interviews

Lines, Lisa, "Interview with Concha Pérez Collado," 13 February 2005, Barcelona.

Newspapers

"A Girl of the Spanish People: A story from the special correspondent of Woman To-day," *Woman To-day*, December 1936, 6.
"The First Women's Battalion," *The Spanish Revolution*, vol. 1, no. 7, 2 December 1936, Barcelona, 4.
Sydney Mail. July 1936–March 1937.
Sydney Morning Herald. July 1936–March 1937.
The Daily Telegraph, Sydney. July 1936–March 1937.
The Osaka Mainichi, Tokyo. July 1936–March 1937.
The New York Times, New York. July 1936–March 1937.

Microfilm Collections

Southworth, Herbert Rutledge, "The Spanish Civil War Collection" or "Herbert Southworth Collection," Research Publications, Inc., University of California, San Diego, 1987.

Monographs

Acier, Marcel (ed.), *From Spanish Trenches: Recent letters from Spain*, Cresset Press, London, 1939.
Bebel, August, *Woman Under Socialism*, translated by D. de Leon, New York Labour Press, New York, 1904.
Borkenau, Franz, *The Spanish Cockpit: An eyewitness account of the political and social conflicts of the Spanish Civil War*, Pluto Press, London, 1937.
Carr, Raymond (ed.), *Images of the Spanish Civil War*, George Allen and Unwin, London, 1986.
Copeman, Fred, *Reason in Revolt*, Blandford Press, London, 1948.
Cuevas, Tomasa, *Prison of Women: Testimonies of war and resistance in Spain, 1939–1975*, translated and edited by Mary E. Giles, State University of New York Press, Albany, 1998.
Engels, Friedrich, *On the Origins of the Family, Private Property and the State*, Foreign Languages Press, Peking, 1978.
Mora, Constancia de la, *In Place of Splendour: The autobiography of a Spanish woman*, M. Joseph, London, 1940.

Foss, William and Gerahty, Cecil, *The Spanish Arena*, The Right Book Club, London, 1938.

Fraser, Ronald, *Blood of Spain: The experience of the Civil War, 1936–1939*, Allen Lane, London, 1979.

Fusi Aizpurau, Juan P., Whelan, Richard et al., *Heart of Spain: Robert Capa's photographs of the Spanish Civil War*, Aperture, New York, 1999.

Fyrth, Jim and Alexander, Sally (eds.), *Women's Voices from the Spanish Civil War*, Lawrence & Wishart, London, 1991.

Gellhorn, Martha, *The Face of War*, Rupert Hart-Davis, London, 1959.

Gregory, Walter, *The Shallow Grave: A memoir of the Spanish Civil War*, Victor Gollancz, London, 1986.

Ibárruri, Dolores, *Speeches and Articles: 1936–1938*, Modern Publishers Pty. Ltd., Sydney, 1938.

Ibárruri, Dolores, *They Shall Not Pass*, International Publishers, New York, 1966.

Low, Mary and Breà, Juan, *Red Spanish Notebook: The first six months of the revolution and the civil war*, Purnell and Sons, London, 1937.

MacDougall, Ian (ed.), *Voices from the Spanish Civil War: Personal recollections of Scottish volunteers in Republican Spain 1936–1939*, Polygon, Edinburgh, 1986.

Mitford, Jessica, *Hons and Rebels: An autobiography*, Victor Gollancz, London, 1989.

Orwell, George, *Homage to Catalonia*, 3rd edition, Secker & Warburg, London, 1954.

Palencia, Isabel de, *Smouldering Freedom: The story of the Spanish Republicans in exile*, Victor Gollancz, London, 1946.

Pettifer, James (ed.), *Cockburn in Spain: Dispatches from the Spanish Civil War*, Lawrence and Wishart, London, 1986.

Porter, David (ed.), *Vision on Fire: Emma Goldman on the Spanish Revolution*, Common Ground Press, New York, 1985.

Rust, William, *The Story of the Daily Worker*, People's Press Printing Society, London, 1949.

Shawcross, Edith, "The Hand that Rocks the Cradle," in Keith Briant and Lyall Wilkes (eds.), *Would I Fight?* Basil Blackwell, Oxford, 1938, 81–102.

Shulman, Alix Kates (ed.), *Red Emma Speaks: An Emma Goldman reader*, 3rd edition, Humanity Books, New York, 1998.

Tisa, John, *Recalling the Good Fight*, Bergin and Garvey, Massachusetts, 1985.

Secondary Sources

Journal Articles

Ackelsberg, Martha A., "Anarchist Revolution and Women's Liberation," *Society*, vol. 25, no. 2, January–February 1988, 29–38.

Ackelsberg, Martha A., "Separate and Equal? Mujeres Libres and Anarchist Strategy for Women"s Emancipation," *Feminist Studies*, vol. 11, no 1., Spring 1985, 63–85.

Buchanan, Tom, "A Far Away Country of Which We Know Nothing? Perceptions of Spain and its Civil War in Britain, 1931–1939," *Twentieth Century British History*, vol. 4, no. 1, 1993, 1–24.

Bunk, Brian D., "Revolutionary Warrior and Gendered Icon: Aida Lafuente and the Spanish Revolution of 1934," *Journal of Women's History*, vol. 15, no. 2, Summer 2003, 99–132.

Bunk, Brian D., "Your Comrades Will not Forget," *History and Memory*, vol. 14, no. 1, Autumn 2002, 65–94.

D'Agostino, Joseph A., "Congress May Reconsider Women-In-Combat Rules," *Human Events*, vol. 59, no. 12, 7 April 2003, 7.

Doyle, Jim, "Paul Preston: Doves of War, Book Review," *Library Journal*, vol. 128, no. 3, 15 February 2003, 152.

Graham, Helen, "'Against the State': A Genealogy of the Barcelona May Days (1937)," *European History Quarterly*, vol. 29, no. 4, 485–542.

Guttman, Jon, "Not All Stories of History's Women Warriors Ended in Martyrdom," *Military History*, vol. 21, no. 1, April 2004, 6.

Hanson, Christopher, "Women Warriors," *Columbia Journalism Review*, vol. 41, no. 1, May–June 2002, 46–50.

Herrmann, Gina, "Voices of the Vanquished: Leftist women and the Spanish Civil War," *Journal of Spanish Cultural Studies*, vol. 4, no. 1, 2003, 11–29.

Holstrom, Nancy, "The Socialist Feminist Project," *Monthly Review*, vol. 54, no. 10, 2003, 38–49.

Kaplan, Temma, "Gender on the Barricades," *Journal of Women's History*, vol. 9, no. 3, Autumn 1997, 177–186.

Kaplan, Temma, "Spanish Anarchists and Women's Liberation," *Journal of Contemporary History*, vol. 6, 1971, 101–110.

Lannon, Frances, "Women and Images of Women in the Spanish Civil War," *Transactions of the Royal Historical Society*, Sixth Series, vol. 1, 1991, 213–228.

Mangini, Shirley, "Memories of Resistance: Women activists from the Spanish Civil War," *Signs*, vol. 17, no. 1, 1997, 171–186.

Muller, Richard R., "Wings, Women and War: Soviet Airwomen in World War II combat. Book Review," *Air and Space Power Journal*, vol. 17, no. 4, Winter 2003, 104–106.

Nash, Mary, "Women in War: *Milicianas* and armed combat in revolutionary Spain 1936–1939," *The International History Review*, vol. 15, no. 2, May 1993, 269–282.

Preston, Paul, "Spain Betrayed?" *The Volunteer*, vol. 23, no. 4, December 2001, 5–8.

Monographs

Ackelsberg, Martha A., *Free Women of Spain: Anarchism and the struggle for the emancipation of women*, Indiana University Press, Bloomington, 1991.

Agulhon, Maurice, *Marianne into Battle: Representation, imagery and symbolism in France, 1789–1880*, Cambridge University Press, Cambridge, 1981.

Aldgate, Anthony, *Cinema and History: British newsreels and the Spanish Civil War*, Scholar Press, London, 1979.

Alexander, Bill, *British Volunteers for Liberty: Spain 1936–1939*, Lawrence and Wishart, London, 1982.

Alexander, Gerard, "Women and Men at the Ballot Box: Voting in Spain's two democracies," in Victoria Lorée Enders and Pamela Beth Radcliff (eds), *Constructing Spanish Womanhood: Female identity in modern Spain*, State University of New York Press, Albany, 1999, 349–374.

Allen, Ann, *Feminism and Motherhood in Western Europe 1890–1970: The maternal dilemma*, Palgrave Macmillan, New York, 2005.

Beevor, Antony, *The Spanish Civil War*, Orbis Publishing, London, 1982.

Blinkhorn, Martin, *Carlism and Crisis in Spain, 1931–1939*, Cambridge University Press, Cambridge, 1975.

Blinkhorn, Martin, *Democracy and Civil War in Spain 1931–1939*, Routledge, London, 1988.

Blinkhorn, Martin, *Spain in Conflict, 1931–1939*, Sage Publications, London, 1986.

Blum, Lawrence A. and Seidler, Victor J., *A Truer Liberty: Simone Weil and Marxism*, Routledge, New York, 1989.

Bolloten, Burnett, *Spanish Revolution: The left and the struggle for power during the civil war*, University of North Carolina Press, Chapel Hill, 1979.

Bolloten, Burnett, *The Grand Camouflage: The Spanish Civil War and Revolution, 1936–1939*, Pall Mall Publishers, London, 1968.

Bolloten, Burnett, *The Spanish Civil War: Revolution and counterrevolution*, University of North Carolina Press, Chapel Hill, 1991.

Bourke, Joanna, *An Intimate History of Killing: Face-to-face killing in twentieth century warfare*, Granta Books, London, 1999.

Brewer, Pat, *The Dispossession of Women*, Resistance Books, Chippendale, 2000.

Brenan, Gerald, *The Spanish Labyrinth: An account of the social and political background of the Spanish Civil War*, Cambridge University Press, Cambridge, 1960.

Brothers, Caroline, *War and Photography: A cultural history*, Routledge, London, 1997.

Broué, Pierre and Témime, Emile, *The Revolution and the Civil War in Spain*, Faber and Faber, London, 1972.

Buchanan, Tom, *Britain and the Spanish Civil War*, Cambridge University Press, Cambridge, 1997.

Buchanan, Tom, *The Spanish Civil War and the British Labour Movement*, Cambridge University Press, Cambridge, 1991.

Calder, Angus, *The People's War: Britain 1939–45*, Cape, London, 1969.

Carr, Raymond, *The Civil War in Spain 1936–1939*, Weidenfeld and Nicolson, London, 1986.

Carr, Raymond, *The Republic and the Civil War in Spain*, Macmillan, London, 1971.

Carr, Raymond, *The Spanish Tragedy: The civil war in perspective*, Weidenfeld and Nicolson, London, 1993.

Christie, Stuart, *A Study of the Revolution in Spain, 1936–1937*, Meltzer Press, London, 1998.

Cleminson, Richard, "Beyond Tradition and 'Modernity': The cultural and sexual politics of Spanish anarchism," in Helen Graham and Jo Labanyi (eds.), *Spanish Cultural Studies: An introduction*, Oxford University Press, Oxford, 1995, 116–123.

Cleminson, Richard and Amezúa, Efigenio, "Spain: The political and social context of sex reform in the late nineteenth and early twentieth centuries," in Eder, Franz X., Hall, Lesley A., and Hekman, Gert (eds.), *Sexual Cultures in Europe: National histories*, Manchester University Press, Manchester, 1999, 173–196.

Coleman, Catherine, "Women in the Spanish Civil War," in Fusi Aizpurau, Juan P., Whelan, Richard et al., *Heart of Spain: Robert Capa's photographs of the Spanish Civil War*, Aperture, New York, 1999, 43–51.

Conlon, Eddie, *The Spanish Civil War: Anarchism in action*, WSM Publications, Dublin, 1986.

Cooke, Miriam, *Women and the War Story*, University of California Press, Berkeley, 1996.

Cooper, Helen M., Munich, Adrienne Auslander and Squier, Susan Merrill (eds.), *Arms and the Women: War, gender and literary representation*, University of North Carolina Press, Chapel Hill, 1989.

Dietz, Mary G., *Between the Human and the Divine: The political thought of Simone Weil*, Rowman and Littlefield Publishers, Totowa, 1988.

Ealham, Chris, "The Myth of the Maddened Crowd: Class, culture and space in the revolutionary urbanist project in Barcelona, 1936–1937," in Ealham and Michael Richards (eds.), *The Splintering of Spain: Cultural history and the Spanish Civil War, 1936–1939*, Cambridge University Press, Cambridge, 2005, 111–132.

Enders, Victoria Lorée and Radcliff, Pamela Beth (eds.), *Constructing Spanish Womanhood: Female identity in modern Spain*, State University of New York Press, Albany, 1999.

Enloe, Cynthia, *Does Khaki Become You? The militarisation of women's lives*, South End Press, London, 1983.

Foran, John (ed.), *Theorizing Revolutions*, Routledge, London, 1997.

Fredricks, Shirley, "Feminism: The essential ingredient in Federica Montseny's anarchist theory," in Jane Slaughter and Robert Kern (eds.), *European Women on the Left: Socialism, feminism and the problems faced by political women, 1880 to the present*, Greenwood Press, Westport, 1981, 125–146.

Gluck, Sherna Berger and Patai, Daphne (eds.), *Women's Words: The feminist practice of oral history*, Routledge, New York, 1991.

Goldman, Nancy Loring, *Female Soldiers–Combatants or Non-Combatants?* Greenwood Press, Westport, 1982.

Goldstein, Joshua S., *War and Gender: How gender shapes the war system and vice versa*, Cambridge University Press, Cambridge, 2001.

Gómez, María Asunción, "Feminism and Anarchism: Remembering the role of Mujeres Libres in the Spanish Civil War," in Lisa Vollendorf (ed.), *Recovering Spain's Feminist Tradition*, The Modern Language Association of America, New York, 2001, 293–310.

Graham, Helen, "Women and Social Change," in Helen Graham and Jo Labanyi (eds.), *Spanish Cultural Studies: An introduction*, Oxford University Press, Oxford, 1995, 99–116.

Graham, Helen and Labanyi, Jo (eds.), *Spanish Cultural Studies: An introduction*, Oxford University Press, Oxford, 1995.

Graham, Helen, *The Spanish Republic at War, 1936–1939*, Cambridge University Press, Cambridge, 2002.

Gregory, Chester W., *Women in Defense Work During World War II: An analysis of the labor problem and women's rights*, Exposition Press, New York, 1974.

Greenwald, Maurine Weiner, *Women, War and Work: The impact of World War I on women workers in the United States*, Cornell University Press, Ithaca, 1990.

Harvard, Robert G., "Introduction," in Federico Garcia Lorca, *Mariana Pineda*, Aris & Phillips Ltd., Warminster, 1987.

Higonnet, Margaret R., "Civil Wars and Sexual Territories" in Helen M. Cooper, Adrienne Auslander Munich and Susan Merrill Squier (eds.), *Arms and the Women: War, gender and literary representation*, University of North Carolina Press, Chapel Hill, 1989, 80–96.

Higonnet, Margaret R. and Higonnet, Patrice L.- R., "The Double Helix," in Margaret Randolph Higonnet, Jane Jenson, Sonya Michel and Margaret Collins Weitz (eds.), *Behind the Lines: Gender and the two World Wars*, Yale University Press, New Haven, 1987, 31–50.

Hills, George, *The Battle for Madrid*, Vantage Books, London, 1976.

Hemingway, Ernest, *The Fifth Column*, Cape, London, 1938.

Hopkins, James K., *Into the Heart of the Fire: The British in the Spanish Civil War*, Stanford University Press, Stanford, 1998.

Huston, Nancy, "The Matrix of War: Mothers and heroes," in Susan Rublin Suleiman (ed.), *The Female Body in Western Culture*, Harvard University Press, Cambridge, 1986.

Hynes, Samuel, *The Soldiers' Tale: Bearing witness to modern war*, Penguin Books, New York, 1998.

Jackson, Angela, *British Women and the Spanish Civil War*, Routledge, London, 2002.

Jackson, Gabriel, *A Concise History of the Spanish Civil War*, Thames and Hudson, London, 1974.

Jackson, Gabriel, *Spanish Civil War: Domestic crisis or international conspiracy?* Heath, Boston, 1967.

Jackson, Gabriel, *The Spanish Republic and Civil War 1931–1939*, Princeton University Press, Princeton, 1965.

Jones, David E., *Women Warriors: A history*, Brassey's, London, 1997.

Junco, José Alvarez, "Education and the Limits of Liberalism," in Helen Graham and Jo Labanyi (eds.), *Spanish Cultural Studies: An introduction*, Oxford University Press, Oxford, 1995, 45–52.

Junco, José Alvarez, "Rural and Urban Popular Cultures," in Helen Graham, and Jo Labanyi (eds.), *Spanish Cultural Studies: An introduction*, Oxford University Press, Oxford, 1995, 82–90.

Junco, José Alvarez and Shubert, Adrian, *Spanish History Since 1808*, Arnold, London, 2000.

Kampwirth, Karen, *Feminism and the Legacy of Revolution: Nicaragua, El Salvador, Chiapas*, Ohio University Press, Athens, 2004.

Kaplan, Temma, "Other Scenarios: Women and Spanish anarchism," in Renate Bridenthal and Claudia Koonz (eds.), *Becoming Visible: Women in European history*, Houghton Mifflin, Boston, 1977, 400–421.

Keene, Judith, "Into the Clear Air of the Plaza: Spanish women achieve the vote in 1931", in Victoria Lorée Enders and Pamela Beth Radcliff (eds.), *Constructing Spanish Womanhood: Female identity in modern Spain*, State University of New York, Albany, 1999, 325–348.

Keene, Judith, "No More than Brothers and Sisters: Women in Combat in the Spanish Civil War," in Peter Monteath and Fredric S. Zuckerman (eds.), *Modern Europe: Histories and identities*, Australian Humanities Press, Unley, 1998, 121–132.

Kern, Robert, "Margarita Nelken: Women and the crisis of Spanish politics," in Jane Slaughter and Robert Kern (eds.), *European Women on the Left: Socialism, feminism and the problems faced by political women, 1880 to the Present*, Greenwood Press, Westport, 1981, 147–162.

Kern, Robert W., *Red Years/Black Years: A political history of Spanish anarchism, 1911–1937*, Institute for the Study of Human Issues, Philadelphia, 1978.

Kurzman, Dan, *Miracle of November: Madrid"s Epic Stand 1936*, G. P. Putnam's Sons, New York, 1980.

Lannon, Frances, "The Social Praxis and Cultural Politics of Spanish Catholicism," in Helen Graham and Jo Labanyi (eds.), *Spanish Cultural Studies: An introduction*, Oxford University Press, Oxford, 1995, 40–45.

Maloof, Judy, *Voices of Resistance: Testimonies of Cuban and Chilean Women*, University Press of Kentucky, Lexington, 1999.

Mangini, Shirley, *Memories of Resistance: Women's voices from the Spanish Civil War*, Yale University Press, New Haven, 1995.

Martínez-Gutiérrez, Josebe, "Margarita Nelken: Feminist and political praxis," in Lisa Vollendorf (ed.), *Recovering Spain's Feminist Tradition*, The Modern Language Association of America, New York, 2001, 278–292.

Mészáros, István, *Beyond Capital: Toward a theory of transition*, Merlin Press, London, 1995.

Milward, Alan, *War, Economy and Society, 1939–45*, Allen Lane, London, 1977.

Moghadam, Valentine, "Gender and Revolutions," in John Foran (ed.), *Theorizing Revolutions*, Routledge, London, 1997, 137–167.

Morris, Francis (ed.), *No Pasarán: Photographs and posters of the Spanish Civil War*, Arnolfini Gallery, Bristol, 1986.

Morris, Lynda and Radfort, Robert (eds.), *The Story of the AIA: Artists International Association 1933–1953*, The Museum of Modern Art, Oxford, 1983.

Morrow, Felix, *Revolution and Counter-Revolution in Spain, including the Civil War in Spain*, Pathfinder Press, New York, 1974.

Mullaney, Marie Marmo, *Revolutionary Women: Gender and the socialist revolutionary Role*, Praeger, New York, 1983.

Nash, Mary, *Defying Male Civilization: Women in the Spanish Civil War*, Arden Press, Denver, 1995.

Nash, Mary, "Ideals of Redemption: Socialism and women on the left in Spain," in Helmut Gruber and Pamela Graves (eds.), *Women and Socialism, Socialism and Women: Europe between the two World Wars*, Berghahn Books, New York, 1998, 348–380.

Nevin, Thomas R., *Simone Weil: Portrait of a self-exiled Jew*, University of North Carolina Press, Chapel Hill, 1991.

Payne, S. G., *The Spanish Revolution*, Weidenfeld & Nicolson, London, 1970.

Paz, Abel, *Durruti: The people armed*, Black Rose Books, Montreal, 1976.

Pennington, Reina, *Amazons to Fighter Pilots: A biographical dictionary of military women*, Greenwood Press, Westport, 2003.

Pennington, Reina, *Wings Women and War: Soviet airwomen in World War II combat*, University Press of Kansas, Lawrence, 2002.

Pierson, Ruth Roach, "Did Your Mother Wear Army Boots? Feminist theory and women's relation to war, peace and revolution," in Sharon MacDonald, Pat Holden, and

Shirley Ardener (eds.), *Images of Women in Peace and War*, University of Wisconsin Press, Madison, 1988, 205–227.

Pink, Sarah, *Women and Bullfighting: Gender, sex and the consumption of tradition*, Berg, Oxford, 1997.

Pollock, Griselda, "What's Wrong with Images of Women?" in Manuel Alvarado (ed.), *Representation and Photography: A screen education reader*, Palgrave, New York, 2001, 76–86.

Preston, Paul, *Coming of the Spanish Civil War: Reform, reaction and revolution in the Second Republic 1931–1939*, Macmillan, London, 1978.

Preston, Paul, *Comrades! Portraits from the Spanish Civil War*, HarperCollins, London, 1999.

Preston, Paul, *Doves of War*, HarperCollins, London, 2002.

Preston, Paul, *Franco: A biography*, HarperCollins, London, 1993.

Preston, Paul, *The Spanish Civil War: Reaction, Revolution and Revenge*, Harper Perennial, London, 2006.

Preston, Paul, *The Spanish Civil War, 1936–1939*, Harper Perennial, London, 2006.

Preston, Paul, *The Spanish Civil War, 1936–1939*, Weidenfeld and Nicolson, London, 1986.

Reid, Evelyn, *Sexism and Science*, Pathfinder Press, New York, 1978.

Reid, Evelyn, *Women's Evolution from Matriarchal Clans to Patriarchal Family*, Pathfinder Press, New York, 1974.

Richards, Michael, *A Time of Silence: Civil war and the culture of repression in Franco's Spain, 1936–1945*, Cambridge University Press, Cambridge, 1998.

Rossiter, Margaret L, *Women in the Resistance*, Praeger, New York, 1986.

Seitz, Barbara, Lobao, Linda and Treadway, Ellen, "No Going Back: Women's participation in the Nicaraguan Revolution and in postrevolutionary movements", in Ruth H. Howes and Michael R. Stevenson (eds.), *Women and the Use of Military Force*, Lynne Rienner Publishers Inc, Boulder, 1993, 167–184.

Shubert, Adrian, *A Social History of Modern Spain*, Unwin Hyman, London, 1990.

Smith, Lois and Padula, Alfred, *Sex and Revolution: Women in socialist Cuba*, Oxford University Press, New York, 1996.

Soudakoff, Nick (ed.), *Marxism versus Anarchism*, Resistance Books, Chippendale, 2001.

Taylor, Sandra C., *Vietnamese Women at War: Fighting for Ho Chi Minh and the revolution*, University Press of Kansas, Kansas, 1999.

Thomas, Hugh, *The Spanish Civil War*, 4th edition, Penguin, London, 2003.

Thomson, Alistair, *Anzac Memories: Living with the legend*, Oxford University Press, Melbourne, 1994.

Tone, John Lawrence, "Spanish Women in the Resistance to Napoleon, 1808–1814," in Victoria Lorée Enders and Pamela Beth Radcliff (eds.), *Constructing Spanish Womanhood: Female identity in modern Spain*, State University of New York Press, Albany, 1999, 259–282.

Van Creveld, Martin, *Men, Women and War*, Cassell & Co, London, 2001.

Vosburg, Nancy, "The Tapestry of a Feminist Life: María Teresa León (1903–88)," in Lisa Vollendorf (ed.), *Recovering Spain's Feminist Tradition*, Modern Language Association of America, New York, 2001, 260–277.

Watkins, K. W., *Britain Divided: The effect of the Spanish Civil War and British political opinion*, Thomas Nelson and Sons Ltd., London, 1963.

Williams, Colin, Alexander, Bill and Gorman, John (eds.), *Memorials of the Spanish Civil War: Official publication of the International Brigade Association*, Alan Sutton Publishing Ltd, Stroud, 1996.

Willis, Liz, *Women in the Spanish Revolution*, Solidarity, London, Solidarity Pamphlet Number 40, October 1975.

Internet Sources

Durgan, Andy, "International Volunteers in the POUM Militias," Fundación Andréu Nin. Expanded version of a paper originally presented to the Conference on the International Brigades organised by the University of Lausanne, 19–20 December 1997. http://www.fundanin.org/durgan1.htm. Accessed on Monday 19 April 2004, 9:20 AM.

Hijma, Bouwe, "List of the Papers of Paul (Pavel) Thalmann and Clara Thalmann 1920–1986." http://www.iisg.nl/archives/html/t/10771255.html. Accessed on Monday 19 April 2004, 10:23 AM.

Radosh, Ronald, "But Today the Struggle, Spain and the Intellectuals", *The New Criterion On-line*. http://www.newcriterion.com/archive/05/oct86/struggle.html. Accessed on Monday 19 April 2004, 10:00 AM.

"The People Armed", AFA Online-FT archive. http://www.geocities.com/CapitolHill/Senate/5602/scwar4.html . Accessed on Monday 19 April 2004, 11:46 AM.

Theses

Piles, Raquel, "The Most Hispanic Thing: An analysis of key texts on Spanish anarchism," Honours Thesis, 1999, Department of History, Flinders University, South Australia, Australia.

Schweich, Rachel, "Revived Voices: Spanish Women's testimonies from the Spanish Civil War," Senior Thesis, May 2000, Women's Studies and Hispanic Studies, Mills College, Oakland, California, USA.

Phipps, Kelly, "Gender and the Language of Struggle: Republican representations of women in the Spanish Civil War," Honours Thesis, April 2003, Gender Studies, Brown University, Providence, R.I., USA.

SPANISH-LANGUAGE SOURCES

Primary Sources

Newspapers

ABC, Madrid. July 1936–December 1937.
ABC, Seville. July 1936–March 1937.
Ahora. July 1936–March 1937.
Claridad. July 1936–March 1937.
CNT. July–December 1936.
Crónica. July–December 1936.
El Diluvio i, Barcelona. July 1936–March 1937.
El Mono Azul. Nos 1 and 4–8, 1936.
"Entrevista a la Anarquista Concha Pérez, CNT," El País, *4 August 2004.*
El Sol. July–December 1936.
Estampa. July 1936–August 1937.
Frente Rojo. July 1938.
Juventud. July–December 1936.
Juventud Comunista. July–December 1936.
La Libertad. July–December 1936.
La Noche. 1936.
La Union, Seville. July 1936–March 1937.
La Voz, Madrid. July 1936–March 1937.

L 'Instant, Barcelona. July–December 1936.
Mujeres, Bilbao. February 1937–December 1937.
Mujeres Libres. July–December 1937.
Mundo Obrero. July 1936–March 1937.
Politica. July 1936–March 1937.
Rello, Mateo "Concha Pérez and Anarchy", *Solidaridad Obrera*, 17 July 2006.
Tierra y Libertad, Barcelona. July 1936–August 1938.
Treball. February 1936.

Pamphlets

La Mujer Ante la Revolución, Publicaciones del Secretariado Femenino del POUM, Barcelona, 1937.
Martí Ibáñez, Felix, *Tres Mensajes a la Mujer*, Barcelona, 1937.

Journal Articles

Goicoechea, Maite, "Mujer y Guerra Civil: La historia que no se contó. Milicianas del 36: Las olvidadas," *Vindicación Feminista*, vol. 26–27, September 1978.

Monographs

Berenguer, Sara, *Entre el Sol y la Tormenta*, Seuba Ediciones, Barcelona, 1988.
Carulla, Jordi and Carulla, Arnau, *El Color de la Guerra*, Postermil, Barcelona, 2000.
Català, Nues, *De la Resistencia y la Deportación: 50 testimonios de mujeres españolas*, Ediciones Península, Barcelona, 2000.
Crespí, Miquel López, *Estiu de Foc: Dietari d'una miliciana*, Columna, Barcelona, 1997.
Cuevas, Tomasa, *Mujeres de la Resistencia*, Sirocco Books, Barcelona, 1986.
"Diario de la Miliciana," in Josep Massot i Muntaner, *El Desembarcament de Bayo a Mallorca, agosto-setiembre de 1936*, Publicacions de l"Abadia de Montserrat, Barcelona, 1987, 393–410.
Estivill, Ángel, *Lina Odena: La gran heroína de las Juventudes revolucionarias de España*, Editorial Maucci, Barcelona, 1936.
Etchebéhère, Mika, *Mi Guerra de España*, Alikornio, Barcelona, 2003.
Hernández, Miguel, *Obra Poética Completa*, 3rd edition, Zero, Madrid, 1977.
Ibárruri, Dolores, *A las Mujeres Madrileñas!*, Partido Comunista Comité Provincial, Madrid, 1938.
Ibárruri, Dolores, *Las Heroicas Mujeres de España*, Editorial Nuestro Pueblo, Madrid, 1937.
Ibárruri, Dolores, Arnáiz, Aurora et al., *Lina Odena: Heroína del pueblo*, Ediciones Europa América, Madrid, 1936.
Iturbe, Lola, *La Mujer en la Lucha Social y en la Guerra Civil de España*, Editores Mexicanos Unidos, Mexico, 1974.
Kaminski, Hans Erich, *Los de Barcelona*, Parsifal Ediciones, Barcelona, 1976.
Los Republicanas: Antología de textos e imágenes de la República y Guerra Civil, Librería Mujeres, Madrid, 1996.
Pàmies, Teresa, *Cuando Éramos Capitanes: (Memorias de aquella guerra)*, Dopesa, Barcelona, 1975.
Parshina, Elizaveta, *La Brigadista: Diario de una dinamitera de la Guerra Civil*, La Esfera Historia, Madrid, 2002.
Usandizaga, Aránzazu (ed.), *Ve y la Cuenta lo que Paso en España: Mujeres extranjeras en la guerra civil: Una antología*, Planeta, Barcelona, 2000.

Secondary Sources

Journal Articles

Moraga, Ángel Luis Rubio, "El Papel de la Mujer en la Guerra a Través de los Carteles Republicanos," *Cuadernos Republicanos*, no. 36, October 1998, 103–111.
Serrano, Julio Pérez, "La Mujer y la Imagen de la Mujer en la Resistencia Antifascista Española: *El mono azul,*" *Mujeres y Hombres en la Formación del Pensamiento Occidental*, vol. 2, 353–366.

Monographs

de Aberasturi, Luis Maria Jiménez, *Casilda, Miliciana: Historia de un sentimiento*, Editorial Txertoa, San Sebastian, 1985.
Alcalde, Carmen, *La Mujer en la Guerra Civil Española*, Editorial Cambio 16, Madrid, 1976.
Alcalde, Carmen, *Mujeres en el Franquismo*, Flor del Viento, Barcelona, 1996.
Alfaro, Fernanda Romeu, *El Silencio Roto: Mujeres contra el Franquismo*, El Viento Topo, Madrid, 1994.
Altolaguirre, Paloma Ulacia, *Concha Méndez, Memorias habladas, memorias armadas*, Mondadori, Madrid, 1990.
Álvaro, Mónica Carabias, *Rosario Sánchez Mora (1919)*, Ediciones del Orto, Madrid, 2001.
Arostegui, Julio (ed.), *Historia y Memoria de la Guerra Civil: Encuentro en Castilla y León*, Consejería de Cultura y Bienestar Social, Valladolid, 1988.
Casanova, Julián, *De la Calle al Frente: El anarcosindicalismo en España (1931–1939)*, Critica, Barcelona, 1997.
Carulla, Jordi and Carulla, Arnau, *La Guerra Civil en 2000 carteles*, Postermil, Barcelona, 1997.
Crespo, Pilar Folguera, "Las Mujeres Durante la Guerra Civil," in Elisa Garrido González (ed.), *Historia de las Mujeres en España*, Síntesis, Madrid, 1997, 515–525.
Di Febo, Giuliana, "Republicanas en la Guerra Civil Española: Protagonismo, vivencias, género," in Julián Casanova (ed.), *Guerras Civiles en el siglo XX*, Editorial Pablo Iglesias, Madrid, 2001, 51–78.
Di Febo, Giuliana, *Resistencia y Movimiento de Mujeres en España 1936–1976*, Icaria, Barcelona, 1970.
Fonseca, Carlos, *Trece Rosas Rojas: La historia más conmovedora de la guerra civil*, Ediciones Temas de Hoy, Madrid, 2004.
Gil, Conchita Liaño et al, *Mujeres Libres: luchadoras libertarias*, Fundación de Estudios Libertarios, Madrid, 1999.
Hetmann, Frederik, *Tres Mujeres: La vida de Simone Weil, Isabel Burton y Karoline von Gunderrodt*, Ediciones Alfaguara, Madrid, 1983.
Julián, Inmaculada, "Dona i Guerra Civil a Espanya (1936–1938): Representació Gràfica," in Mercedes Vilanova Ribas (ed.), *Pensar las Diferencias*, PPU, Barcelona, 1994, 137–148.
Las Mujeres y la Guerra Civil Española/ III Jornadas de Estudios Monográficos: Salamanca, octubre 1989, *Instituto de la Mujer, Madrid, 1991*.
Marín, Dolors, "Las Libertarias," in Ingrid Strobl, *Partisanas: La Mujer en la resistencia armada contra el fascismo y la ocupación alemana (1936–45)*, Virus, Barcelona, 1996.
Márquez Rodríguez, José Manuel and Gallardo Romero, Juan José, *Ortiz: General sin dios ni amo*, Santa Coloma de Gramenet, Hacer, 1999.
Massot i Muntaner, Josep, *El desembarcament de Bayo a Mallorca, agosto-setiembre de 1936*, Publicacions de l'Abadia de Montserrat, Barcelona, 1987.
Nash, Mary, *Las Mujeres en la Guerra Civil*, Taurus, Salamanca, 1989.
Nash, Mary, *Mujer y Movimiento Obrero en España*, D. L. Fontamara, Barcelona, 1981.

Nash, Mary, *Rojas: Las mujeres republicanas en la Guerra Civil*, Taurus, Madrid, 1999.
Quintanilla, Paloma Fernández, *Mujeres de Madrid*, Avapies Madrid, Madrid, 1984.
Ramírez, Francisco Acosta (ed.), *Conflicto y Sociedad Civil: La mujer en la guerra*, Universidad de Jaén, Jaén, 2003.
Rodrigo, Antonina, *Federica Montseny*, Ediciones B, Barcelona, 2003.
Rodrigo, Antonina, *Mujer y Exilio 1939*, Compañía Literaria, Madrid, 1999.
Rodrigo, Antonina, *Mujeres de España: (Las silenciadas)*, Plaza & Janes, Barcelona, 1988.
Rodrigo, Antonina, *Mujeres Para la Historia: La España silenciada del siglo XX*, Carena, Barcelona, 2002.
Scanlon, Geraldine, *La Polémica Feminista en la España Contemporánea (1864–1975)*, Siglo Veintiuno Editores, Madrid, 1976.
Sebares, Francisco Erice, "Mujeres Comunistas: La militancia femenina en el comunismo asturiano, de los orígenes al final del franquismo," in Valentín Brugos et al, *Los Comunistas en Asturias (1920–1982)*, Ediciones Trea, 1996, 313–344.
Semprún, Jorge et al. (eds.), *Mujeres en la Guerra Civil Española*, Salamanca, 1989.
Strobl, Ingrid, *Partisanas: La Mujer en la resistencia armada contra el fascismo y la ocupación alemana (1936–45)*, Virus, Barcelona, 1996.

Conference Papers

Corchero, Josefina Serván, and Muñoz, Antonio Trinidad, "Las Mujeres en la Cartelística de la Guerra Civil," in *Las Mujeres y la Guerra Civil Española/ III Jornadas de Estudios Monográficos: Salamanca, octubre 1989*, Madrid, 1991, 364–370.
Herrera, Maria del Mar Ayuso et al,, "Fuentes para el Estudio de las Mujeres en la Guerra Civil," in *Las Mujeres y la Guerra Civil Española/ III Jornadas de Estudios Monográficos: Salamanca, octubre 1989*, Madrid, 1991, 389–408.
Julián, Inmaculada, "La Representación Grafica de las Mujeres (1936–1938), in *Las Mujeres y la Guerra Civil Española/ III Jornadas de Estudios Monográficos: Salamanca, octubre 1989*, Madrid, 1991, 353–358.
Kampwirth, Karen, "From Feminine Guerrillas to Feminist Revolutionaries: Nicaragua, El Salvador, Chiapas," Paper presented to the Latin American Studies Association Conference, Guadalajara, April, 1997.
Nash, Mary, "La Miliciana: Otra opción de combatividad femenina antifascista," in *Las Mujeres y la Guerra Civil Española/ III Jornadas de Estudios Monográficos: Salamanca, octubre 1989*, Madrid, 1991, 97–108.
Rodríguez, Gema Iglesias, "Derechos y Deberes de las Mujeres Durante la Guerra Civil Española: 'Los hombres al frente, las mujeres en la retaguardia'", in *Las Mujeres y la Guerra Civil Española/ III Jornadas de Estudios Monográficos: Salamanca, octubre 1989*, Madrid, 1991, 109–117.
Las mujeres y la Guerra Civil Española/ III Jornadas de Estudios Monográficos: Salamanca, octubre 1989, Madrid, 1991.

FRENCH-LANGUAGE SOURCES

Primary Sources

Monographs

Blasco, Sophia, *Peuple d'Espagne. Journal de guerre de la madrecita*, translated by Henrietta Sauret, Nouvelle Revue Critique, Paris, 1938.
Thalmann, Clara, *Combats pour la Liberté*, translated by Caroline Darbon, Spartacus, Paris, 1983.

Secondary Sources

Monographs

Nash, Mary (ed.), *Femmes Libres = Mujeres Libres: Espagne 1936–1939*, Pensée Sauvage, Claix, 1977.
Giménez, Antoine, and Les Gimenologues, *Les Fils de la Nuit: Souvenirs de la guerre d'Espagne*, L'Insomniaque and Les Giménologues, Montreuil, 2006.

GERMAN-LANGUAGE SOURCES

Secondary Sources

Monographs

Krasser, Cornelio and Schmuck, Jochen (eds.), *Frauen in der Spanischen Revolution 1936–1939*, Libertad Verlag, Berlin, 1984.

Index

About the Author

Dr. Lisa Lines is a historian and academic editor. Having tutored and lectured at three Australian universities, Dr. Lines is now the Director and Head Editor of Elite Editing, Australia's largest academic editing service. Her qualifications include PhD Social Sciences (History), Honors in History, Honors in Creative Writing, Bachelor of Arts (majors English and History) and Graduate Certificate in Language (Spanish). She is currently completing a PhD in Creative Writing. Her research interests include women's rights and involvement in revolutions.

CPSIA information can be obtained at www.ICGtesting.com
Printed in the USA
BVOW020642191111

276207BV00002B/3/P

9 780739 164921